Winning at Zoning

Winning at Zoning

Dudley S. Hinds
Neil G. Carn
O. Nicholas Ordway

College of Business Administration
Georgia State University

McGraw-Hill Book Company

New York St. Louis San Francisco Auckland
Bogotá Düsseldorf Johannesburg London Madrid Mexico
Montreal New Delhi Panama Paris São Paulo
Singapore Sydney Tokyo Toronto

Library of Congress Cataloging in Publication Data

Hinds, Dudley S. date.
Winning at zoning.

Includes index.
1. Zoning—United States. I. Carn, Neil G., joint author. II. Ordway, O.
Nicholas, joint author. III. Title.
HD260.H56   309.2'12   78–11703
ISBN 0–07–028937–9

1 2 3 4 5 6 7 8 9 0   DODO   7 8 6 5 4 3 2 1 0 9

The editors for this book were W. Hodson Mogan and Joseph
Williams, the designer was Elliot Epstein, and the production
supervisor was Thomas G. Kowalczyk. It was set in Helvetica
by Creative Book Services, Inc.

Printed and bound by R. R. Donnelley & Sons Company.

Contents

Preface

Each year countless Americans find themselves directly involved in matters pertaining to zoning restrictions. Some get involved with zoning because it limits what they may do with property; others get involved because they wish to restrict what other people can do. The chances of getting involved have never been greater. Almost all urban and suburban communities, and many rural ones, now have zoning controls over the use and development of real estate. The controls might be known as a *zoning ordinance,* a *zoning resolution,* or a *zoning bylaw.* They might even be a part of a comprehensive land development code that does not include the word *zoning* in its title. Regardless of the name used, the controls have serious implications for real estate and for anyone concerned with the ownership, development, or brokerage of real estate. Zoning can limit an owner's enjoyment of property and/or the income and sales price that might be derived from it. Zoning can also protect or enhance the benefits that a particular owner might receive by restricting what the owners of surrounding property may do. An understanding of zoning is thus a matter of prime importance to the countless people who become involved with it each year.

The purpose of this book is to help the owners, developers, and brokers of real estate to understand and work successfully with zoning. The need for the book became apparent to the authors during several years of experience in teaching college students, homeowners, and professionals in real estate about zoning. In the course of our teaching, we have made use of several books written for planners, lawyers, administrators, and academics, but we have yet to find one directed to the needs of the people most affected by zoning. We hope that our book will contribute to the meeting of those needs.

Numerous people helped in the production of this book. Jane Hinds provided extensive editorial review, especially in the early stages, and gave encouragement when it was most needed. Robert Dumouchel provided a constructive review of the entire manuscript. Cary Bynum gave valuable advice at several critical stages.

Acknowledgement should also be made of the encouragement, advice, or other assistance received from the following: Dean Kenneth Black, Jr., Janet Cantey, Dean Melvyn Copen, James Cooper, Patricia Dake, Harold Davis, Mary Flock, Richard Forbes, Joyce Hardwick, Pattie Hinds, Elbert Hubbard, Helen Lindsay, Robert Lindsay, Richard Neel, Theron Nelson, Kathy Ordway, William Ross, Marvin Toliver, Paula Tucker, and William Weaver.

Dudley S. Hinds
Neil G. Carn
O. Nicholas Ordway

1
Introduction

"WARNING: ZONING MAY BE HAZARDOUS TO YOUR PROPERTY, POCKET-BOOK, AND WAY OF LIFE." This label is not likely to be found on the cover of any zoning ordinance. Neither is zoning likely to be banned, except in a few places like Houston, Texas, which never have adopted it. Most communities with zoning will probably keep it for a long time. Some people might view zoning as a disease, or at least as a dangerous substance, but for most it is a kind of game. Like a game, it has winners and losers. Unlike a game, there are times when all the players can win and times when all can lose. Most people play at zoning like mediocre amateurs. They are not in tune with reality. In zoning, everyone plays for money—even the amateurs. Those who win often gain increased property values or more lucrative business income. Those who lose may suffer from lower property values or perhaps business failure. If zoning is a game, then it is a serious one. Participants need to know not only the formal rules but also the unwritten principles of strategy and tactics. Unfortunately, many find themselves involved unexpectedly and without preparation. Consider the following examples.

Peter van Amsterhoven, an investor in commercial real estate, acquired a vacant skating rink. After finding no tenant for it for two years, he finally leased it to the Gold Pin Bowling Lanes. Gold Pin had plans drawn for extensive remodeling and began preparations for a grand opening. Upon applying for a permit, the remodeling contractor was told that "bowling" was a "conditional use" in that zone. Gold Pin could not remodel until they received approval from the town council. Approval would take at least two months because the planning commission had to make a recommendation before the council could act, and two public hearings were required.

Jane Watkins won a big sales contest and a trip to Jamaica for two. Now, two weeks before she and her husband Hal are scheduled to leave, they have received a registered letter notifying them of a proposed change in the town zoning map. The owners of the wooded tract behind their home have applied for "S-P Planned Shopping Center" zoning. The date of the public hearing is two days after their scheduled departure. Worried about how big and how close the buildings in the center would be, they wonder if they should postpone their trip.

Ralph Carlisle, an architect, designed a beautiful twelve-story office building for the headquarters of a local firm. The chairman of the board was so proud of it that he was thinking of retiring after its dedication. Four months before the final plans and specifications were supposed to be completed, the city amended the provisions of the "O-2 Office District" to require an additional five-foot yard along the side street for landscaping. The building plans had not allowed for the five-foot yard. Ralph had been aware of the proposed amendment and had tried to convince his client that the plans had to be revised. The client, however, refused to believe that the amendment could apply to a building that was so far along in the design stage.

Ed and Frances Sousa bought a new home that had a room with separate bath, a kitchen, and an outside entrance. They planned to rent it out to help meet the mortgage payments. One week after a tenant moved in, a zoning inspector appeared at the door and informed them that they had an illegal use. A two-family dwelling was not permissible in an "R-1 Single Family District." It seems that the previous owners had built the room for the husband's mother, and such a use was allowed originally because all occupants had belonged to the same "family."

The Sousas, the Watkins, Peter van Amsterhoven, and Ralph Carlisle have never met. They live in different parts of the country, but all have been confronted with a similar problem: how to cope with zoning.

Few actions of government have a more direct effect upon the use and value of real property than local zoning regulations. Yet, whether homeowner, developer, investor, broker, or business tenant, the typical citizen displays an astonishing lack of knowledge about zoning and a pathetic ineptness in dealing with it. Too often each zoning encounter is treated as a separate problem. The knowledge to deal with it is gained hastily and is limited to what seems necessary. Unfortunately, what seems necessary is not always enough. Even corporate executives who are otherwise astute in business can fail miserably in handling a zoning problem.

A citizen who does try to understand zoning is easily frustrated. Most literature on the subject is written for lawyers, city planners, or political scientists. Concerned mainly with law, plans, policies, and other abstractions, it is of little help to the person involved on either side in a neighborhood battle over a zoning change.

With this book we hope to enlighten such a person by explaining clearly what zoning is and how it works. In doing so, we intend to describe it as it is— not necessarily as it ought to be. We are not trying to indoctrinate readers in a particular philosophy of zoning but simply attempting to increase their understanding and effectiveness in grappling with it. Planners, lawyers, public officials, and academicians are welcome to read our book, but our attention will be focused on the other participants.

Who are these participants? There are many different kinds. In addition to the builder or developer, who makes a livelihood by activities that often require zoning decisions, we have the *homeowner* concerned with threats to the neighborhood's stability; the *broker* anxious to close a sale that is contingent upon favorable zoning action; the *merchant* trying to expand in area in order to keep up with a growing business; the *architect* trying to meet the needs of a client; and many others. A book addressed to each of these might result in confusing them all. We are going to concentrate, therefore, on the roles of two major participants: the *developer* and the *objector*.

The developer and the objector are usually thought of as antagonists. To an extent, this is true, but it is far from the whole truth. Their interests overlap more than is generally appreciated. Frequently they can discover enough in common to reach a satisfactory compromise.

Another factor not generally appreciated is the ease with which the same person may switch roles back and forth. Consider Mary Trigg, who would never think of herself as a developer. A fifty-six-year-old widow, she lives in a neat, two-bedroom home in one of the tree-lined streets of Runnymeade Park subdivision. Mary's lot backs up against commercial property that fronts on an arterial street. Last year, she was one of the most outspoken neighborhood opponents to a special-use permit for a tavern on the commercial lot. Does this make Mary an *objector*? Yes, but there is more to it. Mary has been adding to her income by making and selling pottery of original design. And she has been doing this in her home. Over the past five years, the demand for her pottery has grown to the point that she needs a ten-foot addition at the rear of her house to provide space for new kilns. She finds a competent small contractor who is willing to build the addition for a reasonable fee. The contractor draws the plans and applies for a building permit. He provides the permit clerk with copies of the plans, and the clerk gives one set to the Zoning Division. Mary Trigg's property is zoned "single-family." The zoning official must decide whether her pottery making is a permissible "home occupation." If the interpretation is negative, she may appeal the decision to the Board of Adjustment (often called "Board of Appeals"). She may also request an amendment to the zoning ordinance to permit the use. Such requests involve public hearings at which neighbors may well appear to object. If the use interpretation is positive, then the official must check to see if the proposed addition will violate a rear-yard setback requirement. If such is the case, then she must either change her plans or apply to the Board of Adjustment for a "variance." This too involves a public hearing. At the hearing some of her neighbors might appear to object. Mary does not care to admit it, but she is in the role of a *developer*.

Dan Carter is proud to be a developer and a successful one. He has recently obtained an option to purchase a nineteen-acre tract known as the "Brady Estate." For twenty-five years the Brady Estate has been surrounded by substantial homes on one-acre and two-acre lots, but until Mrs. Brady's death last year, it was not available for development. Because of the rapid growth of the community, Dan figures that the best use of the tract would be for approximately 120 condominiums and townhouse units. In order to build these, however, he needs (1) an amendment to the zoning map reclassifying his tract for a higher density and (2) a "conditional-use" approval for a planned-unit development. Both actions require public hearings. The "unreasonable" attitudes of objectors get under his skin, and he often goes fishing the day after one of these ordeals.

Only two months ago, however, he joined with neighboring property owners at another location in successfully opposing a rezoning for a discount department store adjacent to his prestigious boutique shopping center. Next month he is going to another hearing to speak out against a proposed private school on one side of his residence. The headmaster of the school thinks of Dan as an obnoxious, hysterical objector.

The ease with which developer and objector switch roles makes it important for each party to understand both roles. It is also important for each to have insights into the opponent's thinking. So we will try to consider both points of view as fully as possible. As a constant switching back and forth between roles would be awkward, however, we will treat common interests from the viewpoint of a less specific party: the *property owner*, who can be either developer or objector. Where interests conflict, we will take first the *developer's* point of view and then the *objector's*.

Now that we have identified our primary audience, we need to consider how to approach the subject. Mary Trigg and Dan Carter are participants in a complex American game characterized not only by players who often change sides but also by confusing, and frequently changing, rules. Although theoretically regulated by state statutes, constitutional restrictions, and judicial precedent, zoning practices in actuality are highly localized. Only a small minority of cases are ever litigated, and for reasons to be explained later, the decisions in such cases have a limited effect upon subsequent local actions. Thus, a successful encounter with zoning is likely to have little to do with a citizen's knowledge of law or the use of a lawyer and much to do with an awareness of administrative procedures and insights into human nature.

In trying to explain such localized procedures, we are handicapped by the fact that terminology varies between, and even within, states. The terms *planning board*, *planning commission*, and *zoning board* might, in different localities, be names for the same kind of body. A *special-use permit* in one community might be a *conditional-use permit* in another. Indeed, two identical zoning ordinances are seldom found. An academic approach of setting forth general theory and principles, followed by a description of applications, could easily add to the confusion. In this book, therefore, we will use a more pragmatic approach geared to the needs of the novice. We will approach the subject as a property owner encountering zoning for the first time.

We will take our property owner through the text of a typical zoning ordinance, explaining first the use regulations and then the standards pertaining to setbacks, height limits, and other controls over development. After describing what zoning is, we will discuss how it works—its administration, enforcement and amendment and the kinds of human beings involved; the conduct of public hearings and the pitfalls to be avoided in strategy and tactics. We will then explain some of the things that can be done to increase the chances of winning.

Learning how to win at zoning is not easy. It requires lots of digging into dull regulations. There are many details to keep in mind, just as in some card games a player must keep a mental record of all the cards that have been played. We cannot explain everything that needs to be known about winning any more than we could write a book on how to be a championship tennis pro or a Super Bowl quarterback. We will tell what we can and we will try to make it interesting. A reader who does not want to be bothered with fundamentals can skip Chapters 2, 3, and 4 and go directly to Chapter 5. That's when we start explaining how zoning works. A reader who really wants to win, however, had better master the fundamentals.

Learning the fundamentals of zoning is not going to be like marching straight up a flight of stairs. It will be more like climbing a mountain. Sometimes we will need to move sideways and sometimes we may have to backtrack. After explaining part of the zoning text in Chapter 2, for example, we will digress briefly in Chapter 3 to show how the text is related to boundaries on the zoning map. There are many things that should be learned simultaneously. However, there is no practical way in which they can be. The best we can do is to indicate the chapters in which some items will be discussed later. Any reader who wants to flip ahead to read about them should feel free to do so.

Now that some of the complexities have been explained, it is time to start exploring what zoning is. The first step is for the reader to get a copy of the local zoning ordinance—or, better still, copies of two or three local ordinances from nearby communities. Then turn to Chapter 2, and we will explore what zoning is.

2
What Zoning Is

If you are a property owner, then zoning is a local ordinance that limits how your property and your neighbors' may be developed and used. Just exactly what zoning means depends upon the circumstances in which it is encountered. In the previous chapter, we described two mythical property owners: Dan Carter, a professional developer; and Mary Trigg, a one-time developer. Mary, you will recall, was engaged in a home occupation and was trying to add a small room to her residence. Dan was trying to stop a private school from being located next to his house. In his regular business activity, Dan is constantly involved with getting zoning approvals for his various projects, while in her normal pattern of activity, Mary is seldom involved with zoning except to oppose changes in her neighborhood. Mary and Dan will not look at zoning in quite the same way, but both will agree that zoning has two main features: use restrictions (e.g., residential, commercial, home occupation, private school) and development standards (e.g., yards, setbacks, building heights, buffers).

To say that zoning is a regulation of uses and development standards is not enough to tell what it is, however. Private deed restrictions do the same thing. What distinguishes zoning from private deed restrictions is that zoning is based upon the *police power* of government. In some states, a violation of it is akin to a traffic offense and in others it is viewed more seriously as a *misdemeanor*. When Mary Trigg's contractor applied for a permit, questions were raised about the legality of both the proposed addition and the existing home occupation. If her neighbors had not liked her so much, questions might have been raised long ago as a result of their complaints. It was only because of the permit application that the matter came to the attention of the zoning administrator. What if Mary had bypassed the permit procedure and had the work done at nighttime, so that no activity would be visible from the street? Zoning and building inspectors have a knack for tracking down that sort of thing, and neighbors do complain sometimes. If Mary had been caught, she could have been fined and even jailed. People do get jailed for zoning violations, but usually only for repeated offenses. The threat is there, nevertheless, and this is a key feature of the *police power,* which we will now define as "the authority that a government has to regulate human conduct within its boundaries and to punish violators of the regulations."

The fact that zoning is based on the police power has much to do with its form and content. Because the police power is such an awesome one, its use has been ringed with safeguards by both state and federal constitutions and by state statutes. Although the precise limitations differ from state to state, they generally include the following:

1. Any regulation based upon the police power must have a clear and reasonable relationship to the public health, safety, or welfare. Some state courts also accept the "public morals" as a justification.

2. The police power must not be used to "take" private property without just compensation. What constitutes a "taking," however, is not always clear. A reduction in the value of property is not necessarily a "taking."

3. Regulations must comply with the "equal protection" and "due process" requirements of the Fourteenth Amendment to the United States Constitution and with similar requirements of the state constitution.

We will have more to say about *equal protection* and *due process* later. For the moment, let's just think of these terms as meaning that people must be treated equally and fairly. They will be easier to understand after we have described the form and content of zoning.

Now suppose that Mary Trigg has decided belatedly to find out what is in the zoning ordinance. Her first discovery is that the ordinance has two basic parts: a *text* and a *map.* To figure out how her property is affected, she must first consult the *zoning map* to see what zone or zones (usually called *districts*) embrace her lot and the surrounding parcels. In Figure 2-1, Mary's lot (number 17) is designated as "R-3 Single-Family," and the commercial tract behind her is classified as "B-2 Community Business."

The map contains only the symbols for each district, because there is not enough space on most maps to spell out the full designations. This fact can

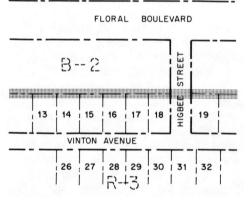

Figure 2-1

be seen clearly in Figure 2-2, which is the zoning map for the Village of Ridgewood, New Jersey.

If there is such a thing as a "typical" zoning map, then the Ridgewood example probably is one. It is hard to be certain, however, about what is typical in zoning. Both map and text come in many varieties. As a professional developer, Dan Carter is never surprised at what he finds. In one community on the periphery of a metropolitan area, no one in the town office seemed to know where a zoning map was. Dan waited until the town clerk came back from lunch and discovered that the sole copy was tacked up on the back of the door to the clerk's supply closet. In more urbanized localities, Dan is able to purchase glossy, three-color printed copies. In some he can buy, for $10 or $15, an atlas with precise zoning boundaries on a large-scale base that shows property lines and street rights-of-way with correct dimensions. Despite their variety, all of Dan's zoning maps have one important element in common: *they are all obsolete!* The typical zoning map is amended so frequently that no map can be depended upon to contain the latest changes. To be certain how a specific parcel is zoned, the property owner must peruse carefully all amendments not yet reflected on the map.

Whatever its exact format may be, the zoning map divides the community into districts bearing designations such as "R-1 Single-Family Residential," "B-1 Neighborhood Business," or "O&I Office and Institutional." As the names and symbols vary from one community to another, it is dangerous to jump to conclusions about their meanings in an unfamiliar ordinance. Instead, they should be checked carefully with the provisions of the text.

The zoning text, like the map, is frequently amended, but less often. Some texts are revised every year or so to incorporate amendments, but this is not always the case. The authors know of one ordinance, adopted in 1955, that has been amended more than fifty times since without appearing in a new edition. To be sure what the provisions are, each amendment must be related to the text in chronological sequence, because some amendments have altered earlier ones. Fortunately, there is no charge for getting a copy of each amendment to this particular ordinance. In some communities, such a charge is made. Textual formats vary from place to place, but there is a surprising degree of uniformity. The principal reason for this is the fact that local governments get their zoning authority from their respective states, but with numerous conditions attached to safeguard against abuses of constitutional rights. Although a few communities have been given the authority to zone by the state constitution, and many more by special state statutes applying to specific localities, most have received authority from general state *enabling acts* affecting all local governments, or all in a particular population category. These general acts bear a strong resemblance to the Standard State Zoning Enabling Act published in 1922 by the U.S. Department of Commerce.

The enabling acts are designed to assure compliance with the "equal protection" and "due process" requirements that we have already mentioned. In a sense, the "equal protection" clause is responsible for the basic concept of zoning. An ordinance that regulated each parcel of land in a different manner would represent a flagrant violation of this requirement. On the other hand, one that attempted to apply the same regulations uniformly throughout the

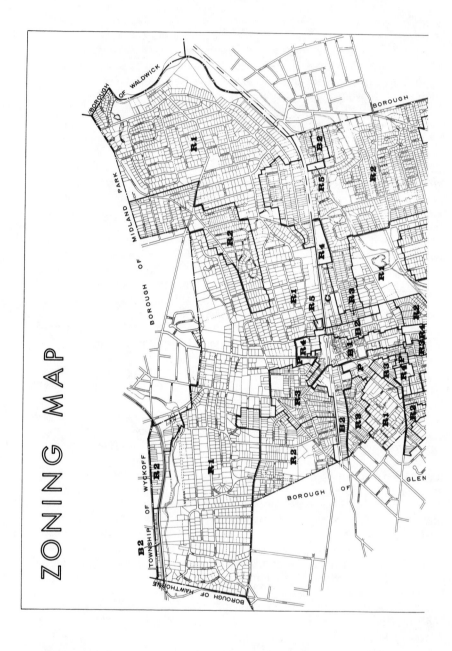

Figure 2-2

community would ordinarily be unworkable. (It should be noted that very small communities have been known to get along with only one zoning district each, but these are simply minor exceptions. For example, Bonwood, Tennesse, was incorporated in the early 1950s solely for the purpose of adopting a zoning ordinance. The area incorporated extended approximately 1500 feet along a major highway and approximately 250 feet on either side. Only one zoning district was created: *single-family residential*.)

Zoning is a compromise between the concept of treating each parcel differently and the concept of completely uniform treatment. It groups similar or compatible uses into classes in the text and similar properties into classes on the map. Although regulations are different between classes or districts, they are, in theory, uniform within any one district. The United States Supreme Court has upheld such classification where justification for the distinctions can be shown. In the landmark case of *Village of Euclid vs. Ambler Realty Company* in 1926, Justice Sutherland, in writing the majority opinion, used a rural analogy to sustain zoning, writing that "A nuisance may be merely a right thing in a wrong place, like a pig in a parlor instead of the barnyard."

The zoning text reflects a concern with constitutionality. It usually begins with a preamble full of generalities intended to justify what follows as having a "clear and reasonable relationship to the public health, safety, or welfare." A typical example of such a preamble is the following:

This Ordinance has been made in accordance with a comprehensive plan designed for the purposes, among others, of lessening congestion in the roads and streets, securing safety from fire and flood and other dangers, providing adequate light and air, promoting the health and general welfare, encouraging such distribution of population and such classification of land uses and distribution of land development and utilization as will tend to facilitate economic and adequate provisions for transportation, communications, roads, airports, water supply, drainage, sanitation, education, recreation or other public requirements. These regulations have been made with reasonable considerations, among others, to the character of the districts and their peculiar suitability for particular uses, and with a general view of promoting desirable living conditions and its sustaining stability of neighborhoods, protecting property against blight and depreciation, and encouraging the most appropriate use of land in the city of Atlanta.

The statement of purpose is usually followed by several pages of definitions of the terms used in the ordinance. (In some texts, the definitions are near the end). These should be studied carefully, because some definitions are highly specialized. Persistence may be needed in finding particular definitions. For example, the term *single-family-attached dwelling* might be found not in that form, but as *dwelling, single-family-attached* or as *attached dwelling, single-family*.

After the definitions, the typical zoning text contains a section listing the districts into which the community is being divided. Often these are merely identified by name and symbol, but sometimes they are accompanied by terse descriptions and statements of purpose. The number of districts included varies widely according to the size and heterogeneity of the community. The section setting forth the districts also contains several other provisions referring to the zoning map, interpretation of boundaries theoreon, and providing for the automatic zoning of annexed territory.

Following the section identifying the districts, the typical ordinance finally deals with regulations. These regulations are of two kinds: *general provisions* and *district provisions*. The order of their presentation varies. As the basic concept of zoning has to do with district provisions, these will be considered first.

District provisions fall into two separate categories: *use regulations*, which specify the uses to be permitted; and *development standards*, which specify permitted heights, bulk and lot coverage of buildings, and required lot area, lot width, lot frontage, yards, setbacks, open space, buffers, and off-street parking and loading. Many early ordinances contained two different sets of districts with a different map for each, one for use districts and one for height, area, and yard districts. Although a few of these might still be in existence, the practice now is to combine the two kinds of regulations. In most texts, the provisions are in prose, but tabular presentations are found in many ordinances.

There are three basic groups of districts: *residential, commercial*, and *industrial*. Suburban ordinances are likely to include *rural districts*, and many ordinances also contain *special districts*, some of which, such as airport-approach districts or floodplain districts, are superimposed on the others. In older ordinances, the districts are arranged in a hierarchy beginning with the most restricted (in terms of uses allowed), usually a single-family category, and proceeding in step-by-step fashion to the least restricted, usually a heavy-industrial category. Often each district permits all uses allowed in the preceding, more restricted districts plus one or more additional uses. Under this arrangement, called *cumulative-use* or *pyramid* zoning, industry is not permitted in residential districts, but residences are permitted in industrial districts. This approach has been altered in recent years by the introduction of a modified "exclusive-use" concept, so that the uses permitted in a given district do not necessarily include all uses permitted in the preceding, "more-restricted" ones. (*Note*: The *exclusive-use* concept should not be confused with *exclusionary* zoning, which is a term denoting discrimination against housing for particular races or income groups).

A common format for the listing of uses is shown in the following excerpt from the zoning regulations of Memphis, Tennessee for the "C-1 Neighborhood Shopping District":

(A) *Use Regulations*. A building or premises shall be used only for the following purposes:

1. Any use permitted in The R-4 Multiple Dwelling District except two-family, townhouses, multi-family dwelling and/or rooming and boarding houses.

2. Theatre, except open-air drive-in theatre; provided however, that no theatre shall be erected or reconstructed unless there is provided on the same lot, or within three hundred (300) feet thereof and within this district, a space for off-street parking which contains an area adequate to accommodate one (1) automobile for every five (5) seats in the theatre.

3. Bank.

4. Bakery employing no more than five (5) persons and when products are sold only at retail on the premises.

5. Barbershop, beauty parlor, chiropody, massage or similar personal service shop.

6. Bicycle sales and repair shop.

7. Business or commercial schools or dancing or music academies.

8. Catering and delicatessen business.

9. Custom dressmaking, millinery, tailoring, or similar retail trade, employing not more than five (5) persons on the premises.

10. Filling station.

11. Garage, storage.

12. Laundromats.

13. Locksmith shop.

14. Medical and dental clinic.

15. Messenger and telegraph service station.

16. Offices.

17. Parking space and lots for the parking of automobiles.

18. Photographer's studio.

19. Private schools including nursery, pre-kindergarten, kindergarten, play and special schools.

20. Receiving and delivery store for wet, dry, or steam cleaning, which shall be done elsewhere.

21. Restaurant.

22. Shoe repairing shop, employing not more than five (5) persons.

23. Shop for the repair of electrical and radio equipment and other similar commodities, employing not more than five (5) persons on the premises, and not involving the conduct of any manufacturing on the premises.

24. Store or shop for the conduct of retail business.

25. Accessory buildings, and uses customarily incident to the above listed uses, including advertising signs and billboards, provided they are erected flat against a wall of a building or within eighteen (18) inches thereof; provided further, however, that signs not exceeding thirty-five (35) square feet in area may be constructed without reference to the above limitations.

Any buildings used primarily for any of the above enumerated purposes may have not more than twenty-five (25) percent of the floor area devoted to storage purposes incidental to such primary use.

Use listings may also be in tabular form, as shown by excerpts from the Tallahassee, Florida, ordinance in Figure 2-3.

The uses enumerated in a text are not exhaustive, and new uses are continually appearing. Unitl the ordinance can be amended to list additional uses, the zoning administrator (usually the building official) is responsible for deciding which category of uses listed has the greatest similarity to the proposed use and, therefore, which districts will permit the new use. Appeals from such interpretations of the administrator can be made to a *Board of Adjustment* (also called *Board of Appeals*), usually a group of lay citizens appointed for staggered terms to serve as a quasi-judicial body.

Figure 2-3 Tabular use listings. Excerpts from ordinance of Tallahassee, Florida.

R-1 Single Family Residential District

1. District Intent

The provisions of the R-1 District are intended to apply to urban areas with low to medium densities, wherein certain educational, religious, non-commercial recreational and other activities compatible with residential development are permitted. The regulations of these districts are intended to protect and preserve the single family residential character and to discourage densities exceeding 3.63 dwelling units per net residential acre.

PERMITTED USES

2. Unrestricted Uses	b. Accessory Uses	3. Restricted Uses
a. Principal Uses		a. Use
(1) Single family dwellings.	(1) Greenhouses, not to exceed two (2) percent of lot area.	(1) Churches and schools.
(2) Parks and playgrounds.	(2) Customary accessory uses and structures, including private garages, clearly incidental to one or more permitted uses and structures.	(2) Golf courses and country clubs excluding miniature or carpet golf and driving ranges.

R-2 Single Family Residential District

1. District Intent

The provisions of the R-2 District are intended to apply to urban areas with low to medium densities, wherein certain educational, religious, non-commercial recreational and other activities compatible with residential de-

PERMITTED USES

2. Unrestricted Uses	b. Accessory Uses	3. Restricted Uses
a. Principal Uses		a. Use
	(1) Customary accessory uses and structures, including private garages, clearly incidental to one or more permitted uses and structures.	(1) Churches and schools.
		(2) Golf courses and country clubs excluding miniature or carpet golf and driving ranges.

Figure 2-3 (continued)

velopment are permitted. The regulations of these districts are intended to protect and preserve the single family residential character and to discourage densities exceeding 4.84 dwelling unit per net residential acre.

RM-1 Single, Two and Multiple Family Residential District

1. District Intent

The provisions of the RM-1 District are intended to apply to urban areas with low to medium densities, wherein a variety of housing types and certain educational, religious, non-commercial recreational and other activities compatible with residential development are permitted. The regulations of this district are intended to protect and preserve the residential character and to discourage densities exceeding 17.4 dwelling units per net residential acre.

USES PERMITTED

2. Unrestricted Uses

a. Principal Uses

(1) Single family dwellings.

(2) Two family dwellings.

(3) Multiple-family dwellings.

(4) Townhouses.

b. Accessory Uses

(1) Customary accessory uses and structures, clearly incidental to one or more permitted uses and structures, including coin operated laundries, recreation buildings and the like.

3. Restricted Uses

a. Use

(1) Churches and schools.

(2) Recreational clubs, intended to serve the surrounding residential area.

(3) Golf courses and country clubs excluding miniature or carpet golf and driving ranges.

(4) Kindergartens, nurseries, and child care facilities.

RM-2 Multiple Family Residential District

	USES	PERMITTED	
1. District Intent	**2. Unrestricted Uses**		**3. Restricted Uses**
	a. Principal Uses	**b. Accessory Uses**	**a. Use**
The provisions of the RM-2 District are intended to apply to urban areas with medium densities, wherein multiple family dwellings are the only permitted housing type and certain educational, religious and non-commercial recreational and other activities compatible with residential development are permitted. The regulations of this district are intended to protect and preserve the residential character and to discourage 25 dwelling units per net residential acre.	(1) Multiple family dwellings.	(1) Customary accessory uses and structures, clearly incidental to one or more permitted uses and structures, including coin operated laundries, recreation buildings, and the like.	(1) Recreational clubs. (2) Golf courses and country clubs excluding miniature or carpet golf and driving ranges. (3) Kindergartens, nurseries, and child care facilities. (4) Churches and schools.

At one time, it was a common practice to list *prohibited* uses rather than *permitted* uses. This practice has lost favor, because it placed on the local government the responsibility for justifying the denial of a permit for a similar but non-listed use. Where *permitted* uses are listed, the burden of proving the similarity of an unlisted use is usually on the developer.

Most uses listed as permitted in a particular zoning district are usually what are known as *uses-by-right*. If a land owner or developer complies with all other requirements, then there is no question about the issuance of a permit for one of these uses. A person can buy property with a known zoning designation and be assured that it can be developed for the uses listed for that district. At one time nearly all uses in zoning ordinances were *uses-by-right*. Over the last twenty years, however, there has been another kind of use appearing with increasing frequency. This is the *conditional use*, which, although listed in a particular district, is permitted only after a public hearing and the approval of a board or commission. Conditional uses may also be called *special uses* or *special exceptions*. The 1970 zoning ordinance of The City of New Kensington, Pennsylvania, for example, refers to them as *special exceptions* that may be granted by the zoning hearing board if specified criteria are met. This board is apparently similar to a board of adjustment. In Atlanta, Georgia, on the other hand, the conditional use is referred to as a *special-use permit* to be granted or denied by the city council.

The following provides an example of the listing of both *uses-by-right* and *conditional uses*:

Uses by Right	Conditional Uses

R-3 HIGH-DENSITY RESIDENTIAL DISTRICT

Uses by Right	Conditional Uses
One-family dwellings	Fire stations
Two-family dwellings	Hospitals
Multiple-family dwellings	Municipal buildings
Churches—places of worship	Nursery/business schools
Dormitories	Nursing/convalescent homes
Fraternity/sorority houses	Off-street parking lots
Libraries and museums	Planned residential development
Parks and playgrounds	Private clubs
Schools and colleges	Rooming/boarding homes
Funeral homes	Utility substations
Accessory uses	
Essential services	

Uses by Right	Conditional Uses

R-4 TRANSITIONAL RESIDENTIAL DISTRICT

Uses by Right	Conditional Uses
One-family dwellings	Hotels and motels
Two-family dwellings	Gift shop, eating places, Pharmacy related to above or primary permitted uses
Three and four-family dwellings	
Cemeteries	Multiple-family dwellings
Dormitories	Off-street parking lots
Fraternity/sorority houses	Personal service
Funeral homes	Planned residential development
Greenhouse/nurseries	Professional services
Home occupations	Research laboratories
Medical clinics	Utility substations
Nursery/business schools	Community garage
Nursing/convalescent homes	
Private clubs	
Public/semipublic uses	
Rooming/boarding homes	
Accessory uses	
Essential services	

C-1 LOCAL BUSINESS DISTRICT

Uses by Right	Conditional Uses
Banks and business offices	Drive-in businesses
Eating and drinking places	Gasoline service stations
Personal services	Multiple-family dwellings
Private clubs	Off-street parking lots
Professional services	Planned residential development
Public semipublic uses	Theaters
Retail business	Community garage
Accessory uses	
Essential services	

C-2 GENERAL BUSINESS DISTRICT

Uses by Right	Conditional Uses
Automobile sales	Animal care
Banks and business offices	Drive-in businesses
Business services	Gasoline service stations

Uses by Right	Conditional Uses
Commercial recreation	Mobile home and trailer sales
Eating and drinking places	Multiple-family dwellings
Hotels and motels	Off-street parking lots
Personal services	Planned residential development
Private clubs	Research laboratories
Professional services	Service garage
Public/semipublic uses	Community garage
Retail business	
Theaters	
Accessory uses	
Essential services	

Distinctions between zoning districts are based primarily upon the uses permitted and secondarily upon the requirements specified for height, yards, area, and other development standards. Some districts differ only in development standards. Thus, although there are only five broad categories of districts—*residential, commercial, industrial, rural,* and *special*—numerous subcategories are not uncommon. For example, a city with a 500,000 population might have as many as twelve residential districts, six commercial districts, three industrial districts, an airport approach district, a floodplain district, and an historical preservation district. For the zoning novice who tries to comprehend the rationale underlying this myriad of districts, the following cautions may be helpful:

1. A zoning ordinance is seldom based on a single comprehensive set of goals, objectives, and policies.

2. It is common for a community contemplating a new zoning ordinance, or an amendment thereto, to draw freely on language, standards, and concepts found in the ordinances of other communities without always having a complete understanding of the rationale involved.

3. Amendments are often made on an ad hoc basis in response to specific pressing problems with little thought as to how each amendment relates to the ordinance as a whole.

4. In short, there is much in a typical zoning ordinance that is there because it is there, and, as arbitrary as it may be, it will remain there until either adequate substitutes are found or the arbitrary provisions are deemed to be unnecessary.

Although zoning has been in vogue in the United States for more than fifty years, present-day ordinances often contain a surprising number of legacies from those of fifty years ago. In fact zoning is such a product of evolution, that some knowledge of its origins is necessary for an understanding of why it is what it is today. Despite the existence of piecemeal ordinances covering portions of cities and selected uses as far back as the late nineteenth century, the ancestor of the contemporary zoning ordinance is generally considered to be the New York City Ordinance of 1916. A fascinating account of the events leading to its adoption is given by Seymour I. Toll in his book, *Zoned American*.[1] These events involved two major areas of controversy: the uncontrolled heights and ground coverage of structures in lower Manhattan and the rapid encroachment of the garment industry on the carriage-trade merchants in Midtown Manhattan. The average American city had no problems on such a scale. Having other problems that might be solved through a similar kind of regulation, however, smaller cities adapted the basic concepts of the New York precedent to their own needs.

During the 1920s, zoning swept the nation's cities like a fad. According to the U.S. Department of Commerce, there were only thirty-five ordinances in 1920, but 981 in 1930, and these covered sixty-seven percent of the nation's urban population.[2] Small towns as well as cities responded, according to John Delafons.

The remarkable popularity of zoning with small communities is shown by the statistics: of the 1,236 ordinances in force in 1932, 563 were for towns of 1,000 to 10,000 inhabitants, and ninety-three were for villages of less than 1,000.[3]

A typical example of a zoning ordinance of the 1920s is the one adopted by Memphis, Tennessee, in 1922.[4] This set of regulations, which is reproduced in Appendix A, although far simpler than those encountered today, had a definite family resemblance. Note, for example, the height limit of thirty-five (35) feet or two and one-half (2½) stories" in the most-restricted residential district. The same standard is in widespread use today, even in communities characterized by single-story dwellings. Note also, however, that the early Memphis ordinance had two different sets of maps: "Use Districts" and "Height and Area Districts." In contemporary ordinances, these are combined.

To appreciate the thinking that went into the ordinances of the 1920s, it is necessary to visualize the land-use and transportation patterns of the decade. The nation entered the twenties with a transportation system still dominated by steam railways and electric streetcar lines. Horse- and mule-drawn conveyances were still ubiquitous, but automotive vehicles, now in mass production, were rapidly taking over the off-rail functions and threatening to usurp some of the functions of rail transportation. Industrial activity was still closely tied to the relatively fixed locations of steam railways, and commercial and residential uses were similarly bound to the fixed locations of trolley-car lines, which converged on the central business district (downtown). In a few very

---

[1] Seymour I. Toll, *Zoned American*, New York: Grossman Publishers, 1969.

[2] Norman L. Knauss, *Zoned Municipalities in the United States*. Washington: U.S. Department of Commerce, Bureau of Standards, Division of Building and Housing, 1931 (mimeographed), pp. 1 and 7.

[3] John Delafons, *Land Use Controls in The United States*, 2d ed., Cambridge, Mass.: M.I.T. Press, 1969, p. 29.

[4] The 1922 ordinance was replaced in 1955. In 1975, work was begun on a replacement for the 1955 ordinance.

large cities, there were subway and elevated lines reinforcing the determinative role of fixed-rail transportation.

Residential areas, except those for the affluent, were characterized by narrow lots, which served to minimize walking distances to streetcar lines and to the retail convenience shops along them. Few homes had mechanical refrigerators, depending instead upon "ice boxes," which had limited capability for keeping perishable foods. It was necessary, therefore, for grocery stores to be close to homes, and the close relationship was not always a pleasant one. The fresh produce and live poultry attracted flies and rodents in addition to emitting obnoxious odors.

Industrial buildings, not having the advantages of air conditioning and modern artificial lighting, had numerous windows that not only transmitted light and air to the inside but also allowed the noise, fumes, and dust given off by the operations performed inside to escape to the outside. Steam power produced by coal-fired boilers was still common, resulting in an industrial atmosphere characterized by soot and the acrid scent of smoke from bituminous coal.

The twenties were not static, however. Annual non-farm housing starts rose from 247,000 in 1920 to more than 800,000 in the years 1923–1927. By 1929 they were back down to 509,000, but this volume was not exceeded again until 1939. Automobile registration rose from 8,132,000 in 1920 to 23,121,000 in 1929. City governments responded to this increase by making large-scale improvements to streets in the form of widenings, straightenings, extensions, repaving, and grade separations at railroad crossings. The private sector responded with filling stations and other automobile-oriented businesses, especially along the newly improved arterial streets. Blocks that were formerly residential began to experience inroads from these new uses that were not tied to streets with trolley-car lines.

In the absence of zoning, a homeowner was disadvantaged in fighting commercial encroachment into a residential area. Only two possible remedies were available, and these were often inadequate. A sometime remedy was the old *common law of nuisance,* which did, and still does, permit a property owner suffering damages through the activities of a neighbor to obtain a court order stopping such activities and, in some instances, to obtain compensation. In practice, the need to pay an attorney, the fact that the burden was on the homeowner to prove damages from the nuisance, and the strong reluctance of judges to restrain alleged nuisances in advance of occurence combined to discourage attempts to use this common law as a remedy.

Another possible remedy was through enforcement of *subdivision deed restrictions.* Deed restrictions are a form of private contract applicable to all lots in a given subdivision. Any purchaser of a lot automatically becomes a party to the contract, which sets forth regulations similar to those found in a zoning ordinance. While useful as a supplement to zoning, deed restrictions have serious shortcomings when used as a complete substitute, as the homeowner of the 1920s discovered. If the offensive use is outside the subdivision proper, then no action can be taken because it is not subject to the restrictions. If inside the subdivision, then action might be taken, but only after hiring a lawyer. If action is not initiated soon enough, then the homeowner might be caught by the doctrine of "laches," which means simply that if you see a violation taking place and do nothing to stop it, then you may forfeit your right to do so.

It is understandable, then, that homeowners embraced zoning as a means of exercising stronger control over neighborhood land uses. Many, in fact, viewed zoning as little more than a device for getting the city to enforce the private deed restrictions. As a result, early ordinances often incorporated the private restrictions in a piecemeal fashion. For example, additional depths for front yards might be required on certain streets over and above what the district regulations specified.

Distinctions Between Residential Districts

Keeping in mind this historical background, we can begin our consideration of the distinctions between districts by looking at the broad category of residential districts. It is common for ordinances to have the following kind of breakdown:

1. One or more districts restricted to *single-family, detached dwellings* and "accessory" uses, the distinctions between the districts being based upon the following requirements: minimum lot area, minimum lot frontage or width, minimum yard dimensions, maximum height, and maximum lot coverage. In some ordinances, there are also distinctions related to minimum floor area, and in many suburban ordinances, there are differences in terms of animals permitted. "Accessory" uses are non-dwelling uses that are incidental to them (garages, storage sheds, greenhouses, for example).

2. One or more districts permitting *two-family* dwellings in addition to *single-family, detached dwelling* and accessory uses and with distinctions based on the same kinds of requirements outlined for the single-family districts.

3. One or more districts permitting *multifamily* (apartment) structures in addition to the single-family and two-family dwellings. The differences between these districts are often related to the following requirements: height, lot area per unit, yard dimensions, maximum lot coverage, and unit types (efficiency, one-bedroom, etc.). In addition, some ordinances make reference to the minimum floor area of each unit, and some distinguish between *garden apartments* (those with direct outside access for each unit) and *flats* (those having access only through a central lobby). The more sophisticated ordinances are apt to differentiate on the basis of "floor/area ratio" and "usable open space," terms that will be explained later. It is not uncommon for some multifamily districts to permit limited retail and hotel usage.

Another basic grouping that is not uncommon, especially in the northeastern United States, is one involving *single-family, attached* dwellings (also called *townhouses, row houses,* and *zero-lot-line development*).

The primary differences between the various residential districts have to do with the kinds of structures ("dwelling types") permitted and represent a legacy from the 1920s that still has strong acceptance today. It involves an implied hierarchy of residential uses in terms of desirability, with the single-family dwelling at the top. In part, this thinking is an outgrowth of the strong emphasis upon the value of real property ownership in our country. Translated from the rural frontier to newly developed subdivision, it results in the treatment of the single-family house and lot as a "homestead" and of the apartment house as an un-American holdover from the feudal system.

Such an attitude did not lack for a substantive basis in the 1920s. Prior to the enactment of zoning, apartment structures were commonly built to yard setbacks no greater, and even less, than those for single-family structures, even though the apartments might be much taller. As the requirements for yards and open space for apartments have been increased over the years, however, the firm bias toward apartments as being "inferior" to single-family development has continued. As Richard F. Babcock put it in his delightful book, *The Zoning Game*, "The primary, if not the exclusive, purpose in the 1920s was to protect the single-family district and that objective is foremost four decades later."[5]

Next to the factor of dwelling type, the most important basis for differentiating among residential districts is density. (A few ordinances use density as the primary basis). This can be expressed as "units per acre," but more frequently, it is specified as "square feet of lot area per dwelling unit." Converting from one approach to the other is simple if it is remembered that one acre equals 43,560 square feet.

Although density is, in reality, an integral part of the use distinctions, it is not always considered as such. In a community where use variances are prohibited, the board of adjustment will sometimes view density not as a component of use but rather as a development standard, which can be varied. Thus, a variance might be granted for apartments at twenty units per acre instead of the normally required fifteen per acre on the grounds that the use, in either case, would be for apartments and that only a development standard would be altered.

Commercial Districts

In the context of zoning, the word *commercial* has a broad connotation encompassing retail and personal services, offices, wholesale activities, and business services. At that end of the commercial spectrum where it borders on residential, there is a fuzziness regarding hotels and certain home occupations, such as music instruction. Similarly, at the end of the spectrum bordering on industrial uses, there is a fuzziness regarding warehousing, major repair activities, sales of heavy merchandise (such as building materials), and some business services (such as printing).

A typical zoning ordinance will contain the following kinds of commercial districts:

1. One or more districts designated according to the area intended to be served, e.g., "Neighborhood Business District."

2. One or more designated according to assumed nuisance level of the uses; e.g., "Limited Retail," "Heavy Commercial."

3. A "Central Business District" if the ordinance is for a community having a downtown area.

[5]Richard F. Babcock, *The Zoning Game*, Madison, Wis.: University of Wisconsin Press, 1969, p. 6.

4. One or more highway-oriented districts, particularly if the ordinance includes suburban areas, to take care of the strips of service stations, fast-food franchises, used-car dealers, and the like.

5. One or more "floating zones" for planned shopping centers.

Other common kinds of districts include, in the suburbs, zones for office and research parks, and, in the cities, zones designed for older residential areas undergoing transition to commercial uses and in which some degree of peaceful coexistence between residential and commercial is desired during the transition.

Distinctions between commercial districts are more complex than those between residential areas. To the extent that they are rational, they reflect an ambivalence resulting from conflicting goals. Illustrating this ambivalence are the following four approaches often used in outlining the commercial districts of a zoning ordinance:

1. The *degree-of-obnoxiousness* approach

2. The *degree-of-necessity* approach

3. The *retail-compatibility* approach

4. The *intensity-of-use* approach

Let us examine each of these approached briefly.

Degree-of-Obnoxiousness Approach

This is an obvious approach involving the categorization of uses according to their degree of obnoxiousness to (a) nearby residential areas and (b) other businesses. "Obnoxious" factors often considered in weighing detriment to residential areas are:

1. Noise

2. Traffic and parking on residential streets

3. Glare (from signs or headlights)

4. Odors and fumes

5. Immorality of activities

6. Boisterous or otherwise unsavory patrons

7. Psychological effects, i.e., the lack of prestige associated with an activity; or its possible connotations of death or sickness; or visual unattractiveness because of gaudy signs, and absence of yards or landscaping; or the open storage of unsightly materials, e.g., old tires and mufflers.

8. Health hazards, e.g., the attraction of flies and rodents.

As zoning involves the granting of permission for a use before it is established, these factors usually cannot be measured. Instead, the uses are classified with the probability of detrimental effects in mind, that is to say, a rough idea of the probability, for the rationale is far from being precise. What happens is that the uses are placed in one district or another according to the experience obtained with the uses in that community or in another community. As a result, some of the decisions may be arbitrary, and others may be based upon obsolete, biased, or otherwise inadequate evidence.

Degree-of-Necessity Approach

This approach looks at commercial uses according to the necessity for having them close to residential uses and to other commercial uses. For example, a convenience store selling milk, bread, and other foods, especially at hours, and on days, when supermarkets might be closed, is more necessary to a residential area than, say, a dress shop. It would therefore be included in a "Neighborhood Business District" classification even though the dress shop (ordinarily a less obnoxious use) might be excluded.

Retail-Compatibility Approach

This approach mainly applies to districts intended to be used in retail areas characterized by diverse ownership of land and buildings—in other words, outside of planned shopping centers. In order for such an area to remain viable for shopping, uses that might tend to disrupt, or otherwise discourage, the flow of pedestrian traffic between shops must be kept out. For example, a service station would not reinforce the other business by generating pedestrian traffic. Furthermore, the vehicles entering and leaving it would provide hazards for pedestrians, thereby discouraging their movements between shops on either side. A furniture store would generally be out of place in the middle of a community business center because of its small volume of pedestrians generated per foot of frontage. Shops specializing in used merchandise might be considered out of place in a high-priced boutique center on the grounds that the kind of pedestrian traffic vital to the boutique shops would be repulsed thereby. The relationships between compatible and incompatible retail uses have been brought together in some excellent tables by Richard Nelson in his book *The Selection of Retail Locations*.[6]

Intensity-of-Use Approach

Relying upon mathematical measurements of a sort, this approach is somewhat more sophisticated than the three previously described. What it does is to limit the extent to which a premises may be used for a particular activity by restricting total floor space, number of employees, hours of operations, capacity of machinery, of other similar factors. For example, laundries and dry cleaners might be permitted as follows:

C-1: *Neighborhood Business District*
Laundry and dry cleaning pick-up establishment where no laundering or dry cleaning is done on premises

[6]Richard L. Nelson, *The Selection of Retail Locations*, New York: F. W. Dodge Corporation, 1958.

C-2: *Community Business District*
    Laundry and dry cleaning establishment employing not more than fifteen persons and having a boiler capacity no greater than fifty horsepower

C-3: *General Commercial District*
    Laundry and dry cleaning establishment having a boiler capacity no greater than seventy-five horsepower

C-4: *Heavy Commercial District*
    Laundry and dry cleaning without special restrictions

For retail establishments such as bakeries, which, in a sense, manufacture what they sell, there is often a requirement in the more restricted districts that all goods must be sold on premises. This, of course, is intended to prevent a predominantly retail use in a residential neighborhood from being converted into a manufacturing operation. Similarly, establishments that both sell and service appliances may be limited in the number of square feet or the percentage of total floor area devoted to the repair activities in an effort to preserve their basic retail character.

A more involved version of floor-area limitations is the device known as *floor/area ratio*, or *F.A.R.* This is simply the ratio between the total floor area of a building and the area of the parcel upon which it is located. For example, an F.A.R. limitation of 5.0 means that on a lot with an area of, say, 20,000 square feet, the total floor area of building(s) may not exceed 100,000 square feet. This device will be discussed in more detail in Chapter 4.

City planners and other city administrators tend to like the intensity-of-use approach because, theoretically at least, it makes it possible to avert the overloading of trafficways, sewers, water mains, and other public facilities. In practice, the restrictions are sometimes difficult to enforce. Imagine telling a retailer that he may not add one more employee or ten additional square feet of floor area to a thriving business!

Example

Now that we have considered several different approaches to the listing of commercial uses, let's look at an actual ordinance and see how the districts differentiated. The Village of Ridgewood, New Jersey, a suburb with a population of 27,547 in 1970, has six commercial districts in its ordinance: B-1, B-2, C, P, OB, and OB-2. The "B-1 Retail Business District" permits, in addition to certain institutional, public, and utility uses, the following:

Antique shops, appliance shops, art studios, art supply shops, automobile display sales rooms without customary servicing as an accessory use, banks and savings and loan associations and similar institutions, barber shops, beauty parlors, bicycle shops, book stores, brokerage houses, butcher shops, camera stores, card shops, cigar stores, cleaning, dyeing and pressing done exclusively for individual retail customers but not including work done for the trade or the wholesale market, clothing and dress shops, confectioneries, coin stores, dance studios, delicatessens, department stores, drapers, drug stores, finance companies, flower shops, furniture and furnishing stores, gift shops, grocery stores, haberdashers, hardware and paint stores, hobby shops, interior decorators, jewelers, leather goods shops, linen stores, liquor stores, music and record shops, novelty shops, office equipment stores, parking lots and buildings as a principal or accessory use, pet shops, photographers, radio and TV sales and repair shops, restaurants, retail bakeries, shoe repair shops, shoe sales stores, sporting goods stores, stamp stores, stationers, tailor shops, taverns and inns, theaters, tobacconists, toy stores, travel and ticket agencies and undertaking establishments; provided, however, that none of the foregoing permitted uses shall carry merchandise other than that intended to be sold at retail on the premises.

All uses must be conducted within the confines of a building.

The "B-2 Retail Business District" permits all of the uses allowed in the B-1 district plus the following:

Apartment hotels, boarding houses, billiard rooms, bowling alleys, buildings used for club, fraternal, recreational, athletic or social purposes, coin-operated self-service laundries and dry cleaning and accessory uses, shop of an electrician or similar tradesman, franchised new-car dealer showrooms and customary accessory uses and used-car lots as an accessory use thereto, provided, however, that there shall not be more than one square foot of area devoted to used-car lot use for each square foot of all buildings devoted to new-car dealer use, furniture mover, hand laundries, hotels, inns, lodging houses, newspaper or job printing plants, shop of a plumber or similar tradesman, telephone and telegraph business offices, and telephone and telegraph equipment offices.

Public garages and gasoline service stations as regulated in Article 5 of this Ordinance, but not including car washing as a principal use.

All uses must be conducted within the confines of a building unless specifically permitted outdoors.

The "C Commercial District" permits all uses allowed in the B-2 district plus the following:

(a) Auto body repair shop, cleaning, dyeing, pressing, tailoring and laundering or like operations done for the trade or on a wholesale basis, jobbing or distributing establishment, storage warehouse, storage yard supplying coal, wood, oil and building materials, welding shop, wholesale business and wood-working shop.

(b) Light machine shop and limited manufacturing, processing and fabrication of products and materials, provided, however, the operations for any such permitted use shall not exceed the limitations imposed by the performance standards set forth in Section 2004 of this Ordinance; also veterinarian hospitals and establishments wholly contained in a soundproof building or buildings.

All uses must be conducted inside a building unless specifically permitted outdoors.

The "P Professional and Office District" is limited to: Business, professional, or administrative offices not engaged in retail or wholesale sales of goods on the premises and not engaged in the repair or servicing of goods thereon.

This district also permits single-family dwellings under certain conditions plus institutional and municipal uses and public utilities.

The "O-B Office Building District" is limited to: Professional or administrative office buildings, banks, savings and loan associations, finance companies, or similar financial institutions or companies.

The district also permits institutional and municipal and municipal uses and public utilities.

The "O-B-2 Office Building District" permits the uses allowed in the O-B district plus:

In additional thereto veterinary hospitals shall be permitted provided the entire operation including animal runs is conducted within the confines of an enclosed sound-proof building.

We leave it to the reader to conclude which approaches were used in differentiating between these districts.

Industrial Districts

A typical zoning ordinance contains two or three industrial districts designated by such imaginative terms as "Light Industrial," "Medium Industrial," and "Heavy Industrial." Distinctions between them are based generally upon the degree-of-obnoxiousness approach, but, in most communities, the result is a somewhat arbitrary set of listings derived from a combination of experience and other ordinances. As of 1976, for example, both Memphis, Tennessee, and Atlanta, Georgia, had industrial listings of "prohibited" uses similar to the listing used in the Memphis ordinance of 1922 that is reproduced in Appendix A.[7] The listings of "permitted" uses for an ordinances with two industrial districts might be as follows:

LIGHT INDUSTRIAL—M-1 DISTRICT

No building or structure or part thereof shall be erected, altered or used, nor land or water used, in whole or part for other than one or more of the following uses:

(1) Any commercial use permitted in a C-5 District.

(2) USES to be conducted wholly within a completely enclosed building, except for on site parking or delivery vehicles which are incidental thereto.

   (a) The manufacturing or processing of such products as bakery goods, candies, cosmetics, dairy products, drugs, perfumes, pharmaceuticals, perfumed toilet soap, toiletries, and food products, excluding sauerkraut, vinegar, yeast.

   (b) The manufacturing, compounding, assembling or treatment of articles or merchandise from the following previously prepared materials: bones, cellophane, canvas, cloth, cork, feathers, felt, fiber, fur, glass, horns, hair, leather, paper, plastics, precious and semiprecious metals or stones, shells, textiles, tobacco, wood (excluding planning mills), yarns, and paint not employing a boiling process.

   (c) The manufacture of pottery and figurines, or other ceramic products using only previously pulverized clay and kiln-fired only by electricity or gas.

   (d) Manufacture of metal products.

   (e) Manufacturing of musical instruments, toys, novelties, and rubber and metal stamps.

   (f) Automotive assembly plant and battery manufacturing.

   (g) Machine shops.

   (h) Assembly of electrical appliances, electronics instruments and devices, radio and phonograph, including the manufacturing of small parts only, such as coils, condensers, transformers, crystal holders, and the like.

   (i) Poultry or rabbit live storage and killing incidental to a retail business on the same premises.

---

[7]As of 1976, both Atlanta and Memphis were engaged in comprehensive revisions of their ordinances.

(j) Plastics manufacturing.

(k) Ice manufacturing.

(3) The following miscellaneous uses:

(a) Boat building and repair.

(b) Railroad freight or passenger stations.

(4) The following uses if approved as a "conditional use":

(a) Concrete and cement products manufacturing.

(b) Brick, tile, or terra cotta manufacturing.

(c) Rock, sand, or gravel distribution.

(d) The manufacturing or processing of fish and meat products and the rendering or refining of fats and oils.

(5) Accessory USES and structures

GENERAL INDUSTRIAL—M-2 DISTRICT

No building or structure or part therof shall be erected, altered, or used or land or water used in whole or in part other than one or more of the following specified uses: (1) Any uses permitted in an M-1 District.

(2) Acetylene gas manufacturing or storage.

(3) Alcohol manufacturing.

(4) Ammonia, bleaching powder, or chlorine manufacturing.

(5) Brick, tile, or terra cotta manufacturing.

(6) Chemical manufacturing.

(7) Concrete or cement products manufacturing.

(8) Freight classification yard.

(9) Oil cloth or linoleum manufacturing.

(10) Paint, oil (including linseed), shellac, turpentine, lacquer, or varnish manufacturing.

(11) Potash works.

(12) Pyroxylene manufacturing.

(13) Railroad repair shops.

(14) Rock, sand, or gravel distribution.

(15) Sodium Compound Manufacturing.

(16) Stove or shoe polish manufacturing.

(17) The following USES if approved as a "conditional use."

(a) Gas manufacturing.

(b) Lamp black manufacturing.

(c) Paper and pulp manufacturing.

(18) Other uses not prohibited by law, not specifically permitted by this Ordinance and which is found to be similar in character to a *use* specifically permitted.

(19) Accessory uses and structures.

In the context of the 1920s, such an arbitrary classification might have been justifiable. In the intervening years, however, there has been much technological progress in manufacturing, thereby making it possible to judge the actual environmental performances of an operation in lieu of relying upon guilt by association. In many communities now, the industrial distinctions are grounded in what are known as "industrial performance standards." Generally these standards consist of quantified limits for various kinds of emissions as measured at the boundary of the parcel on which the activity is occurring. Noise, vibrations, smoke, and odors, for instance, might be limited as follows:

Noise

Every USE shall be so operated as to comply with the maximum performance standards governing noise described below. Objectionable noises due to intermittance, beat frequency, or shrillness shall be muffled or eliminated so as not to become a nuisance to adjacent USES. Sound levels shall be measured with a sound level meter and associated octave band filter manufactured according to standards prescribed by the American Standards Association.

Octave bands in cycles per second	Along property line abutting a residential district between 8:00 a.m. and 6:00 p.m.* Maximum permitted sound level in decibels	Along property line abutting in industrial or commercial district. Maximum permitted sound level in decibels
0–75	72	79
75–150	67	74
150–300	59	66
300–600	52	59
600–1,200	46	53
1,200–2,400	40	47
2,400–4,800	34	41
Over 4,800	32	39

*Permissible sound level between 6:00 p.m. and 8:00 a.m. shall be decreased by 3 decibels in each of the octave bands.

Vibration

Every USE shall be so operated that ground vibration inherently and recurrently generated is not perceptible, without instruments at any point on the property line of the property on which the USE is located.

No vibration at any time shall produce an acceleration of more than 0.1g or shall result in any combination of amplitudes and frequencies beyond the "safe" range of Table 7, U.S. Bureau of Mines Bulletin No. 442. The equations of said bulletin shall be used to determine the values for enforcement.

Smoke

Every USE shall be so operated as to prevent the emission of smoke, from any source whatever, to a density greater than described as Number 1 on the Ringlemann Smoke Chart, provided however, that smoke equal to, but not in excess of, that shade of appearance described as Number 2 on the Ringlemann Chart may be emitted for a period or periods totaling four minutes in any thirty minutes. For the purpose of grading the density of smoke, the Ringlemann Chart as published and used by the United States Bureau of Mines, and which is hereby made, by reference, a part of ARTICLES I to XXXVI shall be the standard. All measurements shall be at the point of emission.

Odors

Every USE shall be so operated as to prevent the emission of objectionable or offensive odors in such concentration as to be readily perceptible at any point at or beyond the lot line of the property on which the USE is located. There is a hereby established as a guide in determining the quantities of offensive odors Table III, Chapter 5, "Air Pollution Abatement Manual" of the Manufacturing Chemists' Association, Inc., Washington, D.C.

To a novice, performance standards might seem to be the answer to the problem of defining industrial classifications. Unfortunately, they have a number of shortcomings. In the first place, not all emissions are as easily quantified as noise, vibration, and smoke; and these, in fact, require more complex forms of measurement than the example would seem to indicate. Second, precise instruments are needed for some of the measurements, and not every community can afford them. Third, the successful enforcement of the standards requires skilled personnel and frequent monitoring. Some smaller communities have met the personnel requirements by contracting for consulting services, but this procedure does not always meet the need for frequent monitoring and for a prompt response to a complaint of violation. Finally, lay members of local boards, commissions, and councils frequently do not understand how to use performance standards. As one objector remarked at a public hearing where performance standards were proposed,

I don't care if I can't see it. I don't care if I can't hear it. I don't care if I can't smell it. I don't care if I can't feel it. I just don't even want to know that it's there!

Rural Districts

Rural districts are included in zoning ordinances for a number of diverse reasons. Some of these reasons are:

1. To provide locations for suburbanites who wish to keep horses and other animals not normally permitted in residential districts.

2. To provide a transitional or "holding" zone for land that will eventually be urbanized but the exact future use of which is not yet clear. (As we will point out later, comprehensive plans are often vague).

3. To protect bona fide farmers from tax assessments based on the market value for future urban uses rather than on the present agricultural value.

4. To conserve areas of scenic beauty, recreational potential, or ecological sensitivity.

5. To permit mineral extraction, sawmills, and agricultural processing without allowing general industrial uses on a permanent basis.

6. To make allowance for necessary rural services facilities such as crossroads stores.

A rural district in an actual ordinance might reflect two or more of these reasons in combination.

Special Districts

Zoning ordinances frequently include districts devised for special purposes that do not fit neatly into the categories of districts already described. For example, some ordinances have one or more *transitional districts* for the purpose of permitting older residential areas to be converted gradually but gracefully to office and institutional use. We will discuss here only three of the more common special districts: *airport approach districts, floodplain districts*, and *historical districts*.

Airport Approach Districts

Airport approach districts (also called *airport hazard zones and airspace safety zones*) are usually superimposed on the other use districts that we have described. That is to say, if a parcel of land is located in a C-3 Commercial District, it may also be in an AH Airport Hazard District, in which case it will be subject to the restrictions of both.

The primary purpose of an airport approach district is to limit the heights of structures so as to protect the safety of aircraft taking off and landing. The Federal Aviation Administration (FAA) regulates such structures even in the absence of local zoning controls, but enforcement is more effective if the federal regulations are incorporated into local zoning. Thus communities adjacent to airports generally adopt the FAA criteria.

In addition to adopting the FAA regulations, some communities also have limitations on uses that might involve concentrations of people. Theaters, churches, schools, and other places of public assembly are often banned within wedged-shaped areas extending outward several thousand feet from the end of each runway. The density of residential development may also be restricted over and above what is normally permitted. Restrictions of this kind are intended to protect the safety of persons on the ground. They are based on the assumption that areas under runway approaches are much more likely to experience crashes than are other areas. Support to this assumption was given by study made in the early 1950s by the President's Airport Commission, often called the "Doolittle Commission" because its chairman was General Jimmy Doolittle. This study included a description of crash locations over a period of several years in terms of the distance and angle of each from the end of the nearest runway. A high proportion of these locations was found to be within the wedge-shaped area extending out approximately 10,000 feet from the end of the runway. The findings were published by the Commission in 1952 in a report entitled *The Airport and its Neighbors*.

The findings of the Doolittle Commission were based on experience with piston-engine, propeller-driven aircraft. The authors are not aware of any up-dating of *The Airport and its Neighbors* to account for the experience with jet aircraft. It should be noted, however, that much of our aircraft activity is still comprised of piston-engine planes.

Jet aircraft have introduced an additional factor to be considered in airport zoning: noise. The noise generated by jet aircraft is far more obnoxious than that caused by piston-engine planes. Eventually most zoning ordinances encompassing approaches to major airports will probably restrict uses and structures located inside of the high-noise areas, so as to minimize human exposure to noise exceeding certain levels. For example, outdoor living areas, such as swimming pools and patios, would be prohibited. Buildings would have to be designed so as to provide acceptable noise levels inside. Despite the fact that jet aircraft have been in use for more than fifteen years, such regulations have had an unenthusiastic reception. Property owners whose ownership antedates airport expansions and jet operations apparently object to being restricted without compensation. Nevertheless, the movement is toward regulation of noise exposure. Various federal agencies such as the Department of Housing and Urban Development have already adopted noise-exposure criteria for projects in which they participate. A developer wishing to build houses in a high-noise area may find that financing is unobtainable. In time zoning ordinances will be amended to incorporate noise exposure controls.

Floodplain Districts

Floodplain (or flood hazard) districts, like airport approach districts, are generally superimposed on the conventional districts. They have three broad purposes:

1. To prevent obstructions to the flow of flood waters along freshwater streams

2. To prevent losses of life and property from:

   a. Freshwater flooding

   b. Tidal flooding

   c. Storm-driven waves along exposed coasts

3. To minimize governmental expenditures for protective works, rescue, relief, and reconstruction

Floodplain regulations vary according to (1) the local importance of each of these purposes and (2) the extent of development already exsiting in flood-plains. Obviously, if a city is largely in a floodplain already, then it would hardly be practical to stop all new building. Floodplain zoning, like zoning generally, often represents a compromise between goals and realities.

Floodplain zoning is based upon an assumed probability of flood occurrence. If it is based on a *twenty-year flood*, for example, then it is designed to restrict development in all areas that would be flooded *on the average* once every twenty years. It would also apply to areas flooded more frequently. It would not, however, apply to areas flooded less frequently. Thus in portions of the floodplain higher than the regulations cover, there is still a risk. In the higher portions of areas subject to a *one-hundred-year flood*, for example, there is a one percent chance of getting flooded in any given year. The assumed flood frequency used in floodplain zoning varies from locality to locality, but there is a trend toward use of the one-hundred-year flood in order to comply with the regulations of the National Flood Insurance Program. Congress established this program in 1968 and set up the Federal Insurance Administration (FIA) to administer it. The FIA has designated all areas having "a one percent annual chance of flooding" as "Areas of Special Flood Hazard." In order for property owners to remain eligible for the benefits of this program their local governments must adopt and enforce regulations approved by the FIA.

For every location within a regulated floodplain, there is a *base flood protection elevation*. This is simply the maximum height of the assumed flood, i.e., twenty-year, fifty-year, one-hundred-year. Along a freshwater river, the base elevation will be higher upstream than it will be downstream. Along a tidal estuary, it will not vary so much, although the existence of road and railroad embankments can lower flood levels somewhat by obstructing the incoming flood waters. To the extent that building is permitted within the regulated area, the lowest floor is normally required to be above the base flood protection elevation unless the structure is flood-proofed.

A typical set of floodplain regulations for a community on a tidal river might be as follows:

Special Flood Hazard Area

This section shall apply to all lands shown on the "Official Zoning Map" as being located within the boundaries of the Special Flood Hazard Area. These boundaries have been delineated on the basis of information obtained from *United States Department of Housing and Urban Development, Federal Insurance Administration*, and represent generally the limits of coastal flooding that can be expected on an average of once each 100 years. Where interpretation is needed as to the exact location of boundaries, the Board of Adjustment shall make the necessary interpretation. The Special Flood Hazard Area is superimposed upon existing zoning districts, and the requirements contained within this section are in addition to the requirements of the respective districts upon which the Special Flood Hazard Area is superimposed. The provisions of this section are not to be construed as permitting any use that is not permitted within those respective districts.

(A) *Purpose.* The purpose of this section is to minimize losses resulting from the occupancy of areas subject to periodic flooding, such losses including; loss of life and property, health and safety hazards, disruption of commerce and governmental services, extraordinary public expenditures for flood protection and relief, and impairment of the tax base, all of which adversely affect the public health, safety and general welfare.

(B) *Requirements.* Within the Special Flood Hazard Area, all structures must be constructed on fill or pilings, or elevated by other means, so that the first floor and basement floor are above the base flood protection elevation of 11.5 feet above mean sea level. Fill used for building sites shall consist of sand, gravel, or other sand foundation materials which will retain structural bearing capacity under saturated conditions. Silts, very fine sands, clays, peat, and other high organic soils subject to compaction or erosion shall not be used. Where wind or water erosion is a factor, fill shall be protected by bulkheads, rip-rap, planting beach grass or other vegetation, or other protective measures.

(C) *Uses Permitted*. The following uses which have low flood damage potential and do not threaten other lands during times of flood shall be permitted within the Special Flood Hazard Area to the extent that they are not otherwise prohibited by this Ordinance or by any other ordinance, and do not require structures, flood control works, substantial filling or grading, or storage of materials. But no use shall be permitted which adversely affects the capacity of the channels or floodways of streams, drainage ditches, or any other drainage facility or system.

(1) Agricultural uses such as general farming, pasture, grazing, outdoor plant nurseries, horticulture, viticulture, and truck farming.

(2) Private and public recreational uses such as tennis courts, driving ranges, archery ranges, picnic grounds, boat launching ramps, swimming areas, parks, wildlife and nature preserves, target ranges, and temporary structures for sale of food and refreshments, arts and crafts.

(3) Lawns, gardens, parking areas, loading areas, and play areas.

(D) *Special Exceptions*. The following uses may be authorized by the Board of Adjustment as special exceptions from the flood hazard requirements. No use may be permitted, however, if it is otherwise prohibited within the applicable zoning district.

(1) Structurally flood-proofed structures, with the first floor below the base flood protection elevation, where the existence of streets or utilities below flood elevations makes compliance with Subsection B impractical, or in other special circumstances. Structural floodproofing shall not be allowed for residences.

(2) Structures accessory to open space or Special Exception Uses.

(3) Circuses, carnivals, and similar transient amusement enterprises.

(4) Drive-in theaters, new and used car lots, roadside stands, signs and billboards.

(5) Marinas, yacht clubs, boat rentals, lighthouses, docks, piers, wharves, groins, sand dunes, bulkheads, seawalls, jetties, and harbor works.

(6) Railroads, streets, bridges, utility transmission lines, and pipelines.

(7) Storage yards for equipment, machinery, or materials.

(8) Kennels and stables.

(9) Other uses similar in character to the above uses.

(10) A residential structure on a lot of one-half acre or less in area that is surrounded, on adjoining lots, by existing structures not built in compliance with the flood hazard requirements.

Historical Districts

Many ordinances now contain provisions designed to preserve areas of particular historical significance. One of the first, that of Charleston, South Carolina, has the following statement of purpose:

The purpose of this article is to promote the educational, cultural, economic and general welfare of the public through the preservation and protection of the old, historic or architecturally worthy structures and quaint neighborhoods which impart a distinct aspect to the city of Charleston and which serve as a visible reminder of the history and cultural heritage of the city, the state and the nation.

The Charleston ordinance, adopted in 1931, superimposes "Old and Historic Districts" on its more conventional districts. In addition to the requirements of the other districts.

No structure within an Old and Historic District may be erected, demolished or removed in whole or in part, nor may the exterior architectural character of such a structure be altered until after an application for a building permit has been submitted to the board of architectural review and approved by it.

The Board of Architectural Review operates tactfully. An applicant who wished to coat his house with aluminum paint to "ward off radiation" was persuaded by the board that lead was a much better buffer, so the man used a leaded paint.

Summary

Earlier, in this chapter, we assumed that one of our mythical property owners, Mary Trigg, had set out to discover what was in her local zoning ordinance. We pointed out that she would have to consult both a *map* and a *text*, and we described a portion of the text: the preamble, the definitions, the listing of districts, and that part of the *district provisions* dealing with use regulations. We discussed the kinds of districts most likely to be encountered in a zoning ordinance and the rationale for them.

The next items to be considered in the text are those provisions setting *development standards*. Before proceeding with development standards, however, we are going to give Mary an opportunity to relate what she has learned about districts in the text to what appears on the official zoning map.

3
A Few Words About Maps and Boundaries

How is my property zoned?

Why is my undeveloped tract zoned 'R-1 Single Family Residential' instead of 'C-5 Warehousing'? It's right next to a railroad.

Why is my lot zoned 'C-1 Limited Commercial' when the property next door is 'C-2 General Commercial'? Why shouldn't I be able to look for the same kinds of business tenants as my neighbor? Why can't the boundary be moved one hundred feet to the west to include me in 'C-2'?

We have a nice single-family neighborhood, and I thought that all of it was zoned for single-family only. Last week a builder started putting up apartments on the vacant lots along the boulevard. We found out that those lots had been zoned for apartments ever since the zoning ordinance was adopted twenty years ago. How could that be?

Questions like these are serious concerns for property owners. Zoning affects the value of property. Having the "right" zoning on one's own property or the "wrong" zoning on a neighbor's property can make quite a difference in the income received from a lease or sale. The answers to such questions are not always easy to find, but the search for them is easy to begin. It starts with a look at the official *zoning map*, as our fictional pottery maker, Mary Trigg, discovered in Chapter 2.

The *zoning map* and the *zoning text*, as we pointed out in Chapter 2, are both parts of the *zoning ordinance*. Both are legally adopted, and neither one is useful without the other. In Chapter 2, we described different kinds of districts as set forth in the text of an ordinance, and we discussed the provisions of those districts. Now we need to turn our attention back to the map, which ties the textual provision to specific parcels of land.

The zoning map specifies precisely the location of district boundaries. The boundaries, in turn, enclose the geographic areas where the regulations of a particular district apply. The boundary lines on the map, therefore, are every bit as rigid as any wording contained in the text. In order to change a boundary, it is necessary to obtain an amendment to the map in much the same manner as one would go about getting the text amended. A change in the map, however, has a special name: *rezoning*.

Rezoning is a matter of such significance to property owners that several later chapters of this book will discuss in detail the nature of the process and the kinds of strategy and tactics used. In this chapter, we are going to concentrate on an explanation of why boundaries and districts are depicted as they are on the map.

The typical zoning map has a pattern of districts and boundaries that reflects diverse origins. In part it is a product of rational planning, and in part it is a recognition of what was already existing when the map was adopted. In large part it is the result of numerous amendments made in response to changing conditions and/or pressures from developers, speculators, and property owners. As the reasons for the boundaries are more easily understood than those for the district designations, we will explain them first.

We will begin by referring back to Mary Trigg's problem. Mary, you will recall, wants to make pottery in her home, which occupies Lot 17 in Runnymeade Park subdivision (see Figure 2-1). Lot 17 and all other lots along Vinton Avenue are zoned "R-3 Single-Family." Behind Mary's lot is commercial property fronting on Floral Boulevard. It is designated on the zoning map as "B-2 Community Business." The boundary between the "R-3" district and the "B-2" district runs right along Mary's rear lot line. If she could get the boundary shifted forward on her lot so that the back portion of her residence would be in the "B-2" district, then perhaps her problem could be solved. Unfortunately for Mary, the chances of getting the boundary shifted are not good. According to accepted practice in drawing boundaries, the boundary behind her property is in a good location and should not be moved.

To understand why Mary's boundary and others are placed where they are, one must keep in mind the fact that zoning is basically a product of the 1920s that has been modified in subsequent years. In Chapter 6, Flexible Zoning, we will describe some important changes since the 1920s.   For the moment, however, we will stick to the basics of *traditional* zoning, still a major factor in the typical ordinance. Under the traditional concept of zoning, a community is divided into districts depicted on the map. Within each district, the regulations apply uniformly to all parcels. Between any two districts, the regulations are different, even though the differences may be slight. For example, two different residential districts might have identical provisions regarding uses but slightly dissimilar ones with respect to depths of front yards. Between a residential and an industrial district, on the other hand, the regulations are quite different. Some people consider any two districts with similar regulations to be "compatible" and any two with dissimilar regulations to be "incompatible."

Whether similar or dissimilar, two adjacent districts on the zoning map are separated by a boundary that is, with minor exceptions, rigid and absolute. What is permitted on one side of the line is not necessarily permitted on the other. The owner of property on one side of a boundary may be allowed a more valuable set of uses than the owner of property on the other side. The kind of development permitted on one side might be detrimental in some respects to the kind permitted on the other. Thus the exact location of the boundary between two districts can be a matter of great concern to a property owner. Much of the controversy in zoning arises out of attempts to alter zoning boundaries.

Every zoning boundary is a potential battle line between two contending groups, one of them attacking the boundary, and the other defending it. As is the case with military battle lines, some zoning boundaries are easy to defend and others are easy to break through. Planners and others who draw zoning boundaries are constantly looking for features that will provide stable boundaries and minimize conflict. Thus, boundaries are frequently found along major physical barriers such as railroads, steep ravines, sharp ridges, and freeways (but usually not conventional streets). No boundary is completely invulnerable to assault, but those based upon such prominent physical features are generally considered to be the easiest to defend.

A glance at a typical zoning map will quickly reveal the fact that most boundaries do *not* follow strong physical features, simply because there are not enough such features in the right locations, and because prominent individual property lines normally exist somewhere other than along these convenient physical features. Most boundaries follow property lines, and, where possible, they usually follow *rear* property lines. In traditional zoning, great weight is given to *like facings* of uses, meaning that properties facing along a street are ordinarily zoned in the same way. This practice sometimes takes on the status of a principle. Whether principle or merely practice, however, the recognition given to *like facings* in drawing boundaries along rear property lines is understandable. In our urban society, a street address often connotes status. The owner of property on one side of a street wishes to prevent any use on the other side that might threaten the street's prestige. Property is customarily approached from the front by guests, customers, potential tenants, and potential buyers. The uses and condition of property on the other side of the street are readily apparent to them and may affect their willingness to visit, rent, or buy. Uses to the rear, however, are not so readily apparent.

To some extent the reliance on like facings reflects some of the conditions of the 1920s that were holdovers from earlier decades when stables, manure, garbage, and service alleys for the collection of same were at the rear of a lot, and when the fronts of homes had porches for outdoor living. Although stables are gone, alleys are no longer in vogue, and outdoor living has moved to the backyard or to an open area owned in common with neighbors, the practice of preserving like facings remains a popular one for commercial as well as for residential uses.

Boundaries that preserve like facings are usually easier to defend than those that do not. In Figure 3-1, for example, three corners of an intersection are zoned "commercial" and used for service stations. The fourth is zoned "residential." This kind of relationship is ordinarily difficult to defend. If the owner of the aparment building on the "residential" lot applied for a change in the zoning map to a "commercial" classification, the request would likely be granted.

Unfortunately, it is not always possible for boundaries to follow rear property lines. It can be seen in Figure 3-1 that part of the boundary between C-2 and R-3 follows side lot lines. No matter which side lines are followed, the boundaries will be, to a great extent, arbitrary. Their only defense is that "the boundaries have to be drawn somewhere."

There are also difficulties in trying to maintain *like facings*. In older cities where lot dimensions are less likely to be uniform, there are problems associated with lots of unequal depths. In Figure 3-2, for example, a zoning boundary following rear lot lines would extend commercial zoning deeply into Lots 6 and 8, which have side lines common with residentially zoned lots.

In some cities this kind of situation is handled by locating a boundary a uniform distance from, and parallel to, the street on which the commercial uses

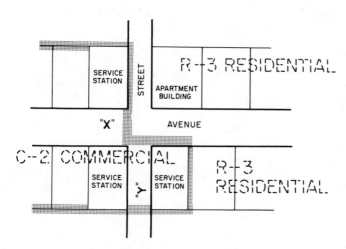

Figure 3-1

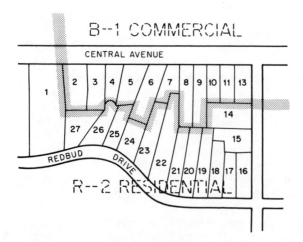

Figure 3-2

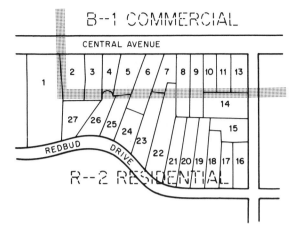

Figure 3-3

front, as shown in Figure 3-3. The text of the ordinance then permits the extension of an allowable use a specified distance across the boundary on lots that are split by the boundary. Irregular property lines create zoning problems that are not easily cured. For example, residential lots partly adjacent to, or divided by, a commercial zoning boundary are prime candidates for commercial rezoning when the residential use becomes poorly maintained or obsolete. Once a single residential lot is rezoned for commercial use, there is great incentive for owners of adjacent residential properties to ask for such zoning whether or not there is sufficient demand for commercial space to support their requests. This "domino effect," frequently fed by unfounded speculation, can severely damage the stability of a much larger residential area.

Double-Frontage Lots

Other difficulties are presented by double-frontage lots. These are lots that abut streets at both the front and the rear. Figure 3-4 indicates some of the problems that they can create in the delineation of zoning boundaries. The owners of Lots 1, 2, 3, and 4 have good arguments for commercial zoning, but if their requests are granted, then the property on the south side of Spring Creek Lane is adversely affected, and further requests for commercial zoning might be generated.

Unlike facings do not always justify rezoning, however. If Union Avenue is a boulevard with a wide median that is thickly planted with shrubbery, then Lots 1, 2, 3, and 4 might reasonably be left in a residential classification. Similarly, if a landscaped buffer, together with a guarantee against driveway entrances, could be provided along the Spring Creek Lane frontage of Lots 1, 2, 3, and 4, then those lots might be zoned commercially without adverse

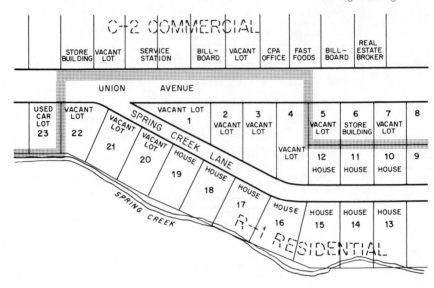

Figure 3-4 Some effects of double-frontage lots.

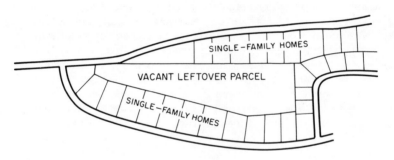

Figure 3-5 Land-locked parcel.

effects on the lots on the other side of Spring Creek Lane. Such buffers will be discussed further in Chapter 6.

Odd-Shaped Parcels

The delineation of boundaries is sometimes complicated by the existence of oddly shaped parcels. For example, the parcel in Figure 3-5 is what is some-times referred to as a "land-locked parcel." Although strictly speaking this is not a correct designation. The only access to a street is along a narrow frontage. Such a situation results from piecemeal subdividing or from land that is simply left over after everything else has been subdivided. Such parcels frequently become the subjects of requests for special zoning treatment. If zoned for single-family use, the owners may complain that they are too large for such use but at the same time incapable of subdivision into smaller lots because they do not have proper street access.

In a controversy involving such a parcel, someone is sure to suggest it be purchased for a park. Few communities can afford to meet the many requests for parks to solve zoning problems, and the adjoining-lot owners are seldom interested as long as they can stop any rezoning.

As an example of the kind of "no win" situation that can be encountered in preserving like facings, consider the following fictional case.

The crossroads settlement shown in Figure 3-6 is annexed to a village. Now it must be zoned. The entire planning board agrees that the business area at the intersection of Elm Grove, Croftsburg Highway, and Edgewood Road should be classified as "C-2 Community Business," but they cannot agree on exactly where to draw the boundaries. There are three possible solutions, all having shortcomings. In Figure 3-7, the boundary encloses only the main concentration of business and professional uses. The owners of Lots 3, 4, 5, and 16 could reasonably object to this arrangement on the grounds that their lots would be left facing a commercial district and would be unsuitable, therefore, in the long

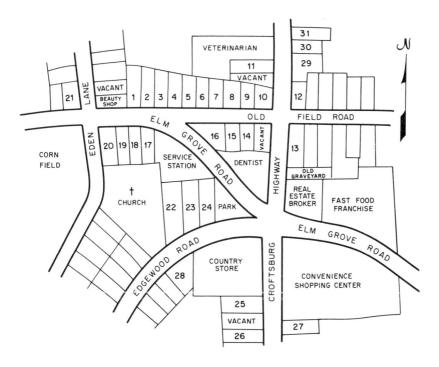

NOTE: ALL LOTS NOT OTHERWISE INDICATED CONTAIN RESIDENCES

Figure 3-6

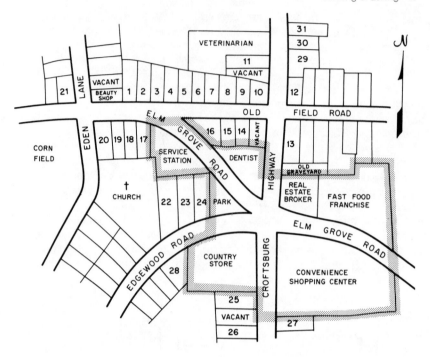

NOTE: ALL LOTS NOT OTHERWISE INDICATED CONTAIN RESIDENCES

Figure 3-7

run for residential usage. The owners of Lots 23, 24, and 25 could lodge similar objections with respect to the country store and the convenience shopping center.

In Figure 3-8, the commercial district has been enlarged to overcome the objections raised to Figure 3-7, but this has created new problems. Lots 1 and 2 are sandwiched between the beauty shop and the commercial zoning on Lot 3. Lot 15 borders the commercial district on two sides. Who wants to live on a parcel like that? Lot 22 is not only next to a church that is growing rapidly with suburbia, but now it is also next to the C-2 district on the other side as well as at the rear. The vacant parcel between Lots 25 and 26 was already facing in part the back of the convenience shopping center. Now it also abuts the commercial zoning on Lot 25. Is it likely that anyone would build a house on it?

In Figure 3-9, the C-2 district has been greatly expanded, but all problems have not been eliminated. The veterinarian does not like the thought of conducting a *nonconforming* use immediately adjacent to a business zone. On the other hand, the owners of Lots 29, 30, and 31 would oppose putting the veterinarian in C-2. The owner of Lot 11 agrees with the veterinarian because she objects to being left between the veterinarian and the C-2 boundary. To the south, Lot 27 now faces in part a commercial zone across the streeet in addition the side exposure that it already suffered at the rear of the shopping center. There are also questions for the future. What is going to happen to the church property when the congregation outgrows it and moves to another location? What will be the fate of the cornfield?

Although the preceding example deals with annexed territory that had not previously been zoned, it also illustrates the "domino effect" that can sometimes occur when a residential lot is rezoned as "commercial" in an area with irregular platting. The effect can be especially difficult to control if commercially zoned frontage is expanded to a residential street and zoning officials subsequently feel obligated to consider like facings. Activity of this sort is frequently referred to as "commercial encroachment," although an "encroachment" as defined in real property law does not actually occur.

Strip Zoning

Defensible boundaries, as Figures 3-6 through 3-9 illustrate, can be hard to find. One change often leads to another. Nowhere is such a chain reaction more aparent than it is in *strip zoning*, a term usually applied to a continuous

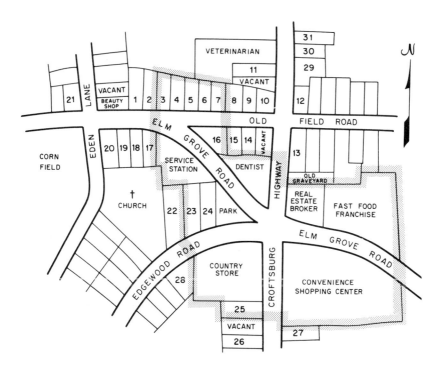

NOTE: ALL LOTS NOT OTHERWISE INDICATED CONTAIN RESIDENCES

Figure 3-8

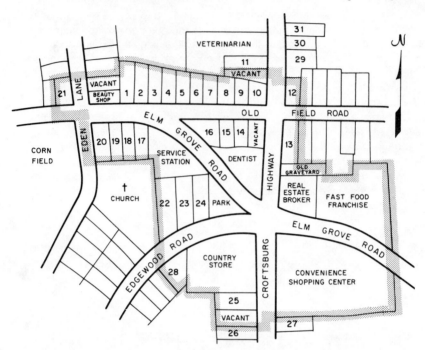

NOTE: ALL LOTS NOT OTHERWISE INDICATED CONTAIN RESIDENCES

Figure 3-9

ribbon of commercial zoning along an arterial street. It is an anathema to many people for several reasons. In the first place, it presents nightmares for traffic engineers and general confusion for motorists. Typically it is characterized by uncontrolled driveway entrances and exits (called "curb-outs" by engineers and planners) and almost continuous left-turn movements. Secondly, the strip commercial zoning is often wasteful of land and frontage.

In Figure 3-10, the entire strip is zoned "commercial," but much of it is either vacant or in residential use. The market demand for such frontage may not catch up with the supply for decades; in the meanwhile, the suitability of the vacant and residential parcels for any noncommercial use is seriously impaired if not destroyed. Strip zones also present aesthetic problems; they are usually characterized by a jumbled mixture of advertising signs, concrete and asphalt paving, ugly buildings, and minimal landscaping (including artificial grass and plastic plants).

The ill effects of strip zoning can sometimes be avoided by forcing uses into planned clusters. Many uses, however, are difficult to fit into planned clusters, so the strips will probably remain with us for a long time. Meanwhile, we must contend with the problems associated with them. Figure 3-11 illustrates a common problem. The total frontage of the commercial district is 1000 feet. Is this a strip or a cluster? What arguments would developers or property owners have for expanding the commercial district by adding one lot at either end? What counter arguments could be made? Generally the developer would argue that the extension of the boundary to include one more lot would not constitute *strip zoning*; it would simply be a minor addition to a compact cluster. He might also claim that the entire arterial was "going commercial" anyway and was therefore unsuitable for other uses. The counter arguments might be that the boundary had to be drawn somewhere if the entire arterial were not to be strip-zoned for commercial uses and that if this request were granted, then there would be a weak defense against further extensions. Furthermore, it might be said that the existing cluster was not a planned cluster and that any extension of it would be an extension of uncontrolled access to the highway. The highway frontage could remain suitable for residential uses if uncontrolled strip zoning could be avoided.

Transitional-Use Provisions

Strip zoning is not the only potential problem associated with drawing boundaries along side lot lines. In Figure 3-12, the boundary follows the rear lines

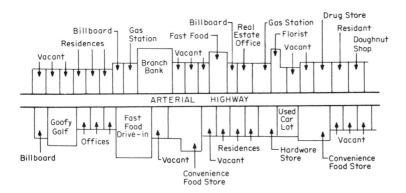

Figure 3-10 Typical land uses in a strip-commercial district.

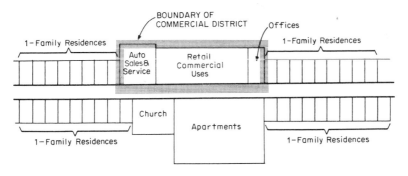

Figure 3-11

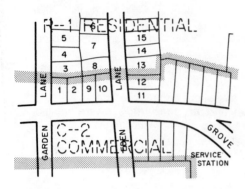

Figure 3-12

of commercial Lots 1, 2, 9, and 10 and the side line of commercial Lot 12. The rear lines of Lots 1, 2, 9, and 10, however, are the side lines of residential Lots 3 and 8. The owners of those lots, as well as the owner of Lot 13, can understandably argue for inclusion in the commercial district. The owners of Lots 4, 7, and 14 might be understanding, but they would probably oppose such an argument.

Some communities have tried to alleviate the problems associated with boundaries along side lines of lots by incorporating *transitional-use* provisions in their zoning texts. For example, a text might contain the following language:

Transitional Uses in "R" Districts

In any "R" (Residential) District, a transitional use will be permitted on a lot the side lot line of which adjoins, either directly or across an alley, any commercial or industrial district.

Thus, in Figure 3-12, Lots 3, 8, and 13 are eligible for "transitional uses." Although they remain zoned for "single-family residential," they may be used for a limited number of other uses not normally allowed in a single-family district. These uses might include offices, institutions (such as a club or a kindergarten), and off-street parking (properly landscaped).

A *transitional-use* provision may also be worded so as to ease what would otherwise be an abrupt change from one set of height limits, or front-yard requirements, to another. Such a provision might resemble the following example:

C-2 Community Commercial District

FRONT YARD: No front yard is required except where property on the same side of the street within the same block is in a residential district or a more restricted commercial district, in which event the stricter requirement shall govern.

Transitional Zoning in General

In addition to the transitional-use provision, there are at least two other techniques that involve transitions in zoning. The term *transitional zoning* is often thought of as a technique of drawing district boundaries in a step-down fashion so that (1) single-family districts do not adjoin apartment districts, commercial districts, or industrial districts; (2) two-family districts do not adjoin commercial districts or industrial districts; and (3) apartments do not adjoin industrial districts. Figure 3-13 illustrates one such application of this concept.

Implicit in this kind of transitional zoning is an assumption that apartments, and even two-family dwellings, are somehow less desirable than single-family houses, and that having sixteen families in an apartment building next to a shopping center is less detrimental than having one family in a single-family home in the same location. An application of transitional zoning is sometimes referred to erroneously as "providing a buffer." In recent years there has been a trend toward the substitution of requirements for true buffers in the form of walls and landscaping between dissimilar districts as an alternative to the use of transitional zoning.

As we mentioned in the preceding chapter, *transitional zoning* can also be thought of in terms of a transition over time. A district established for this purpose might permit offices and institutions in a residential area but require that residential setbacks and height limits be observed and that landscaping and buffers be provided.

Rationale for Districts

Like the boundaries which enclose them, the districts shown on a zoning map have more than one explanation. A new zoning map is usually proposed shortly after a community has adopted a new comprehensive plan. The planners who draw the original proposal tend to look upon zoning primarily as a device for implementing the comprehensive plan, and their proposed map reflects this attitude. In theory the planners are correct. The various state enabling acts that permit local communities to adopt zoning require that zoning be based upon a comprehensive plan (or master plan). The Standard State Zoning

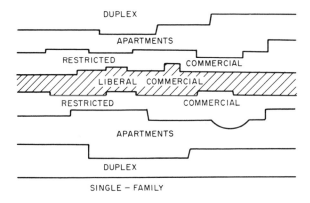

Figure 3-13 Transitional bands along both sides of a liberal commercial district.

Enabling Act, published by the U.S. Department of Commerce in 1922, and the prototype for most state zoning acts, contains the following:

Such regulations shall be made in accordance with a comprehensive plan . . .

In actuality, the plan requirement often means little more than a payment of lip service. In many states, the courts have held the zoning map itself to constitute the comprehensive plan. Even where the plan is treated less cynically, however, it is not a simple task to relate it to the zoning map.

At best, a comprehensive plan is a general statement of community objectives and policies expressed both in writing and on a map. The map (commonly called a *land-use plan*) illustrates a future pattern of land use. To some people, this future pattern constitutes an official set of objectives that should be attained if possible. To others, it merely represents one of several possible arrangements that would accomplish the goals of the comprehensive plan. However it is viewed, the *land-use plan* is much less specific in nature than the *zoning map*. Boundaries between different uses on the plan are not drawn to the same degree of precision as zoning boundaries and are often conjectural. Consequently, the plan should not serve as a literal blueprint for establishing zoning boundaries, even though planning officials may be legally bound to use it as a guide. The comprehensive plan is not only general in nature; it is also long range. Twenty or twenty-five years is a frequently used time span. Shorter-range planning is on the increase, but many plans still concentrate on describing what a community should be like twenty-five years hence, with little thought being given to intermediate objectives. Such a plan is of scant help as a guide to immediate problems. For example, let us suppose that the City of Jefferson has just annexed a blighted area known as "Willow Bend."

Willow Bend contains 420 acres, approximately 110 of which are used industrially. A little over 200 acres are used for low-income dwellings, most of which are owner-occupied, and the remainder is in streets, railroads, and vacant parcels. Some of the industrial uses are small-scale operations mixed in with the residential uses. Several rail lines crisscross the area. For all practical purposes Willow Bend is stagnant. The City of Jefferson annexed it only because Willow Bend had no sewers and constituted a health menance to Jefferson residents. Now the city faces the problem of how to zone Willow Bend. The comprehensive plan has designated the whole area for industrial use by the year 1995. Should it be zoned industrially now? If so, what assurance is there that industrial development will occur? What will be the fate of the low-income homeowners who live there now? If they continue to live there, what will happen to the environmental quality of their neighborhood, which is already less than satisfactory? The Jefferson zoning ordinance does not permit residences in industrial districts, and those already in existence may not be enlarged, substantially altered, or rebuilt in the event of serious damage. Jefferson's decision will probably involve a compromise between the long-range objectives of the comprehensive plan and present-day reality.

Even in less complex situations, the planners who draw the proposed zoning map must give some recognition to what already exists on the ground. If, for example, the Village of Brookhaven contains large areas developed for one-and-one-half-story homes on lots 75 feet wide and 140 feet deep with front yards of 35 feet and side yards of 15 feet, then it is a good bet that the planners' proposal will contain a district with such requirements in the text. On the proposed map, the areas already developed basically in compliance with that district will be zoned accordingly. Such practice would be in accord with the Standard State Zoning Enabling Act, which, in addition to the comprehensive plan requirement, also states:

Such regulations shall be made with reasonable consideration, among other things, to the character of the district and its peculiar suitability for particular uses, and with a view to conserving the value of buildings and encouraging the most appropriate use of land throughout such municipality.

After a proposed new zoning map is presented by the planners who drafted it, there is apt to be a series of public hearings at which property owners voice objections. Numerous changes are made in response to these objections before the map is adopted. The resulting document, then, even at the time of its adoption, already contains compromises that may conflict with the objectives of the comprehensive plan.

After a new zoning map is adopted, the process of making frequent amendments to it begins. Not only are boundaries altered, but whole new districts are created on the map. For example, several separate areas might be zoned on the new map "C-1 Commercial." Helen Jones, who owns vacant land zoned "R-1 Residential," may be successful in getting the map changed so as to create an additional "C-1" zone encompassing her property even though it is not contiguous to one of the other areas so zoned. If there are objections to some of the uses permitted in "C-1," then the town council might compromise by creating a new kind of district in the text of the ordinance. The new district, permitting some but not all of the uses permitted in "C-1," might be designated as "C-1A." Although the Jones land would be the only area initially indicated on the map as "C-1A," amendments designating other areas in the same way would be sure to follow.

Spot Zoning

The change of the Jones' property from "R-1" to "C-1" or "C-1A" might be dubbed *spot zoning*. This is an emotional term with sinister connotations and a favorite tactical smear at public hearings, but often its use is justified. Strictly used, *spot zoning* is the act of drawing or redrawing district boundaries so that one small parcel is in a district all by itself. Often this act results in a small island of apartment, commercial, or industrial zoning surrounded by single-family residential areas. Hence, its emotional content. True, *spot zoning* flies in the face of the basic constitutional justification for zoning as a device for classifying similar properties and similar uses and then regulating development in a *uniform* manner within each classification. Spot zoning obviously represents anything but uniform treatment.

A big problem in dealing with spot zoning is in distinguishing between an example of honest-to-goodness spot zoning and a use of the term merely as a smear. With respect to a 10,000-square-foot lot surrounded by a single-family residential district, there can be no doubt that, if commercial rezoning is under consideration, then *spot-zoning* is an appropriate term. Regarding a fifty-acre tract, few objective observers would use such an epithet. In the one-acre to ten-acre range, however, there is much basis for disagreement. Some communties have attempted to define the minimum area and dimensions that any area must have before it might be considered for any change of zoning except to a classification already existing on adjoining land.

Under some conditions "spot zoning" may be virtually unavoidable if a community employs an "exclusive-use district" for specific uses that have unique locational problems or that tend to generate emotional reactions. For example, if a funeral parlor is not considered an appropriate use in any commercial or residential district, it might therefore be permitted only in a "Funeral Parlor District" in which no other uses are included. As a result, the zoning for every funeral parlor will appear on the zoning map as a "spot zone."

Whether by spot zoning or by less dastardly amendments, the typical zoning map is changed frequently. Sometimes the amendments reflect revisions to the community's comprehensive plan. More often, they are made without regard to the plan. Even the best plan quickly becomes obsolete in our society because circumstances can change rapidly and suddenly. If a plan is not revised continually, then the zoning map will likely be revised anyway without the guidance that the plan might provide. This is not to say that all amendments made in disregard of a plan are necessarily made in response to changing conditions. Many of them are motivated solely by the desire for personal gain by particular property owners and by the desire for political power by certain office holders. Regardless of the motivations, however, the patterns present in a typical zoning map cannot be explained entirely without some reference to the many amendments that have been made to it.

Summary

In this chapter, we have introduced a fictional property owner to some of the complexities involved in drawing and redrawing zoning boundaries. We have discussed briefly the relationship of the zoning map to the comprehensive plan. More will be said on this subject in later chapters. We have also touched upon some of the frustrating problems encountered in trying to establish defensible boundaries in awkward circumstances. Sometimes these problems can be lessened, if not overcome, through the application of development standards. In the next chapter, we will introduce our property owner to development standards, a vital part of the regulations contained in each zoning district.

4
Development Standards

The districts that are depicted on a zoning map are not only devices for imposing different use controls on various groupings of properties, but are also a means for applying different sets of standards that regulate how buildings and uses may be placed on a site. A property owner who is a novice at zoning will find that these *development standards* are generally more difficult to comprehend than the use provisions. They are about as exciting as multiplication tables and much more formidable, but they are terribly important to property owners and developers.

For a professional developer, a thorough understanding of development standards provides an advantage in battling with the zoning administrator over the interpretation of provisions. Getting a favorable interpretation might mean the ability to build four more apartment units or one more story in an office building in projects costing a million dollars or more. Every little increment is important.

For a property owner like Mary Trigg, who wants to add a ten-foot by ten-foot room to her home for a pottery kiln, the question presented by the development standards is not whether she will be able to build a bigger or a smaller addition but whether she will be able to build at all. In her case, the standards are critical. She ought to be able, therefore, to gain a clear understanding of how the standards affect her by turning quickly to one particular page in the ordinance and reading it, but this is not necessarily the case. For someone who wants to do more than build a simple addition to a house, the interpretation of development standards can turn out to be quite complicated.

Development standards are, by their very nature, obtuse. It is unfortunate, that such important restrictions are frequently made even more obtuse by their form of presentation. Dull to read, and often confusing, development standards are not even confined to one location in the text. What seems to be a clear-cut rule in one paragraph may be contradicted by another paragraph many pages away. Typographical errors are not uncommon. The term *curved line* might appear erroneously as *curbed line*. An entire line might be omitted in the middle

55

of a complex regulation. The typical ordinance not only has been amended many times; it has also been amended too hastily on occasion. Zoning administrators are usually aware of these flaws and can clear up a reader's confusion as to what a standard means.

Development standards are more complex than use regulations. The simplest standards are those found in the districts designed for one-family and two-family homes. Typically they include the following:

Minimum area of lot expressed in square feet or acres

Minimum yard setbacks (front, rear, and side) in feet

Minimum lot width at front building line in feet

Maximum height of building in stories and/or feet

Maximum percentage coverage of lot by buildings

Maximum heights for fences, walls, and hedges

Some ordinances also contain minimum requirements for floor area, and many contain off-street parking requirements.

As is the case with use regulations, development standards may be expressed either by means of statements or in tabular form. The following excerpt from the ordinance in Champaign, Illinois, exemplifies a widespread practice of stating development standards separately for each district. The statements usually appear right after the statements on use regulations.

Excerpt from Zoning Ordinance of Champaign, Illinois

Section 5. Area and Yard Regulations. The following regulations shall govern the intensity of use of land and the required yards in the R-1B District:

(a) *Intensity of Use*. Every dwelling erected, converted, enlarged or structurally altered in the R-1B District shall be located upon a lot having an area of not less than 6,500 square feet and an average width of not less than 65 feet. This regulation shall not be interpreted to prevent the erection of a single-family dwelling on a platted lot or tract having less area or width than required herein if the platted lot or tract was of public record on the date this amendatory ordinance became effective as to such lot or tract.

(b) *Front Yard*. There shall be a front yard of not less than 25 feet. Lots fronting on two non-intersecting streets shall have the required front yard on both streets.

(c) *Side Yard*. There shall be a side yard, on each side of the lot, of not less than ten per cent of the width of the lot, or six feet, whichever is the smaller, except that on corner lots the side yard on the street side of the lot shall be not less than 15 feet.

(d) *Rear Yard*. There shall be a rear yard of not less than 20 per cent of the depth of the lot, or 25 feet, whichever is the smaller.

Note that development standards are referred to here as "Area and Yard Regulations." They may also be called "Height, Area, and Yard Requirements," "Lot, Yard, and Height Requirements," or any of several other terms.

A tabular presentation of development standards might resemble the example in Figure 4-1 from Charleston, South Carolina.

Standards for multiple-family, commercial, and industrial districts frequently include:

Minimum area and dimensions of lot

Minimum yards and setbacks for structures and activities

Maximum heights of structures and hedges

Maximum lot coverage and minimum open space

Maximum floor/area ratio

Maximum residential density

Minimum off-street parking and loading

Buffers of minimum dimensions

Minimum distances from other specified uses

Minimum floor area

Minimum landscaping

Maximum numbers and sizes of advertising signs

Maximum numbers of entrances and exits, and minimum geometric design standards

Now how does a property owner relate these standards to the development of a vacant lot for a particular use? The first step is to obtain an accurate survey of the property showing all boundaries and dimensions. In using this, the reader should understand that the *front lot line* or *property line* is usually the same as the *right-of-way* for the street. In zoning terminology, the word *street* includes not only the roadway for vehicles but also an area of varying width on each side that may be used for sidewalks, trees, grass, and utility lines. See Figure 4-2.

The second step is to check the standards for *area* and *dimensions* to determine if the lot is big enough for the development contemplated.

Area and Dimensions of Lot

All, or nearly all, ordinances specify a minimum lot *area* for each residential use, the minimum varying from district to district. Many ordinances contain area standards for nonresidential uses. Along with the requirement for a minimum area, there is frequently a minimum for the *width* of the lot or parcel. Some ordinances also specify a minimum *frontage*, which is not always the same as width. *Frontage* is measured along the right-of-way boundary of the street, or streets, bordering the lot. *Width*, on the other hand, is usually measured at the front building line, which is set by the front-yard requirement. (See Figure 4-3.) Width can also be measured in other ways, so it would be wise to consult the definition section of the ordinance before reaching a conclusion. If the parcel is a corner lot, or if it faces two parallel streets, the definition of width must be checked to find out whether or not the owner has a choice as to which dimension is the *width*.

Figure 4-1 Example of tabular format—Charleston, South Carolina.

ZONE District Designation³	Front Yard- Minimum Depth	Side Yards-2/ Minimum Widths			Rear Yard- Minimum Depths	Min. Lot Area per Family in Sq. Feet Type Dwelling Unit			Max. % of Lot Occ. Prin. Bldgs.	5/ Max. Height Limits	Accessory Bldgs. to Residences- Setback Required		Additional Dwellings distance from Front Lot Line 4/
		Total	South or West	North or East		1-Fam.	2-Fam.	Multi- Fam.			From Front Street	From Side Street	
SR-1	35'	18'	12'	6'	35'	9000	NA	NA	35%	35' 2½ stories	70'	35'	Not Allowed
SR-2	25'	18'	12'	6'	35'	6000	NA	NA	50%	35' 2½ stories	70'	25'	Not Allowed
SR-3 1/	NR	18'	12'	6'	3'	6000	NA	NA	35%	50' 3 stories	70'	12'	100'
SR-4 1/	NR	15'	9'	3'	3'	4000	NA	NA	35%	50' 3 stories	70'	9'	80'
SR-5 1/	NR	10'	7'	3'	3'	2500	NA	NA	35%	50' 3 stories	60'	7'	70'
STR 1/	25'	18'	12'	6'	35'	6000	4500	NA	50%	35' 2½ stories	70'	25'	100'
DR-1F 1/	25'	15'	9'	3'	30'	4000	3000	2250	50%	50' 3 stories	70'	25'	80'
DR-1 1/	NR	15'	9'	3'	3'	4000	3000	2250	35%	50' 3 stories	70'	9'	80'
DR-2F 1/ 6/	25'	10'	7'	3'	25'	2500	2000	1650	50%	50' 6/ 3 stories	60'	25'	70'

District	Front Yard	Side Yard			Rear Yard	Lot Area			Lot Coverage	Height			
DR-2 1/6/	NR	10'	7'	3'	7'	2500	2000	1650	35%	50' 6/ 3 stories	60'	7'	70'
DR-3 1/6/ *DR-4	NR	10'	7'	3'	7'	2500	2000	1650	50%	50' 6/ 3 stories	60'	15'	70'
**LB1/	NR	Side yard requirements for residences same as for DR-IF District. None specifically required for businesses			Dwellings 20' Other NR	2500	2000	1650	Resid. dwellings 50% Businesses NA	3 x least dist. between front line of bldg. & centerline of street on which it fronts. See conditions of exception section.			
**GB1/	Dwellings 15' Bus. NR	Side yard requirements for residences same as for DR-IF District. None specifically required for businesses			NR	1500	1500	1500	Same as LB District Above	Same as LB District Above	60'	15'	70'
**LI 1/	All structures 15'	Residential: 2 side yards, each at least 5 ft. in width. Industrial and business: none specifically required.			Dwellings 20' Other NR	1500	1500	1500	Residential dwellings 50% Other NA	Same as LB District Above	50'	15'	70'

ZONE District Designation[3]	Front Yard- Minimum Depth	Side Yards-[2] Minimum Widths			Rear Yard- Minimum Depths	Min. Lot Area per Family in Sq. Feet Type Dwelling Unit			Max. % of Lot Occ. Prin. Bldgs.	[5] Max. Height Limits	Accessory Bldgs. to Residences- Setback Required		Additional Dwellings distance from Front Lot Line 4/
		Total	South or West	North or East		1-Fam.	2-Fam.	Multi-Fam.			From Front Street	From Side Street	
**H.I.	25'		Minimum 25-ft. wide side yard required on side adjoining residences or residence districts		20'	NA	NA	NA	NA	Same as LB District Above	NA	NA	NA
Old & Historical					REFER TO AND APPLY OVERLAPPING ZONE REQUIREMENTS AND REFER TO ARTICLE III OF THE ZONING ORDINANCE.								

Notes:

1. Attached Single-family Dwellings Permitted. Refer to Article V of the Zoning Ordinance Text for special provisions of standards and regulations for one-family attached dwellings, Town or Row houses where permitted. Also refer to Article II to determine number of such units permitted in each use district.

2. Under no conditions shall the minimum distance between residences not joined by a common wall be less than three feet.

3. In any district, it shall be unlawful to construct a porch, piazza or balcony so that the same extends in whole or in part over a public street, lane, court, or other public right-of-way without specific permission from the city executive body and compliance with all applicable city ordinances.

4. Additional Regulations Concerning Accessory Buildings in Residential Zones:

   In any residential zone the area covered by accessory buildings shall not exceed 10% of the area of the lot (to the nearest 200 square feet) upon which the principal building is located.

   If allowed in the schedule of major area regulations, additional dwellings at the rear of a lot must meet the following conditions:

   a. The minimum side yard requirements of the zone district shall be afforded the additional dwellings;

   b. An additional 70 per cent of the required lot area per family shall be afforded each additional rear lot dwelling or apartment garage;

   c. The per cent of the lot to be occupied by all buildings shall not exceed thirty-five per cent of the entire lot area;

   d. The least distance between the main building and the garage apartment or additional dwelling shall not be less than twenty-five (25) feet;

   e. A garage apartment shall not be closer than twenty (20) feet to the rear property line and shall comply with the distance from front lot line requirements listed in the schedule of major area regulations.

5. See Article entitled "Exceptions and Modifications".

6. See special height and area modifications for residential structures in excess of fifty (50) feet ("high rise") in Article VII.

   Abbreviations: NA—Not Applicable, NR—Not Required.

*7. See special height and area provisions for this classification, which are set forth in Sec. 51-36.

**8. In LB, GB, LI and HI districts, a hotel, motel, apartment motel, multi-family dwelling consisting of more than twenty units, or other similar structure for lodging purposes shall be considered a business, and shall not be subject to residential requirements set forth in this table.

60

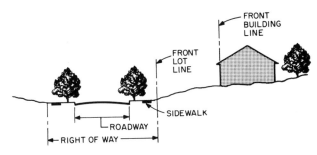

Figure 4-2

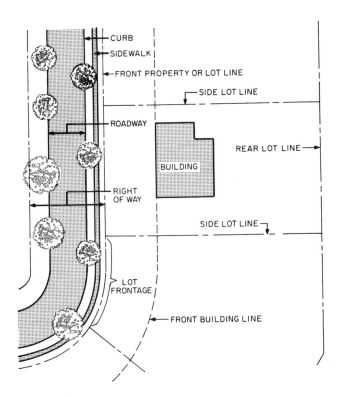

Figure 4-3

It is customary for the regulations to permit substandard *lots-of-record*, that is to say, lots legally in existence prior to their becoming substandard, to be used in conflict with the basic requirements for area and dimensions, but as we will explain later, limits are often placed upon the intensity of their use.

Area, like width, may involve questions of definitions. A corner lot, for example, can have less area than first seems apparent because of the existence of an arc at the property line. See Figure 4-4.

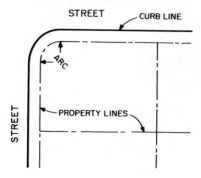

Figure 4-4

There may also be problems with utility easements on the lot with streets that have been designated for future widening. Some ordinances require that the area included in the easements and in the future street widening be excluded in whole or part from the calculations of lot area and dimensions.

Area standards have two forms. One is a basic minimum for any development at all. The other is a control over the intensity of use through restraints on density, floor/area ratio, and lot coverage. The basic minimum is generally expressed in terms of square feet, while intensity controls are expressed in a variety of ratios and percentages. These will be described after we have considered some rules limiting the placement and shape of the buildings on a given parcel.

The Zoning Envelope

After the minimum requirements for area and dimensions of the lot have been ascertained, the next step is to discover what spaces may be occupied by buildings. Before proceeding, however, it is necessary to understand a definitional difference between two kinds of buildings. One kind is referred to as a *principal building* (or *main building*), which is simply a building within which the major use of the property is located e.g., a house in a residential district. The other kind of building is called an *accessory building* and is a structure such as a garage or storage shed that is ancillary to the main use. This distinction is important to know because the regulations for the two are often different. In many districts, only one principal building is permitted on a given lot.

The cubic space within which the principal building may be placed is sometimes referred to as "the zoning envelope." This is simply an imaginary, rigid tent inside of which the building may be put in any location so long as it does not penetrate one of the imaginary surfaces.

Figure 4-5 depicts a highly simplified zoning envelope. Most have more complex shapes determined by several interacting standards. Let us now examine each of these standards separately, beginning with those that outline the base.

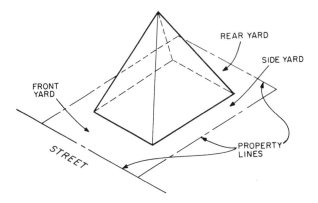

Figure 4-5 Depiction of simplified zoning envelope.

Yards and Other Setbacks

One of the major functions of a zoning ordinance is to regulate the spacing (a) between streets and buildings, together with outside activities, and (b) between buildings and other buildings. This is done in the stated interest of exposing building interiors to natural lighting and ventilation, inhibiting the spread of fire from one structure to the next, and minimizing conflicts between street traffic and off-street activities. It may also be done in the interest (either explicit or implicit) of (1) preventing construction that would complicate future street widenings or (2) creating aesthetically pleasing open space (although as we shall see later, requiring space to be open from ground to sky does not guarantee that it will be aesthetically pleasing). The standards for *yards* and other *setbacks* perform this function by establishing the base of the zoning envelope and its horizontal limits in general.

Figure 4-6 depicts a lot for a single-family house and the various yards referred to in zoning ordinances.

Perhaps some clarification is in order at this point. Although Figure 4-6 shows yards as *areas*, and zoning texts sometimes refer to *yard areas*, the requirements normally specified for a yard are in terms of a linear dimension. That is to say, the ordinance will require a front yard having a minimum depth of so many feet and a side yard having a width of so many feet. Here are some typical yard requirements:

Front Yard. There shall be a front yard having a depth of not less than thirty-five (35) feet.

Side Yard. There shall be two side yards, one on each side of the building each having a width of not less than ten (10) feet. Where a lot is located at the intersection of two (2) or more streets, the width of the yard along the side street shall not be less than twenty (20) feet. No accessory building shall project beyond the yard line on any street.

Rear Yard. There shall be a rear yard having a depth of not less than thirty (30) feet or twenty (20) percent of the depth of the lot, whichever amount is smaller, but in no case shall it be less than twenty (20) feet in depth.

In some ordinances, a corner lot is subject to the front-yard requirements of both streets. Another common provision is one that adjusts the required front yard to take into account existing buildings. For example, the text might read as follows:

There shall be a front yard of not less than 40 feet, except that where existing buildings on the same side of the street and within 200 feet of either sideline of the subject property form an existing setback line, new buildings shall conform to the existing setback line; provided, however, that no building shall have a front yard of less than 30 feet and no building need have a front yard greater than 50 feet.

Some ordinances provide a degree of flexibility in the side-yard requirements by specifying a minimum width on either side and also a minimum for the sum of the two side yards, as in the following example:

There shall be two side yards and no side yard shall be less than 15 feet; provided, however, that the aggregate width of the two side yards, combined, shall equal at least 33 feet.

A developer should always read the definitions of *yards* before trying to apply the requirements to a specific situation. Some ordinances, for example, measure the front yard from the center line of the street rather than from the edge of the right of way. It is also important to look elsewhere in the ordinance for *exclusions* from yard standards. Balconies and outside steps are not treated consistently. In some ordinances these projections might be exempt from the requirements.

Basic yard requirements are not always imposed upon nonresidential districts. In the early years of zoning, yards were considered essential for the health and safety of *residential* areas but merely as ornamentation for other areas. As the courts generally did not accept aesthetics as a justification for zoning restrictions, the yard requirements for nonresidential uses had to be based upon future street widenings or upon proximity to residential uses. Such attitudes have gradually been changing. Yards, however, have traditionally been required for residential uses in nonresidential districts, and many ordinances have long contained special yard provisions applicable to any nonresidential building on a lot adjoining a residential district. For example:

Every principal building may be built without any side yard, provided, however, that where a side yard in the B-1 Retail Business Zone District shall abut the side yard of any residential zone, there shall be provided a minimum side yard of 12 feet. In the event that

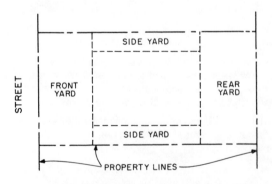

Figure 4-6 Yards in a single-family district.

a side yard be provided for a structure within the B-1 Retail Business Zone District, said side yard shall be not less than 12 feet.

Front yards are often dealt with in similar fashion. On a corner lot in a commercial district, the developer of an office building might find that the building must meet residential front-yard standards on the side street because a residential district adjoins the rear lot line. In addition, more and more ordinances seem to be incorporating general requirements for basic yards in nonresidential districts. Such provisions are especially common in districts that encompass planned commercial or industrial developments, in those where an image of prestige is being promoted, and in those containing neighborhoods that are in transition from residential to commercial use.

Although our main concern at this point is in defining the zoning envelope for a principal building, the reader should be aware that the yard standards may also be applicable to fences, walls, hedges, signs, parking lots, open-air sales and storage, swimming pools, and accessory structures generally. Detached accessory buildings, by the way, are often treated more leniently than principal buildings. For example, in a district requiring a forty-foot rear yard and a fifteen-foot side yard for the principal building, a detached accessory building might be permitted within five feet of the side or rear property line.

The reader should also be aware that the basic yard requirement is not the only kind of setback applicable to a principal building. There may be an additional setback mandated at ground level to allow for future widening of a street. A triangular setback area might be specified as a corner lot to preserve *vision clearance* for motorists approaching the intersection. Sometimes, this setback applies only to the first story. There may also be standards for setbacks, either at ground level or at upper-floor levels, that vary with the height of the building. These variable setbacks will be described in conjunction with the height standards.

Building Heights and Variable Setbacks

For zoning purposes, the height of a building can be measured in feet, in stories, or in both ways. It is measured from a starting elevation that is often known as *grade*. On perfectly level terrain, the *grade* elevation would be obvious, but seldom is this the case. A steeply sloping site may have differences in elevation at ground level of fifteen feet or more. As the average height of a building story is roughly ten feet, the way in which the grade is defined can make a difference in the number of stories permitted. In many ordinances, a story can be constructed *below grade* on a sloping lot without using up any of the allowable height. Thus, the definition of this base elevation is an important determinant of the zoning envelope. In some ordinances the grade is simply the average *existing elevation* (*natural grade*) across the front building line; in others, it is the proposed *finished elevation*. Here are a few examples of other definitions of grade:

1. The average elevation of the ground level at the foundation wall of the building.
2. The level of the public sidewalk opposite the middle of the front of the building.
3. A. For buildings have walls adjoining one street only, the elevation of the sidewalk at the center of the wall adjoining the street.

B. For buildings having walls adjoining more than one street, the average of the elevation of the sidewalk at the centers of all walls adjoining the streets.

C. For buildings having no wall adjoining the street, the average level of the finished surface of the ground adjacent to the exterior walls of the building. Any wall approximately parallel to and not more than fifteen feet from a street line is to be considered as adjoining the street. Sidewalk grades shall be as established by the office of the Director of Public Works.

In some zoning ordinances, the basic grade is not defined; the definition contained in some other municipal ordinance, such as the building code, is used.

Once the property owner has established the beginning elevation for the height limits, then it is time to consider the limits themselves. They are of two kinds: *absolute* and *variable*. In one-family and two-family districts, the limits are usually *absolute*. That is to say, they consist of fixed numbers of stories or feet that may be exceeded only by getting a hardship variance or by erecting one of the listed exceptions (flagpoles, church steeples, water towers, cupolas, etc.). The definition of "height" must be read to find out just what parts of the building are included in the limitation. Frequently height is measured to the highest point on a building. In cases of gambrel, gable, or hip roofs, however, it is sometimes measured to the mean height level between the eaves and the ridge.

In residential districts, a common limit is "2½ stories or 35 feet." Here are two sample definitions of "half-story":

Half story means the space within or under a sloping roof, the floor area of which does not exceed two-thirds of the floor area of the story immediately below it and which does not contain an independent apartment.

Story, half. A story under a gable, hip, or gambrel roof, the wall plates of which on at least two (2) opposite exterior walls are not more than two (2) feet above the floor of such story.

Provisions for districts that permit buildings of over three stories frequently contain variable requirements for heights and setbacks, either as substitutes for the absolute height limits or in addition to them. For example:

Buildings Exceeding 45 Feet in Height. If a building exceeds 45 feet in height, then the building, or that portion of the building above 45 feet, shall be set back from the required side and rear yard lines one additional foot for each two feet of building height above 45 feet. This additional setback requirement shall not be interpreted to require a side yard in excess of the required front yard.

Although stated as a requirement for additional setbacks, this, in a sense, is also a variable height requirement, because the height is ultimately limited by the feasibility of providing the added setbacks. Note the phrase, "or that portion of the building above 45 feet." This implies that the variable setbacks do not need to be applied to the base, only to the upper levels. In some ordinances, the additional setbacks are not required at the front of a building for a height not exceeding a specified multiple of the street width. Above that height, no portion of the structure is allowed to exceed the limits imposed by an imaginary plane inclined at a specified angle. A simplified version of this is shown in Figure 4-7. In this example, no portion of the building is permitted

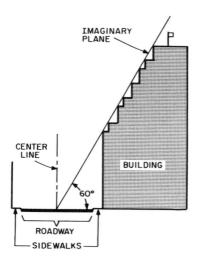

Figure 4-7 Example of front setback based upon inclined plane.

to be closer to the street than an imaginary plan inclined at an angle of sixty degrees with the street and extending upward from the center line of the street. A control of this sort encourages a "ziggurat" profile on a building.

Controls making use of inclined planes can be very complex, requiring expert help in dealing with the zoning administrators. Keep the following example in mind when reading Chapter 5 on how zoning works and the importance of interpretation:

Height and Bulk Control Regulations. Between a height equal to one (1) times the controlling width of fronting streets and a height equal to two (2) times the controlling width of fronting streets, buildings shall be erected as follows: Along street lines so as not to penetrate a seventy (70) degree street line setback plan except that an aggregate width of penetration not to exceed fifty (50) percent of the frontage of the lot shall be permitted so long as a single width of penetration does not exceed one hundred (100) feet.

Along side lot lines, which are not street lines, so as to be no closer than five (5) feet to the side lot line or to remain within a seventy (70) degree side setback plane, whichever requires the greater setback, except that an aggregate width of penetration not to exceed twenty (20) percent of the depth of the lot shall be permitted so long as the width of a single penetration does not exceed seventy (70) feet. The street line setback plane shall not be penetrated by a projection of the building which also penetrates a side setback plane.

Along rear lot lines which are not street lines, so as to be no closer than fifteen (15) feet to the rear lot line or to remain within a sixty (60) degree rear setback plane, whichever requires the greater setback, except that an aggregate width of penetration not to exceed fifty (50) percent of the width of the lot shall be permitted so long as the width of a single penetration does not exceed seventy (70) feet. The side setback planes may not be penetrated by a projection of the building which also penetrates the rear setback plane.

Walls surrounding courts by as much as seventy (70) percent shall set back from opposite walls so as to fall beneath a plane inclined upward at sixty (60) degrees from the horizontal and beginning at the base of the opposite wall of the court.

When there is an alley along a side or rear lot line, setback shall be measured from the centerline of such alley as vertically projected to the level of the required setback and setback planes shall have their bases along the center of such alley as vertically projected to height equal to one (1) times the controlling width of fronting streets.

Above a height equal to three (3) times the controlling width of fronting streets, no additional setback is required, provided however, that any setback line established between one (1) and two (2) times the controlling width of fronting streets shall not be penetrated.

A much simpler example is the next one, which applies to a central business district:

HEIGHT LIMITS. No building hereafter erected or structurally altered shall exceed the cubical contents of a prism having a base equal to the area of the lot and having a height two (2) times the width of the street on which the lot abuts; provided however, that a tower with a base not exceeding twenty-five percent (25%) of the lot area may be constructed without reference to the above limitations.

If the lot abuts on two (2) streets of unequal width, then for the purpose of calculating the cubical contents, the wider of the two streets shall control for a distance of two hundred (200) feet measured at right angles back from such wider street, provided that such two hundred (200) feet shall be within the "C-4" Central Business District.

Note the exemption ". . . a tower with a base not exceeding twenty-five percent (25%) of the lot area. . . ." This is a control over *lot coverage,* which is the next development standard to be discussed.

Intensity of Development

After the basic zoning envelope has been defined for a parcel, there are still other controls that usually must be applied before the property owner can know just how large a building may be placed on the site. These controls have to do with the *intensity of development* and regulate the proportion of the site that may be covered by buildings (*lot coverage*); the ratio of total floor space to total area (*floor/area ratio*); and in multiple-family districts, the number of dwelling units per acre (*density*). *Lot coverage* is normally a simple and direct control, expressed as a maximum percentage of total lot area. (Remember, however, that easements may or may not count as part of total lot area.) Figure 4-8 illustrates how the simple form works. In some ordinances, the lot coverage permitted varies according to the height of the structure. For example, the standard might diminish from thirty percent for a two-story structure down to only eight percent for one thirty stories in height.

In addition to the maximum lot coverage, it is not uncommon to find specified a minimum area that must be kept in "open space." The definition of "open space" varies from ordinance to ordinance, but generally it includes landscaped area and area devoted to recreation, and sometimes it excludes parking space and driveways. The *open space* requirement may be stated in terms of a ratio to the total floor area in the building or, for residential development, in terms of so many square feet per dwelling unit.

The requirements for *off-street parking and loading* can also be critical, in some situations, in determining lot coverage. On a site with an odd shape or rugged topography, a building that needs a generous provision for parking might be more limited in its site coverage by the area required for parking than

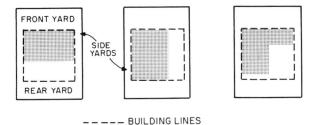

----- BUILDING LINES

Figure 4-8 Illustrating how the same lot coverage can be applied in different shapes. In this example, each shaded area represents 30 percent coverage.

by the direct *lot coverage* control. Parking requirements will be discussed more fully toward the end of this chapter.

Floor/Area Ratio

Floor/area ratio, also called *floor/lot ratio* and simply F.A.R., represents an attempt to control the intensity of site development with a maximum of flexibility. It is defined as the ratio between (*a*) the total floor area in the building, or buildings, on a site and (*b*) the total area of the site itself. Thus, a floor/area ratio of 2.0 would permit 40,000 square feet of floor space on a site of 20,000 square feet. A ratio of 2.5 would permit 50,000 square feet of floor space on a site of the same size. Figure 4–9 shows three of the many options available to the owner of a lot that is subject to an F.A.R. of 4.0. In each of the three illustrations, the lot size is the same: 100,000 square feet. Thus in each case, the maximum floor area allowed is 400,000 square feet. In Figure 4-9a, the owner has covered the entire site with a four-story structure containing 100,000 square feet per floor. In Figure 4-9b, half of the site has been covered. As there are only 50,000 square feet on each floor, the building in Figure 4-9b can be as tall as eight stories. In Figure 4-9c, the entire site has been covered with a one-story structure, using up to 100,000 of the 400,000 square feet of floor area permitted. The remaining 300,000 square feet have been put into a tower that is twelve stories in height. This height is possible because the tower covers only one-fourth of the base and each level has only 25,000 square feet.

In these examples, we have discussed floor area as if it included all of the area covered by the building multiplied by the number of stories. In doing so we have overly simplified the term, because the definition of *floor area* normally excludes some space from the limitations. The exact nature of the exclusions varies among ordinances, but here are some representative examples defining *floor area:*

1. The gross horizontal areas of the several floors of a building, exclusive of garages, basements, open porches, and equipment and service areas measured from the exterior face of the exterior walls of a building.

2. The sum of the gross horizontal areas of one or more floors of a building excluding cellar, attic, garage, open breezeway, open porches, and terraces.

3. The gross horizontal area measured from the exterior faces of the exterior walls, the exterior faces of supporting exterior columns for any floor not enclosed by exterior walls, the centerline of any party wall separating two buildings, or as measured from the exterior face of a projection, the area of which is included in this definition. In particular FLOOR AREA shall include the following:

   (1) Exterior corridor space from which access is gained to dwelling and/or sleeping units.

   (2) Floor space in penthouses and attics.

   (3) Floor space used for mechanical equipment.

   (4) Floor space in accessory buildings.

   (5) Elevator shafts and stairwells at each floor.

   (6) Floor space in interior balconies or mezzanines.

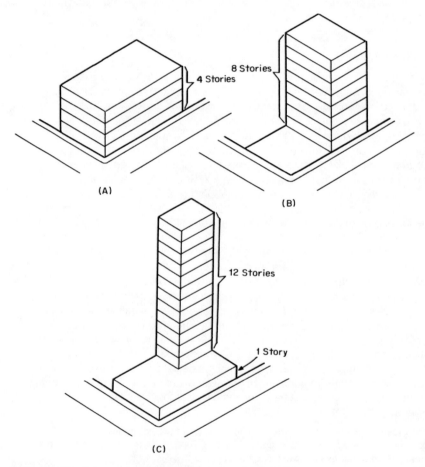

Figure 4-9 Three examples of options when F.A.R. is 4.0.

FLOOR AREA shall NOT include:

(1) Exterior unenclosed private balconies.

(2) Unenclosed ground floor space.

(3) Permitted covered or enclosed parking areas.

4. Floor-Area:

    A. *Commercial, Business, and Industrial*: The sum of the gross horizontal area of the several floors of a building measured from the centerline of walls separating two buildings but not including attic space with headroom of less than seven (7) feet, basement space used for retailing, uncovered steps or fire escapes, accessory water towers or cooling towers, accessory off-street parking spaces, or accessory off-street loading berths.

    B. *Residential*: The gross horizontal areas of the several floors of a dwelling, exclusive of garages, basements and open porches, measured from the exterior faces of the exterior walls of a dwelling.

Again we are reminded of the need to study the definitions.

As an encouragement to builders to put extra features into their developments, some ordinances grant F.A.R. *bonuses*. For example, in a downtown district where yards and open space are not normally required, a bonus might be granted for the provision of ground-level open space. The use of a "carrot" in addition to the traditional "stick" is known as *incentive zoning*. Besides the use of an F.A.R. bonus, it can involve other bonuses, such as a density bonus for a residential development that provides extra amenities. *Incentive zoning* will be discussed more fully in Chapter 6.

The restrictions on floor/area ratio regulate some aspects of intensity but not all. They are most effective in limiting the intensity with which cubic space is used by buildings. They are effective only indirectly in regulating the intensity with which a site is used by human activity. Of course, the greater the floor area, the greater the opportunity for human activity; but the degree to which the floor area is utilized can vary considerably. A floor in an office, for example, can be occupied mainly by people or mainly by filing cabinets. The most direct control over activity would be one limiting the number of persons present at any given time—employees, customers, residents, and visitors. Fire prevention codes impose such restrictions on restaurants and other gathering places, but a fire code carries with it an awareness of danger that a zoning ordinance lacks. For most purposes limits on occupancy are not practical and, in a democratic society, perhaps not desirable. There is another indirect form of control, however, that can be used in residential districts; this is a regulation of the *density* of dwelling units per acre.

Density Controls

Dwelling units vary in size, and so do the families occupying them, but most ordinances attempt to regulate density by limiting the number of *dwelling units* per acre. In fact, we know of no specific ordinances in the United States that attempt to do it any other way. We have heard it proposed that limitations be based upon the number of *bedrooms* per acre, and perhaps somewhere there is an ordinance that incorporates this feature. Not being aware of it, however, we will stick to the typical variety.

The typical zoning text specifies either a *maximum* number of *units per acre* or a *minimum* number of *square feet of lot area per family*. One acre is equal to 43,560 square feet. Thus we have the following conversions:

Maximum Dwelling Units Per Acre (d.u.'s/ac.)	Minimum Lot Area Per Family In Square Feet
2	21,780
3	14,520
4	10,890
6	7,260
8	5,445
10	4,356
15	2,904
20	2,178
30	1,452
40	1,089
60	726
80	544.5
100	435.6

Rounding off these numbers can be deceptive. For example, if the ordinance requires 4400 square feet of lot area per unit, then ten units cannot be placed on a one-acre site; only nine may be built. On two acres (87,120 square feet), nineteen may be built.

The word "acre" can also be deceptive. Sometimes the term "net acre" is used. This excludes the area taken up by streets and other specified uses. Whether the simple word "acre" means "gross acre" or "net acre" can make a big difference in the number of units permitted.

Earlier in the chapter, we discussed basic area standards. Nearly all zoning ordinances also use area standards as a means of controlling the *density* of residential development. In single-family districts, the flat minimum set for each lot controls the number of dwelling units per net acre. In districts permitting more than one family, the basic area required for the first unit on a site is often greater than that specified for each additional unit, as indicated in the following example:

Lot area per family:

(a) A lot occupied by a single-family dwelling shall contain an area of not less than six thousand (6,000) square feet and an average width of not less than fifty (50) feet.

(b) A lot occupied by a two-family dwelling shall contain an area not less than six thousand (6,000) square feet and an average width of not less than fifty (50) feet.

(c) A lot on which a multiple dwelling is erected shall contain a width of not less than one hundred (100) feet and an area of not less than nine thousand (9,000) square feet for a three (3) dwelling unit, plus two thousand five hundred (2,500) square feet for each additional dwelling unit.

(See also the tabular presentation from Charleston, South Carolina, in Figure 4-1.)

The justification for this is that the area needed for one unit includes the required yard areas. The yards needed for more than one family do not increase proportionately with additional units; therefore, the total lot-area-per-family need not be raised proportionately.

Buffers, Parking, and Loading

Controls over floor/area ratio, density, and lot coverage are not the only constraints on the intensity of development. The developer sometimes discovers that the shape and topography of a tract seem to conspire with controls over parking, loading area, buffers, and open space so as to limit the intensity permitted to a much greater extent than had been anticipated. Requirements for open space have already been mentioned. We refer to them again because they are sometimes overlooked in the developer's basic density calculations, leading to unhappy consequences.

Another constraint on the intensity of use is the requirements for off-street parking and loading. Standards for the number of parking spaces are generally expressed as ratios to dwelling units, to seating capacity, to floor area, or to numbers of employees. Loading spaces are usually related to total floor area for various kinds of uses.

It is not enough to know how many spaces are needed. The size of each space is also important, and the definition of a "parking space" or "loading space" is not always the same in different ordinances. Some ordinances require larger spaces than others. Even the same ordinance may have different minimums for different kinds of uses.

In addition to the standards for number and size of spaces, ordinances often contain other parking restrictions, such as prohibition against parking in any required front yard. Commercial parking might be banned within so many feet of a single-family district. As parking lots increase the runoff of rainwater, there may be requirements for retention reservoirs to permit a more gradual discharge of water after heavy rains. Some ordinances have mandatory provisions for the landscaping of parking lots. Many also prohibit access across residential districts to serve parking for nonresidential uses.

Buffers

Buffers, in the form of fences, walls, hedges, earthern berms (low artificial ridges), and/or a wide band of trees and shrubbery, are often required along the property lines of a nonresidential development that adjoin a residential district. As the width specified can be as much as fifty feet, or even more, a developer needs to give careful attention to what these requirements might do to the anticipated placement of buildings. The neighbors, on the other hand, need to inquire into what assurance, if any, there is for satisfactory maintenance of the buffer. Many a beautiful buffer has deteriorated in only a few years from lack of water, fertilizer, and wall maintenance and from failure to clean out accumulated trash. When the wall is on the developer's side of the property line, and the landscaping on the other, there is a natural tendency for the developer to ignore maintenance. See Figure 4-10.

Airport Approach Restrictions

As we pointed out in Chapter 2, zoning ordinances often contain special restrictions on heights and uses in the vicinity of airports that extend out 10,000 feet or more from the ends of runways. These restrictions are superimposed on the restrictions of the regular zoning districts. An ordinance should always be checked to see if there are such provisions, and if they are applicable, before any commitment is made to develop or invest in property.

Multiple Buildings and Accessory Structures

So far we have described development standards for the *principal building* on a lot. In many, if not most, districts, only one principal building may be placed on a lot. Where more than one is allowed, provision must be made for the spacing between the buildings. Regulations for this spacing can be quite complex.

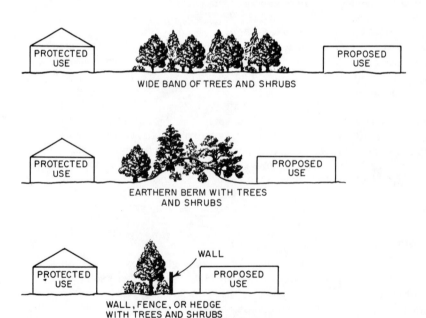

PROTECTED USE   PROPOSED USE

WIDE BAND OF TREES AND SHRUBS

PROTECTED USE   PROPOSED USE

EARTHERN BERM WITH TREES AND SHRUBS

WALL

PROTECTED USE   PROPOSED USE

WALL, FENCE, OR HEDGE WITH TREES AND SHRUBS

Figure 4-10 Examples of buffers.

District Provisions and General Provisions

Most development standards for property in a given zoning district are grouped together in one place in the zoning ordinance, but not all of them are. A property owner who relies entirely on the *district provisions* can count on trouble. Regulations that supplement or modify the district provisions are found in several other sections of the typical zoning ordinance. Some of the more common subjects covered include off-street parking, sign controls, airport height limits, limitations on the number of buildings per lot, locations of accessory structures, general exceptions to the height limits, storage of recreational vehicles, visibility clearances at intersections, and exceptions to front-yard requirements. Though often called *General Provisions*, these regulations can appear under a variety of names, among which are *Supplementary District Regulations, Exceptions and Modifications*, and *Exceptions to Development Standards*.

As an example of the importance of general provisions, let us consider the C-2 Commercial Service District in Atlanta, Georgia. This district, which permits service stations among other things, has the following front-yard requirements.

Front Yard. There shall be a front yard having a depth of not less than forty (40) feet. No product may be stored, displayed, or offered for sale within a required front yard, and on a corner lot within the required side yard along a side street.

Now the novice might conclude that this provision would prohibit the sale of gasoline, or the location of gasoline pumps, within forty feet of the front lot line. What the novice does not know is that it is not enough to read the above regulation on page 40 of the ordinance. It is also necessary to turn to page 60 under an article entitled "GENERAL AND SUPPLEMENTARY REGULATIONS" to find that the front-yard requirement in the district regulations does not apply to gasoline pumps and that, indeed, the following lesser requirement governs:

Service station pumps and pump islands may occupy a required yard provided that no portion of said pump or pump island may be closer than twelve (12) feet to any street line. Service station canopies may occupy a required yard provided that no portion of said canopies may be closer than six (6) feet to any street line.

In addition to front-yard exceptions, there are usually exceptions to height limits for spires, steeples, cupolas, elevator housings, and the like. Balconies and steps may be exceptions to all yard and lot-coverage requirements. Not all exceptions favor the property owner, however. Some impose stricter controls. For example, in a section entitled *Building Lines* additional setbacks might be required along specified streets.

Even the section of the ordinance dealing with *definitions* can sometimes contain regulations that have been incorporated right into the definitions. Consider the following examples:

Camp Sites

Camp sites are areas which are located on high ground in an S-1 district. They should have a good access road, fresh water, and when feasible an electrical supply with several outlets which campers may tap into. The areas should be segregated into parcels with the specific purposes of serving either mobilized camping facilities such as trailers, and non-mobilized facilities such as tents. In addition adequate vehicle parking space should be provided for each camp site. The City may assess a small fee such as $1.00/day on the mobilized campers to cover the cost of the electric service provided. (*City of New Kensington, Pennsylvania*)

Gasoline Station

Buildings and premises where gasoline, oil, grease, batteries, tires and automobile accessories may be dispensed at retail, and where in addition minor servicing and repair may be made, and cold drinks, candy, tobacco and similar goods sold as accessory to the principal use. Uses permissible at a gasoline station do not include major mechanical and body work, painting, welding or other work involving noise, glare, fumes, or smoke, or automobile storage or sales areas. (*Concord, New Hampshire*)

Hobby Shop

An accessory use which is not conducted for renumeration but solely as a hobby, pasttime or means of education or entertainment. Such activity shall be carried on entirely within a building and only between the hours of 7 a.m. and 10 p.m. (*Phoenix, Arizona*)

Home Occupation

An occupation conducted in a dwelling unit, provided that:

a. No person other than members of the family residing on the premises shall be engaged in such occupation.

b. The use of the dwelling unit for the home occupation shall be clearly incidental and subordinate to its use for residential purposes by its occupant, and not more than one-third (1/3) of the floor area of the dwelling unit shall be used in the conduct of the home occupation.

c. No home occupation shall be conducted in any accessory building.

d. No commodity nor stock in trade shall be kept or sold upon the premises.

e. No sign or other evidence of the conduct of a home occupation shall be visible outside the dwelling unit.

f. No mechanical equipment is operated except such as normally used for purely domestic or household purposes; and provided further that in the pursuit of such home occupation, no equipment shall be used which creates noise, vibration, glare, fumes, odors, or electrical interference detectable to the normal senses off the lot, if the occupation is conducted in a single-family residence, or outside the dwelling unit if conducted in a single-family residence. In the case of electrical interference, no equipment or process shall be used which creates visual or audible interferences in any radio or television receiver off the premises or causes fluctuations in line voltage off the premises. (*Tallahassee, Florida*)

Substandard Lots-of-Record

Zoning is an ordinance that balances future plans with present reality. It must deal with the problem of pre-existing lots that may be too narrow, too shallow, or too small in area to be in compliance with the regulations. Lots that were legally separate parcels prior to the passage of the ordinance are usually called "lots-of-record," and even if they are substandard, some use of them must be permitted. Often, however, this use is more limited than the district permits generally. For example, in a district permitting low-rise apartments, a substandard lot-of-record might be limited to a single-family residence. In some ordinances, two or more substandard lots of record that are contiguous and in a single ownership must be used in combination and may not be sold separately.

Advertising Signs

Controls on advertising signs are often found grouped together in a special article of the text. Sometimes they are even in an entirely separate ordinance. Sign regulations can be elaborate, and we will not attempt to explain them here. We will, however, touch on a few important points. Perhaps the most important point to be made is the distinction commonly found between *general advertising signs*, on the one hand, and what are variously called *point-of-purchase*, *owner identification*, or simply *business signs* on the other hand. The latter are directly related to a business activity on a site. The provisions regulating a business sign are based upon the assumption that some sort of sign at the location of the business is necessary both to the operator and to the general public. If business is to succeed, and if the public is to be served, then new customers must know where to find a bakery, a restaurant, or a shoe repair shop. At least one sign is needed for each business, and it must be on the same site. This assumption of necessity still leaves open the questions of how many and what kinds of signs are needed, how big they should be, and what kinds of lighting should be permitted. The regulations for business signs deal with these questions, often making distinctions between signs in different zoning districts. Signs are categorized as *roof* signs, *flat-wall* signs, *projecting* signs, *free-standing* signs, *window* signs, and *mobile* signs. They are also classified as *temporary* or *permanent*. Provisions are made for each category including the number to be permitted for each business and street frontage and the extent to which flashing, or intermittent, lighting will be allowed.

General advertising signs are normally treated more strictly than are business signs on the assumption that they are not as necessary in particular locations. A business sign is an accessory structure or use. A general advertising sign, however, may be treated as the *principal structure* and *principal use* on a lot.

Summary

Development standards in zoning are numerous and diverse. Most can be found in the provisions for each district, but others are scattered throughout the text. Careful study is needed by property owners and developers to ascertain just what the standards are and how they relate to each other.

5
How Zoning Works

Dan Carter, a developer, has an option to purchase the nineteen-acre tract known as the "Brady Estate." For twenty-five years, the tract has been surrounded by substantial homes on one-acre and two-acre lots. Now that the tract is finally available for development, single-family homes on such large lots no longer seem to be the most profitable use. Dan wants to get the tract rezoned from "R-1 Single-Family" to "R-5 Single-Family." The "R-5" district permits lots as small as 6000 square feet. It also permits, as *conditional uses*, the townhouses and condominiums that Dan hopes to build.

Fred and Hilda Potts have heard of Dan's plans. They are militantly opposed. As co-presidents of the Maplewood Homeowners Club, they have alerted all eighty-three member households to what they view as a serious threat. In preparing for their defense against Dan, the Potts bought a copy of the latest revision of the zoning ordinance, both text and map, and began studying how it applied to Maplewood. They were upset at finding several apparent violations of the ordinance in their neighborhood. In addition to opposing what Dan wants to do, they intend to confront the zoning administrator with the apparent violations and try to improve the effectiveness of zoning enforcement.

Meanwhile, across town in Runnymeade Park subdivision, Mary Trigg has been trying to get a building permit for a ten-foot by ten-foot addition to the rear of her house to provide space for a new pottery kiln. She had employed a contractor who drew the plans and applied for the permit. Now the zoning administrator is holding up issuance of the permit because of two questions: (1) Is Mary's pottery making a permitted use? (2) Would the addition violate the rear-yard requirement? Mary decides to go down and talk to the zoning administrator.

All four of the people in these examples are about to become involved with the processes of zoning administration. One, Mary Trigg, has had limited experience with zoning and knows little about how it works. Two, Hilda and Fred Potts, have had a fair amount of experience. On the average of once every two years, their civic club opposes something at a public hearing. Still, there is much that they do not understand. The fourth person, Dan Carter, is well aware of how zoning works. In fact, he is not so concerned with how it works as he is with *how he can make it work* to his advantage.

The ability to make zoning work to advantage should be a goal of every property owner. It is not a goal that can be attained overnight, however. We have already discussed the complexity and lack of uniformity in the regulations themselves. The administration of zoning is similarly complex. Zoning is administered and influenced by human beings with a variety of motivations, attitudes, intelligence, and sensibilities. Two identical zoning ordinances adopted in different communities would not be administered in exactly the same way. The property owner needs to understand why that is so and how to adapt to the local system. This understanding is as much a need for the objector as it is for the developer.

The property owner also needs to understand that zoning involves more than one process. There is a process for getting a permit, a process for getting a violation corrected, a process for appeals, a process for obtaining or opposing a variance, a process for getting or stopping a rezoning, and other processes according to how a particular ordinance reads. Depending upon which process is involved, a property owner's initial experience with zoning can begin at one of several levels in the government. As the three examples cited at the beginning of this chapter represent fairly common ways in which people become involved with zoning, it might help to see just what experiences they have in going through various zoning processes. Let's start with Mary Trigg.

Mary Trigg's experience begins right on the front line of zoning with the people who review building plans, issue permits, and track down violations. In Mary's case, her contractor went to the city *building department* and applied for a *building permit*. In doing so, he submitted several copies of the construction plan for the proposed addition. He also submitted several copies of a *plot plan* showing the dimensions of Mary's lot, the location of her house, and the location of the proposed addition. The permit clerk sent one copy of the construction plan and one copy of the plot plan to the *zoning division*. Employees of the zoning division reviewed the plans and noted that: (1) the proposed addition would violate the rear-yard requirement; and (2) the use for a kiln might indicate a nonpermissible home occupation. The contractor suggested to Mary that she had better have a talk with the *zoning administrator*.

What can Mary expect when she meets the *zoning administrator*? Before answering that question, we should point out that not all zoning administrators are called by that name. Nor are they all in the same kind of organization. In our example, the zoning administrator is a division chief within a building department, which is also responsible for administering the electrical code, the plumbing code, and the building code as well as the zoning ordinance. In some communities, there is a separate zoning department. In small towns, zoning administration may be the responsibility of the town clerk. Whatever the title or the form of organization may be, the zoning administrator has considerable power and flexibility in interpreting the ordinance, as Mary will discover.

Few ordinances are so tightly written that they cover all situations without the use of administrative discretion. Some leave great latitude to enforcement personnel as a result of oversights or errors in wording. For example, the definition of "grade" may not be clear for a sloping lot that fronts on two different streets. Depending on how the zoning administrator interprets "grade," the developer might be allowed one more or one less story in a proposed building. If the administrator interprets "grade" as being along the lower of the two streets, one less story might be allowed. On the other hand, if the "grade" is deemed to be along the higher street, then one more story might be allowed.

In a "C-1 Business" zone, the ordinance might require all merchandise to be sold and displayed in a "completely enclosed" building. What is a completely enclosed building? If the front of a store is made up largely of folding doors that are opened early every morning and not closed until late at night, is the store completely enclosed? Some front-line officials might so interpret it. Decisions of administrators can be appealed, but appeals take time, and time can be critical.

It is important, then, to know just what kind of people one is going to encounter in the front lines. This is something that each developer or objector will need to ascertain, because there are no firm generalizations that we can make. In formal education, for example, zoning officials range from high-school dropouts to the holders of degrees in engineering and architecture. We will make some subjective observations, however. It has been our experience that the administrators of zoning tend to be people who pride themselves on being "practical" rather than "theoretical" and who view the ideas of planners with some scepticism.

In many communities, officials have a built-in bias in favor of granting building and zoning permits. This bias stems from two facts of life in local government. One is that the combined fees from all permits (building, electrical,

A. "GRADE" IS ALONG LOWER STREET

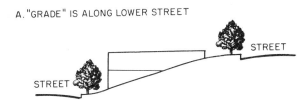

B. "GRADE" IS ALONG HIGHER STREET

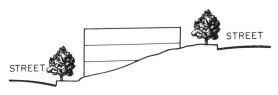

Figure 5-1 Two alternative interpretations of "grade" on double-frontage lot.

plumbing, zoning) can be substantial. They may even be in excess of the expenditures required for running the department. Being able to produce a "profit" for the general municipal coffers can be a matter of pride, and even a source of power for the official. The other fact of life is the strong dependence of most local governments on the real property tax as a source of revenue. More buildings add to the tax base and, therefore, help to produce more revenue without the need for an unpopular increase in the tax rate. (Never mind the possibility that the new buildings might also add to the need for increased expenditures.) Building and zoning officials sometimes take pride in the value of buildings added to the local tax base each year and may not wish to jeopardize new construction by being "overly strict" in interpreting ordinances.

Mary Trigg's first step is to visit the zoning administrator and try to get the ordinance interpreted in her favor. They have a lengthy conversation, and the administrator is obviously sympathetic, but he will not approve the issuance of a permit. He tells her, however, that she may appeal his decision to the *board of adjustment* (the *board of appeals* in some communities), so Mary fills out an application for an appeal and begins thinking about how to present her case.

Board of Adjustment

Although some zoning ordinances provide for appeals directly to the local governing body, the usual provision is for a *board of adjustment* (or *board of appeals*). This board is made up of several residents of the community appointed for overlapping terms by the local governing body. It is difficult to generalize about the kind of people appointed, but often they are in businesses or professions having some connection with building or real estate. Builders, architects, and attorneys, for example, are likely appointees. A *board of adjustment* is sometimes referred to as being a "quasi-judicial" body, meaning that it has some of the characteristics of a court of law. At the meetings of some boards, business is conducted much like that of a court. Witnesses are sworn and the merits of applications are often argued by lawyers. All boards are not so formal, however.

Board members generally serve without pay or for only a nominal amount, their reward being the satisfaction of performing a civic duty. This duty is not always a pleasant one. Members who are professionals or proprietors of small businesses may be subjected to pressures from important clients, customers, or lenders to lean toward the approval of particular applications. A member who is not completely scrupulous might welcome the opportunity to curry favor with potential clients or customers by gaining the reputation of being "reasonable" or "practical."

In addition to appeals from administrative decisions, a *board of adjustment* normally considers two other kinds of matters:

1. Applications for *special exceptions*, the conditions for which are spelled out in the text of the ordinance, for uses, such as telephone exchanges and electric power substations, that must sometimes be permitted in otherwise incompatible surroundings for

reasons of public necessity or convenience. (This *special exception* is a more limited kind of permission than is the conditional-use permit. Unfortunately, some ordinances confuse the terms by making them synonymous.)

2. Requests for *variances* from the literal application of the ordinance on the grounds that, because of conditions peculiar to the property in question (or to it and a few others), such literal application would result in unnecessary hardship.

At the moment, however, we are interested only in the hearing of an *appeal*.

Mary is notified that her appeal will be heard at a meeting set for three weeks hence. During this period, her neighbors receive notices in the mail telling them of the matter to be considered and of the time and place of the board's meeting. The ordinance for Mary's community might even provide for a temporary sign to be posted in her front yard as a means of giving notice. Mary's neighbors begin calling her to discuss the matter. They do not object to her pottery making or to her proposed addition. They do object to the appeal, however. They fear that, if granted, it might lead to other, and less desirable, home occupations. They tell Mary that they would go along with her proposal if she could get it approved as a *conditional use* with strict conditions attached. But the zoning administrator has already explained to Mary that the ordinance does not permit such a conditional use in her district. Mary decides to go ahead with the appeal.

At the hearing, Mary again receives a sympathetic response. The members of the board of adjustment make it clear that they would like to help her. On the other hand, they are impressed with the administrator's reasoning and with the neighbors' objections. They could rule either way. Let's see what Mary's next steps would be with either outcome.

ASSUMPTION A: The Board Rules in Mary's Favor

If the board of adjustment rules Mary's pottery making to be a permissible use, then her next step is to apply for a *variance* from the rear-yard requirement so that she can build the addition. She will apply for the variance in much the same manner in which she applied for the hearing of her appeal. She might have to pay a fee of perhaps $25 at the time of application. This amount varies from place to place. The neighboring property owners will be notified in much the same way that they were notified of the appeal, and the hearing will be held by the same *board of adjustment* that heard the appeal.

Requests for *variances* are by far the largest category of items considered by the average board of adjustment and the most important of the board's responsibilities. The need for variances arises out of the fact that all zoning districts are to some extent arbitrary. Properties that are supposedly similar are placed in the same category and regulated uniformly. This practice nearly always results in the inclusion of at least a few properties that are quite different from the others. For example, a large section of town might have been sub-divided into lots 80 feet wide and 150 feet deep. When the zoning ordinance was adopted, one-third of these lots contained homes. Each had front and rear yards of at least 40 feet in depth and side yards of at least 15 feet in width. These existing yard dimensions were used as the basis for the requirements

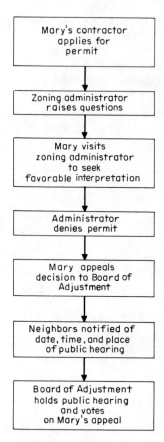

Figure 5-2 Mary Trigg's progress.

in the zoning district that was created for the neighborhood. In general, the standards are reasonable, but *on some properties the requirements cannot be met*! Two or three parcels of record might be only 90 feet in depth. A literal enforcement of the yard requirements (40 feet in front and 40 feet at the rear) would leave only 10 feet front-to-back for a house, clearly an unreasonable condition. Some relief must be granted to the property owner if the ordinance is not to be confiscatory. Other parcels of record might be unusually narrow (say, 40 or 45 feet in width). On these lots, the side-yard standards would be impracticable. Still other lots could be triangular in shape. On these, all yard provisions might be impediments to a reasonable use of the property.

Topography also can be a factor. A lot having a steep slope from front to back might present difficulties in connecting to a sewer. If the public sewer line is under the street instead of in an easement at the rear of the lot, then the legal front building line could conceivably be below the grade of the sewer. Some amelioration of the yard requirement might be the only reasonable solution to this problem.

The examples just cited seem clearly to call for variances, but not all situations are what they first seem to be. A lot that is substandard in width may be the result of the sale of a strip along one side to the owner of the adjacent lot. If this transaction took place after the effective date of the zoning regulations, then any resulting hardship would have to be considered "self-created" and not a justification for a variance.

Even if some kind of variance appears to be justified, there may be a serious question as to the *extent* to which the ordinance should be varied. If nearly all residences in a neighborhood have widths of sixty-five feet, and are located on lots that are one hundred feet in width, then should the owner of a lot that is seventy-five feet in width be granted a variance sufficient to construct a house sixty-five feet wide, or would justice be done if one fifty feet wide could be built? If a substandard lot is in a two-family district, then should the variance be enough to permit a two-family dwelling, or is a single-family dwelling all that the variance should allow? How much weight should the board give to possible detrimental effects that the neighboring property might suffer if the variance were granted? A board that is too liberal with variances can undermine the intent of the ordinance; one that is overly strict can perpetuate severe injustices.

State enabling legislation usually provides guidelines for a board of adjustment to follow, but a board may have considerable leeway in applying the guidelines. In some states, boards of adjustment are in the habit of granting "use variances." That is to say, they give property owners permission to put property to a use not otherwise permitted. This might be an apartment house, or perhaps even a retail establishment, in a single-family district. Many private citizens fail to appreciate the amount of discretion vested in the board. They concentrate their attention on the procedure for *amending* the ordinance and overlook the possibility that *varying* the regulations may have the same result.

In practice, boards of adjustment can differ greatly from one community to another in the degree of strictness with which they approach the subject of variances. Before bothering to submit a request for a variance, a property owner would do well to investigate the board's reputation for strictness. It is not enough to look at the statistics on approvals and disapprovals, however. Some boards may have reputations of such strictness that relatively few requests are made. The few that are made are clearly justified, so the percentage of applications that are approved is high. On the other hand, a board that grants only sixty percent of the requested variances may actually be fairly liberal. Its reputation may encourage requests of dubious merit, and those rejected may be only those that are the most blatantly unjustified.

A board that takes a strict stance will generally adhere to the following rules:

1. There must be a showing of hardship based upon unusual conditions in the size, shape, topography, or orientation of the property.

2. The unusual conditions must be peculiar to the property in question or to not more than a few properties in the zoning district. (A general condition would be a subject for action by the elected governing body of the community.)

3. The hardship alleged must be on the property itself. Personal hardships caused by other factors are not to be considered.

4. The hardship must not have been self-created by the present owner or by any previous owner subsequent to the effective date of the zoning regulations in question.

5. It must be clear that a literal application of the regulations would deprive the owner of a reasonable use of the property.

6. The relief granted should be only what is sufficient to permit a reasonable use.

7. The relief granted should not cause substantial detriment to nearby property or to the public good.

8. Under no circumstances should a variance be granted for a use or structure not otherwise permitted in the zoning district in which the property lies.

A board of adjustment adhering to these strict guidelines would not grant a variance to Mary Trigg. There is simply no hardship on her property that would deprive her of a reasonable use of it. In many communities, however, the boards require only a showing of "practical difficulty or unnecessary hardship," and in one of those localities Mary might well obtain her variance.

Let us assume that Mary does get a variance. Her next step is to inform her contractor, so that he can obtain the building permit. The contractor will post the permit in a conspicuous place on Mary's property and begin work. This is necessary so that any inspector driving by can see it. If no permit could be seen, it might be assumed that the work was taking place illegally. During the course of construction, one or more inspectors will visit the site periodically to make sure that the work that has been done is in compliance with the approved plans. Upon completion of the addition, a final inspection will be made. If the findings are favorable, then a *certificate of occupancy* (also called *occupancy permit*) is issued, and Mary can use the addition for the kiln.

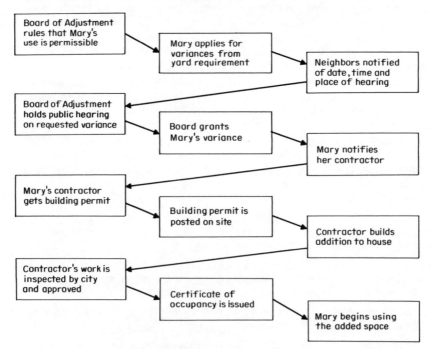

Figure 5-3 Mary Trigg's progress under Assumption "A".

Although seemingly straightforward, the inspection process is not always simple. Many problems can arise. For example, owners will sometimes attempt to "bootleg" illegal alterations of a building in defiance of the zoning law by doing all work at night. Even where a permit exists, the inspectors must be alert. For example, Fred White owned a two-story apartment building. The building contained eight units on the two main floors and one additional unit that was in a semi-basement with a ground-level entrance. This was possible because the building was on a corner lot and the side street was on a slope. The zoning ordinance normally permitted only eight units, but, because the ninth unit had been created prior to the effective date of the zoning restriction, its continued use was legal.

The basement did not extend under the entire building, and Fred got a permit to excavate and finish a basement under the remainder of the structure in order to provide storage space. Before the work was completed, an inspector dropped by without prior notice and saw that brand-new bathroom and kitchen fixtures were being unloaded and moved into the "storage space." Further checking revealed that Fred was in the process of creating an illegal apartment. Who would have expected that the inspectors would pay such close attention to the creation of a storage room?

Mary Trigg would never think of trying to cheat on zoning. When she gets her permit, everything will be legal and ethical. When and *if* that is. We have been assuming a favorable outcome on Mary's appeal of the zoning administrator's decision. Suppose this assumption is wrong. Suppose the board of adjustment upholds the administrator's interpretation that pottery making is not a permissible use.

ASSUMPTION B: Mary's Appeal is Denied

If Mary's appeal is rejected, she may have several possible alternative actions to pursue, depending upon how her ordinance reads.

1. She might retain an attorney and appeal to a court of law. As there are several points in zoning processes where this action might be taken, we are going to hold off our discussion of appeals to the courts until we have finished describing the nonjudicial processes. Judicial appeals will be discussed in Chapter 8.

2. If her ordinance permits, Mary might apply for a *use variance*. This application would be heard by the *board of adjustment* in much the same way that we have already described for the hearing of a variance from the yard requirements.

3. She might apply for a *conditional-use permit* if her ordinance listed "pottery making" as a conditional use in her district. But we have already said that this is not the case.

4. She might apply for an amendment to the *text* of the ordinance to list "pottery making" as a permitted use, or she might apply for an amendment to the *map* to move the zoning boundary so that at least the rear portion of her residence would be zoned as "B-2 Community Business" (assuming that the B-2 district permitted the pottery making).

The procedures that Mary will go through in her efforts to amend the ordinance are similar to what Dan Carter will experience in trying to get approval for developing the Brady Estate. They are also basically the procedures with which Fred and Hilda Potts will have to contend in opposing Dan's plans. We will therefore consider both Mary's and Dan's cases together. First, however, we have some unfinished business with the zoning administrator. Hilda and Fred have discovered several apparent zoning violations in their neighborhood, and they intend to confront the administrator with them. Here is what they have found:

1. On six lots along Crestwood Drive (where nobody belongs to the Maplewood Home-owners' Club) there are homes built recently in seeming disregard of the forty-five-foot front-yard requirement in Maplewood. The lots do fall off sharply from the street back toward a ravine, but Hilda and Fred cannot understand why the permits were granted without first requiring the builders to go through the variance process.

2. Just outside the boundaries of Maplewood subdivision, there is a ten-acre tract on which a general contractor has an office building, several sheds, and a large open area where equipment and materials are stored. The tract is zoned "R-1 Single Family Residential," just like Maplewood. Fred and Hilda cannot understand how such a thing could exist in a residential zone. They especially cannot understand how the stepped-up activity of late could be permissible. In the past six months, there has been a lot of welding taking place at night. Long-time residents say that the welding is a new development.

So, Hilda and Fred go to see the zoning administrator. Although the administrator is not exactly enthusiastic over their visit, he is not hostile either. The Potts family is actually helping him in one of his most difficult tasks: the finding and correction of violations. Even in the best-run and most highly systematic department, this task is difficult. Violations are found in a number of ways. Inspectors look for them routinely as they go about their other duties in the field. In some communities, the police help by spotting construction activity where no permit is posted. Applications for business licenses[1] are cross-checked to determine if the businesses represent zoning violations. Many violations come to light, however, only as a result of complaints from neighbors.

Violations are not always easy to correct. Local governments normally have two kinds of remedies available to stop violations. One is through the prosecution of a violator on charges of committing an offense or misdemeanor, resulting in a possible fine or jail sentence upon conviction. Ordinances usually provide that each day's continuation of a violation constitutes a separate offense. The other kind of remedy is through the seeking of an injunction or writ of mandamus to cause the violation to cease, and, if appropriate, to cause the premises to be restored to a condition not in violation.

In practice, violators are usually treated with great restraint. Property rights are respected in our society, and public opinion demands that restrictions on them be enforced sensitively. Zoning violators rarely go to jail. In fact the zoning

[1] *Business-license* regulations sometimes overlap with zoning. They can limit the locations of activities such as bars, package stores, and bingo parlors. They can also restrict hours of operation, size of operation, and use of display signs. As these items may also be regulated by the zoning ordinance, the owner of a business may need to deal at the same time with two different sets of officials. Thus, the zoning administrator must coordinate enforcement with the licensing official. Licensing regulates a business; zoning regulates real estate. As a business usually occupies real estate, some confusion between the two kinds of restrictions is understandable. The confusion sometimes leads to zoning provisions that are, in reality, licensing regulations.

inspectors will ordinarily try very hard to get voluntary compliance without charging the property owner with an offense. Thus violations can linger on for some time after they are reported and before they are corrected.

Nonconforming Uses and Structures

Now let's look at the two specific complaints made by Hilda and Fred. "The contractor's operation," explains the zoning administrator, "is a legal, nonconforming use." What does that mean? Well, a zoning ordinance represents a compromise between a desired pattern of uses and the need to accommodate a substantial investment already in existence. In order to comply with the constitutional prohibition against taking private property without just compensation, some allowances must be made for the retention, at least temporarily, of uses and structures existing at the effective date of the ordinance but not permitted by the ordinance. These are usually categorized as follows:

1. *Nonconforming uses of land* with incidental structures, e.g., used-car lots, drive-in movie theaters.

2. *Nonconforming uses in conforming buildings,* e.g., a dress shop in a residence.

3. *Nonconforming uses in nonconforming buildings,* e.g., service station in a residential district.

4. *Advertising signs*.

Some ordinances permit nonconforming uses and structures to remain indefinitely unless the structure is destroyed to the extent of a specified proportion of its replacement cost (say, sixty percent). They generally do not permit the use to be increased in extent or the structure to be altered substantially so as to increase its useful life. They also do not permit the use to be reestablished after having been discontinued for a specified period of time (usually either six months or one year).

Other ordinances go further and require a phasing out of both uses and structures that are nonconforming. The length of the period provided for the phasing out is supposed to allow ample time for the *amortization*[2] of investment and varies from two to five years, for most uses of land with incidental structures, to twenty years or more for substantial buildings. *Amortization* is a term that refers to the recovery of the remaining value of a structure over a period of time. The intent of amortization is to lessen the immediate economic loss from the zoning restriction to the property owner.

The zoning administrator must somehow keep up with where all of the nonconforming properties are and make sure that they are not enlarged, not reestablished after being destroyed or vacated, and not allowed to continue past the deadlines set for their discontinuance. In some communities this task is handled efficiently and in others ineptly.

In the case of the general contractor's yard that Hilda and Fred Potts have complained about, the zoning administrator pulls out a file that contains evi-

[2]*Amortization* in zoning does not have the same precision in meaning that the term has in finance or accounting.

dence of much correspondence with the contractor. It appears that the contractor must eliminate the nonconforming uses and structures within eight years. It also appears that there has been a running battle between the contractor and the zoning inspectors going on for the past twelve years. The contractor is constantly trying to expand activities on the site, and the inspectors are continually stopping the additional use. The nighttime welding is a new development that the zoning administrator was not aware of. It would appear to be an illegal expansion of the nonconforming use, and it will be investigated immediately.

What if Hilda and Fred are not pleased with interpretation given by the administrator to the nonconforming use provisions? They may appeal the interpretation to the *board of adjustment* and then to the courts.

Restrictive Covenants (Deed Restrictions)

Regarding the other complaint made by Hilda and Fred, the zoning administrator is of no help whatsoever. The administrator concedes that the six houses on Crestwood Drive might be in violation of the restrictive covenants recorded with Maplewood Subdivision but insists that they are not in violation of the zoning ordinance. The zoning ordinance does not require forty-five feet for a front yard—only thirty-five feet. It seems that the city has no authority to enforce the greater restrictions under its police power. The restrictive covenants are strictly an agreement between private parties, and a violation can be corrected only through action brought in a civil court by one or more of the parties to the agreement. If the city should happen to be a bona fide party to the agreement, then it too could initiate a civil action. It could not, however, use its police power to withhold a permit.

Amendments

Now that Fred and Hilda have had their discussion with the zoning administrator, we will turn to their other problems: the Brady Estate. Dan Carter wants to do two things that involve zoning processes: get the Brady Estate rezoned from "R-1" to "R-5" and get conditional-use approval for a planned-unit development (PUD). The rezoning that Dan seeks is technically an amendment to the map portion of the zoning ordinance.

Every zoning ordinance contains provisions for amendments to it, and the typical ordinance is amended frequently. Amendments to the map, which are much more common than amendments to the text, are the most frequent sources of zoning controversies in most communities. Amendments may be originated by the local governing body, by the planning commission (board), by the planning department, or by property owners. Most are originated by applications of property owners to the *planning commission*. This body (also called *planning board* and *zoning commission*) is made up of citizens who are appointed by the governing body and who usually serve without compensation. They are responsible for holding a public hearing on each application (after due notice of such hearing has been published) and for making a recommendation to the governing body based upon (a) the findings made at the public hearings and (b) the amendment's ostensible relationship to the community's "comprehensive plan." In many communities they are assisted by a staff of professional planners, sometimes representing a *planning department*. In larger communities, the *planning department* may actually substitute for the planning commission.

Following the recommendation by the planning commission, the proposed amendment must be acted upon by the local *governing body* before it becomes part of the ordinance. Local governing bodies have many names: *city council, board of aldermen, board of selectmen, board of supervisors, county board of commissioners, county court,* and others. In some communities, more than a simple majority is required in order for the governing body to enact an amendment that has received an adverse recommendation for the planning commission.

Both Dan Carter and Mary Trigg will begin the rezoning process in the same way. Although the land area involved in each case is different, and Mary's request is for a simple boundary change, while Dan's is for a complete change in classification of a large tract, the actions that each seek are basically the same. Dan will probably have to pay a much larger filing fee than Mary, but both will face the same timing deadline. The applications will probably have to be filed several weeks in advance of the hearing dates in order to allow time for: (a) notice to be given to the public in general and nearby property owners in particular (see Figure 5-4); and *(b)* reviews of the two requests by the professional planning staff and recommendations thereon. See Figure 5-5.

Notice of a zoning hearing is usually given through an advertisement in a newspaper. The advertisement is frequently supplemented by the posting of a sign on the property that is the subject of the request or by the mailing of individual notices (often by certified mail) to the owners of property within a specified radius (say 300 feet). In some communities, the applicant may be

Figure 5-4

responsible for giving individual notice to the neighboring owners. The applicant might even be required to obtain a written response from each of these owners indicating approval or disapproval. The views of owners of nearby property are sometimes given a higher status than those of more distant ones.

These procedures that we have described are generally those that Dan Carter faces in getting a hearing for his rezoning request. If Mary Trigg applies for an amendment to the *map*, she will face the same procedures. If, however, she decides to seek an amendment to the *text* so as to add "pottery making" as a permitted use in her district, then the only notice given will be a city wide notice. As the amendment would affect all R-3 districts in the city, there would be no sign posted on her property and no individual notices given to her neighbors. In fact, she might even avoid a filing fee by persuading a friendly member of the City Council to initiate the proposed change.

Whether the proposed amendment is to the text or to the map, there will be a recommendation from the professional staff to the lay Planning Commission and, following a public hearing, a recommendation from the Planning Commission to the City Council. The recommendations may be for approval, for disapproval, or for approval in part. For example, if Mary requests that the zoning boundary be shifted so that the rear 100 feet of her lot is in the B-2 district, the recommendation might be that the boundary be moved only 75 feet. In some communities, Dan Carter's request for a rezoning to "R-5" might be met with a recommendation that it be rezoned to "R-4". Then, too, the recommendation might be that action be deferred on the particular property in question while a study is made of a larger area surrounding it. Such a deferral, however, might be a delaying tactic rather than the reflection of a bona fide concern for the larger area. It is common for ordinances to specify a waiting period before a rejected application may be refiled (say eighteen months). If the opposition is heavy, someone sympathetic to the applicant might move to initiate the deferral in order to buy time.

The Political Nature of Zoning

In requesting their amendments, Mary and Dan are entering a political process. The further along the process they move, the more political it becomes. If "politics" is the art of government, then the entire process is in fact political. The zoning process is also political in a less formal sense. The arts of influence and compromise, pressure and concession, play an important role in the decisions ultimately reached.

Zoning is part of the total process of local government. It would be unrealistic to expect it to be any less "political" in nature than local government generally. Elected officials usually desire to be reelected. Their decisions on zoning, as on other matters, are bound to be colored by that desire. Anyone wishing to get property rezoned and anyone wishing to prevent a rezoning must contend with that simple truth. It explains much of the inconsistency found in the actions of councils and boards of commissioners. The recommendations of professionals are important, but the final action is inevitably political in nature.

Elected officials generally seek to keep all parties to a zoning dispute happy if reasonably possible. For example, in the City of Fairmont there was a low-

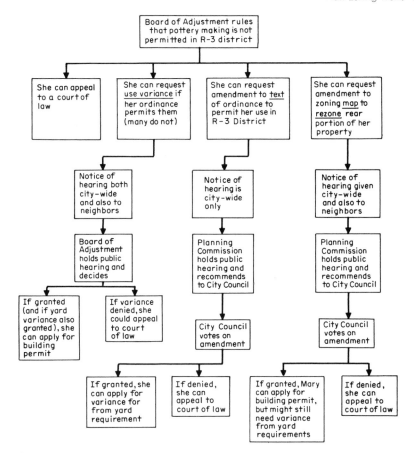

Figure 5-5 Mary Trigg's progress choices under Assumption "B".

income neighborhood of homeowners whose homes were on lots only thirty feet wide. Side yards were two to three feet in width. Although the zoning was entirely for single-family use, the neighborhood was in existence before there was a zoning ordinance, and several lots contained nonconforming uses. The planning board received an application to rezone one of these narrow lots for retail commercial use. The professional planner recommended against it on the grounds that it was a clear example of attempted *spot zoning* and that it would set a precedent for further changes of the same sort.

At the public hearing held by the planning board, the applicant, an elderly man named John Evans, explained that he had experienced a stroke. Since having the stroke, he had been unable to work. He hoped to obtain a small income by opening a very small grocery in his living room. Several neighbors were present. They were opposed to commercial zoning but in favor of allowing Evans to operate a grocery if it could be accomplished in some other way. The planning board could think of no way to do this. They pointed out to the neighbors that zoning dealt with property and not with individuals.

The matter then went to the city council. There was an attorney from an influential veterans' organization present to represent Evans. The attorney argued that Evans was a veteran and a fine, upstanding citizen and that he deserved better treatment. One member of the council suggested that the property be rezoned to commercial but that it revert to a single-family zoning at such time as Evans ceased to own it, to live on it, or to operate a grocery on it. The professional planner objected that this was highly irregular action. The city attorney was asked for an offhand opinion. He said that it was a permissible thing to do. The city council rezoned the property accordingly.

On the day following the council's action, the planner sought out the city attorney for an opinion as to how such a unique rezoning should be indicated on the official zoning map. "Just forget about it," was the answer. City attorneys often advise the city that any reasonable action taken is legal until the courts overturn it. Many opinions are political rather than legal in nature, as is illustrated in the example involving John Evans.

Although zoning does, in theory, deal with land and structures and not directly with the particular persons owning them, it is not uncommon for personalities and personal problems to influence decisions. (Boards of adjustment, as well as elected councils and commissions, are susceptible to such influences.) If an applicant is elderly, or in a wheelchair, or suffering from a terminal illness, a board of adjustment may be inclined to grant a variance even if it can find nothing unusual about the property itself. If the applicant for a rezoning is a prominent citizen with an excellent reputation, then the city council might be tempted to grant a request that it would not usually approve, ignoring the possibility that the solid citizen might die suddenly, go bankrupt, or simply sell the property to someone less responsible.

Councils and commissions also tend to reflect the prejudices and fears of their constituents. Irrespective of its merits, an application involving a cemetery, mental hospital, alcoholic rehabilitation center, nursing home, funeral home, home for disturbed children, liquor store, or drug treatment center is apt to meet with a cold reception. Death, mental illness, old age, drugs, and alcoholism are unpleasant subjects, and the average property owner opposes any nearby rezoning that would serve as a reminder of one of these unpleasant subjects. Additionally, other applications may be denied on the basis of commercial reasons. For example, discount stores, bargain stores, thrift shops, and other retail outlets featuring low prices or used merchandise can instill in owners of nearly property a fear that these uses will lower the quality of the area in the eyes of the public.

Bribery and Other Covert Influence

Bribery is an unpleasant subject, and we wish we could say that it did not exist in zoning. Every now and then, however, there appears a news story about the indictment or conviction of a council member or county supervisor in connection with a zoning bribe. Obviously, some bribery takes place. How much we do not know. It is illegal and unethical. It is also unnecessary. The authors have seen too many zoning matters decided on their merits to believe that any applicant must feel coerced into paying a bribe to get approval for a proposal that has merit. If such a coercion does seem to exist, and if it is specific and concrete, then it should be reported to the district attorney. If it is only a vague feeling or a result of rumors, then the applicant might do well to forget about property in that community and go elsewhere.

A more difficult problem is the kind of covert influence that may be legal. Local elected officials are interested in future votes, future campaign contributions, and future appointnments through patronage. This means not only that they woo voters and potential contributors directly but also that they seek the favor of congress persons, governors, U.S. senators, and the many political operatives who have influence with the holders of higher offices. Such operatives may be in a position to influence the outcome of a zoning application through private persuasion. There might be a political debt to be collected, or there may be the implied prospect of a future favor. Nothing might be asked of the applicant at the time, but at a later date, a sizable campaign contribution might be solicited. Sometimes the applicant can gain added influence simply by retaining the "right" attorney (i.e., one with known political ties). We do not recommend the use of covert influence in any case. If an application is justified, then it should receive approval on its merits.

Summary

Zoning administration is a collection of processes involving several different groups of people who represent varied backgrounds, motivations, intelligence, and sensibilities. Administrative organization and procedures are not the same in every community. Neither are the kinds of people involved. Basically, however, there are three kinds of processes encompassed by traditional zoning: the *enforcement process* in the hands of appointed administrators; the *process for appeals and variances* for which a board of adjustment is responsible; and the *amendment process* for which elected officials in the form of a council or board of commissioners (supervisors) are responsible. These processes are constrained by constitutional and legislative controls, but the people involved, being only human, can be influenced by politics and emotions.

We have not yet finished with Mary's and Dan's pursuit of their amendments to the ordinance. In addition to the formal procedures, there is a body of strategy and tactics for public hearings that each must master in order to be successful. The discussion of strategy and tactics merits an entire chapter. As this discussion is applicable to hearings for conditional-use requests as well as for the traditional amendments (and as both Mary and Dan might become involved in such requests), we are going to describe conditional uses and some other devices that have added flexibility to zoning in the next chapter before going on to the discussion of strategy and tactics in Chapter 7.

6
Flexible Zoning

The permits, appeals, variances, and amendments discussed in the preceding chapter are basics in what we described in Chapter 1 as the "game of zoning," but there is much more to the game than the basics. In much the same way that the forward pass opened up the game of football, some innovations have opened up zoning to make the game much more flexible. Our fictional characters, Mary Trigg and Dan Carter, hope to make use of this added flexibility. Dan expects to obtain *conditional-use* approval for a *planned-unit* development, so that he can build townhouses and condominiums in the middle of a single-family neighborhood. In the previous chapter, Dan was trying to get the Brady Estate rezoned from "R-1" to "R-5." The R-5 district permits the planned grouping of townhouses and condominiums as a conditional use. So once Dan gets the rezoning, he will go through another similar procedure to gain approval of the conditional use. (In some communities, he might be able to combine both procedures.)

Mary Trigg also hopes to win something by employing a conditional use. She has been told by a member of the city council that she has little chance of getting the text of the ordinance amended so as to list "pottery making" as a *permitted use* in the R-3 "single-family" district but that she might be able to get it listed as a *conditional use*. If Mary is successful in getting such an amendment, then she will request specific approval of such a use on her property.

As we pointed out in Chapter 2, a *conditional use*, unlike a *permitted use*, or *use-by-right*, is authorized only after a public hearing and the approval of a board or commission. Its advantage to a developer is that it can allow uses that would not otherwise be sanctioned. We did not discuss conditional uses in detail in the previous chapter, because we wanted to concentrate on the processes of traditional zoning. The conditional use is not part of traditional zoning; it is one of several devices that represent significant deviation from the concepts of traditional zoning. Some of the other devices include the *planned-unit development*, the *floating zone*, *incentive zoning*, *contract zoning*, and the

97

map amendment with reverter clause. Together these devices are sometimes called *flexible zoning*.

Flexible zoning has been grafted on to traditional zoning in an effort to overcome some of the rigidities of traditional zoning and to make the regulations relevant to changing patterns of development. If zoning can be viewed as a Model T Ford that has undergone frequent modifications over the years to keep it in style, then this chapter has to do with innovations similar to disc brakes, automatic transmission, power steering, electrically controlled windows, air conditioning, and FM radios. Most zoning ordinances today still strongly reflect a basic structural principle of the ordinances of the 1920s: *predictability* or *certainty* as to how land may be used and as to where uses may be put. Compromising this inherited structure, however, is a set of modifications made over the past twenty years to introduce more *flexibility*. There are good arguments for having these modifications, but they are not easily fitted to the original product.

To the property owner, the various devices providing flexibility represent a mixed blessing. On the one hand, they sometimes make it possible for a developer to do things in locations, or in ways, otherwise taboo while giving neighboring property owners a degree of protection that they would not otherwise have. On the other hand, some flexible techniques severely restrict the future utility of the property and, consequently, the ability to dispose of it easily.

Karla Peterson, for example, bought a half-acre parcel fronting on Highway 48 from Ben Everett, an apartment builder. The half-acre parcel had been part of a larger tract on which Ben had built 300 garden apartments. Karla thought that it would be a good site for a convenience food store, but the zoning was "RM-10 Apartments." Under traditional zoning regulations, she would have had but one choice—apply for an amendment to the zoning map to rezone her property as "B-2 Highway Commercial." Opposition would have been great, because a single-family subdivision abutted the parcel on one side and also because the "B-2" district permitted many uses other than convenience food stores. There was another choice, however. The original zoning ordinance had been amended to permit a convenience food store as a *conditional use* in the "RM-10" district. A public hearing was required, but the opposition was pacified and the permit granted because the following conditions were attached:

1. The only commercial use permitted was the convenience food store.

2. The store was prohibited from operating between the hours of 11:00 p.m. and 7:00 a.m.

3. The size of the store was limited to a maximum of 1500 square feet.

4. Landscaped buffers were required on three sides.

Karla built the store and leased it to a chain for a period of twenty years. At the end of the third year, the chain went bankrupt and the store was closed. Meanwhile, another chain had established a store at a superior location 1500 feet down the highway. The market for Karla's store evaporated and she was stuck with a building limited by zoning to a single retail use. No one wanted to lease it, and no one wanted to buy it.

The subject of flexible zoning is a controversial topic, and it is an area of zoning that is constantly evolving. We will not attempt to touch upon all aspects of flexible zoning, but we will present a general overview of flexible devices that a typical reader might encounter in a zoning problem. Other devices are in use in some communities, and new ones are being developed. In Chapter 11 we will describe some of the latest concepts.

Conditional Use

The most widely used mechanism for adding flexibility to zoning is probably the *conditional use* (also called *special-use permit* and other names). There is no particular reason for describing it first, but it does present a good example of the contrast between traditional zoning and flexible zoning. If a use is listed in the text of an ordinance as a "conditional use," then it will be permitted only if specified conditions are met and (usually) only after a public hearing has been held and approval has been given by the local governing body, which may attach additional conditions or even reject it outright as being unsuitable under any conditions.

Such a practice is in direct contrast to traditional zoning theory, according to which all zoning permission is preannounced. That is to say, all property owners are supposed to be able to look at the zoning map and the text of the ordinance and ascertain exactly how they may use their properties and exactly how their neighbors may use theirs. One may then buy or build or lease with assurance of what may or may not happen.

In actuality, the practice has often departed from the theory. In some communities, boards of adjustment, acting behind a facade of traditional zoning, have granted use variances and special exceptions liberally, thereby adding great flexibility. In many suburban counties, the governing bodies (boards of commissioners or supervisors) have placed large acreage in "agricultural" or "low-density residential" zones and then rezoned tracts to "commercial" or "medium-density residential" or "industrial" freely upon request. In a rapidly growing locality, the pressures for flexibility are strong. The conditional-use device represents an effort to provide flexibility in an orderly and aboveboard manner (although this is not always the case).

The conditional use is an orderly and aboveboard device to the extent that:

1. Uses that are permitted conditionally are listed as such for everyone to see in the text of the ordinance.

2. Conditions are clearly spelled out in the text.

3. There is an established procedure to be followed, including a public hearing, and owners of surrounding property are notified as to exactly what is proposed.

4. Conditions added as an outcome of the public hearing are clearly and rationally related to the peculiar conditions or the particular site and use.

Unless these qualifications are met, a conditional use could very well be illegal.

The kinds of conditions attached to an approval of a conditional use often include:

1. Limits on total floor area.

2. Limits on floor area devoted to particular uses, such as the area devoted to the sale of used merchandise or to the repair of merchandise.

3. Limits on location of activity (e.g., a shop for the sale of new appliances might be permitted to display used appliances but only in the rear third of the building).

4. Limits on hours of operation.

5. Limits on capacity (e.g., a self-service laundry might be restricted to twenty washers and five dryers, each of a maximum size).

6. Special restrictions on signs.

7. Restrictions on location and number of windows and doors and requirements for air conditioning.

8. Architectural controls, including both appearance and height.

9. Landscaped buffers and setbacks.

If applied judiciously, the conditional-use device can help in adapting a zoning ordinance to the needs of a rapidly changing society. It can be abused, however, and it can also be overly used. After all, the basic concept of zoning is that similar properties and similar uses are to be regulated uniformly. Carried to the extreme, conditional uses could result in having separate regulations for every parcel of land. Arbitrary decisions based upon whim and emotion could become rampant.

Pete Corelli, for example, owned a block of shops in a strip-commercial area zoned "C-1." His parking was inadequate, but his tenants did well. The building was on the side of the street used by commuters on their way home from work, and many of them stopped en route to buy. Then a parallel freeway was completed a few blocks away, and the commuter traffic fell off drastically. Pete's tenants moved out, and he could not replace them with activity permitted in "C-1." He applied for a change in zoning to "C-2." The city council denied the change. Again he was turned down. He managed to fill some of the vacant space by lowering the rents substantially, but most of the space stayed empty. Finally he found a good tenant that he thought was allowed in "C-1"—a dance studio. The zoning administrator said, "No, a dance studio is a 'C-2' use."

As another year's waiting period had elapsed, Pete reapplied for a rezoning to "C-2." This time, perhaps, the assurance of a specified tenant would placate the neighbors. It didn't. The professional planners recommended that the change be denied, again pointing out all of the objectional uses that could be installed on the property under "C-2" zoning and reminding all concerned that there was no guarantee that one of these would not replace the dance studio in the future. The planners also pointed out a few potential problems with the studio, including noise and late-hour operations. The planning board held a public hearing and recommended to the city council that the application be denied.

At the city council meeting the mayor looked for a compromise. She suggested that the text of the ordinance be amended to include a "dance studio" as a conditional use in the "C-1" district. This necessitated another public hearing by the planning board. The hearing was held and the board recommended against the amendment. The city council adopted the amendment over the board's objections. The mayor informed Pete that he could now apply for the conditional-use approval, which would require still another hearing by the planning board and another action by the council.

The planning board gave in and deferred to the apparent wishes of the city council. They recommended approval of the conditional-use permit for the dance studio in Pete's building subject with the following conditions attached: air conditioning, no windows, and no operation between 11:00 p.m. and 9:00 a.m. At the city council meeting where final action was to be taken, the neighbors were out in force. They had decided belatedly that the dance studio was unsuitable even with the restrictions. The city council acceded to their wish and denied the request. Pete was too stunned to respond.

Pete's experience highlights a prime danger in flexible zoning: unpredictable and capricious behavior by elected officials. When any part of a zoning process is taken from the hands of appointed administrators (who, even with their use of discretion, must follow procedures containing built-in safeguards) and given to elected officials who must maintain popularity with the public, then the property owner's uncertainty is bound to increase.

In addition to the danger of capricious action, the *conditional-use* concept carries with it some problems of a more practical nature for the zoning inspectors. Under traditional zoning, inspectors can sometimes spot violations from their autos, because they are aware of what zoning district they are riding through and they are familiar with the regulations for that particular district. Not so with conditional uses. Each conditional use could have a different set of restrictions. The inspector must know not only the general regulations for the zoning district but must also be informed as to the special restrictions for each conditional use in order to evaluate a possible violation.

The inspectors often find requirements for buffers and landscaping especially difficult to enforce. There is little difficulty in seeing that they are met initially, but their continued maintenance is another matter altogether. Failure to irrigate or fertilize or combat fungi can result in the demise of plants. Failure to cut weeds and clean out trash in a landscaped strip can destroy its intended function. There is no easy way for an inspector to distinguish between voluntary landscaping and the landscaping that is required, and the average local government simply does not have the resources to police the maintenance of the required landscaping.

Some problems with buffers stem from ill-advised or poorly thought-out plans. The selection of materials, both natural and artificial, is not always realistic. Unless there is a firm guarantee of good, continued maintenance, then materials should be selected according to their ability to withstand the forces of weather, neglect, and vandalism. Fences and walls should not require frequent painting. Neither should they be easily destroyed by children. Plants should be drought-resistant. Trees placed close to property lines should not be chosen from varieties that have root problems. The authors know of one case involving an applicant who, after getting a conditional use approved over the bitter and lengthy opposition of the next-door neighbor, deliberately selected trees known for their uncontrollable roots for planting along the boundary of the neighbor's property. Had zoning inspectors not made him replace them with a less destructive variety, the foundation of the neighbor's home would have been undermined within a few years. On the other hand, neighbors can also be spiteful. In another instance, a motel owner was required to provide a buffer with trees along a side street in connection with an expansion of the motel. The landscaping greatly increased the attractiveness of the motel, and a jealous competitor hired teenagers to poison the trees at night. The trees were replaced but were poisoned again. After the third planting, the police set up a stakeout and resolved the problem.

Despite its limitations, the *conditional use* seems to have become an accepted device for adding flexibility to zoning. In this chapter, it provides us with a relatively simple introduction to the subject of flexible zoning in general.

Floating Zones

A *floating zone* is a district that is included in the text of a zoning ordinance but not shown on the map initially. In order to get an area so designated on the map, it is necessary to go through the amendment process, but for a floating zone the process is more restricted than it is for an ordinary rezoning. The would-be developer must submit a proposed site plan showing the location and design of buildings, the parking layout, entrances and exits, lighting, drainage, and buffers, among other things. Often a favorable report demonstrating the economic feasibility of the development must be submitted. If approved, with or without additional conditions attached, the floating zone is added to the zoning map.

Once the map has been amended so as to add a floating zone to a particular location, then the zone is no longer "floating" with respect to that location. The textual provisions of the district are applicable to the area included. *But*, the provisions contained in the text are not the only restrictions on the development and use of the property! The approved site plan, and any conditions attached to it, also regulate what may and may not be done. Every thing permitted in a floating zone is, in a sense, a conditional use given blanket approval as part of the site plan. Thus, no two floating zones shown on the zoning map have exactly the same regulations.

Floating zones are products of post-World War II suburbanization. They reflect the needs of suburbia for large-scale developments (especially shopping centers) and the inability of planners and decision makers to preannounce the proper sites for such developments on official zoning maps. To illustrate this inability, let's imagine the suburban township of Hollyford. Hollyford was just beginning to be invaded by urbanization and, wishing to handle it properly, hired a firm of planning consultants. The consultants prepared several studies and reports and presented the township with a report and a beautiful, multicolored map entitled "Comprehensive Land Use and Development Plan." Among other things, the plan indicated in red where all future commercial uses should be. The southwest corner of Ruston Boulevard and Washington Highway was one of the favored locations for a major shopping center, so the 100-acre Kerr tract was colored in red (see Figure 6-1). The plan was adopted by the Hollyford council, and then the zoning map was completely revised to reflect the plan. On the zoning map, the Kerr tract was designated as "C-3 Community Retail."

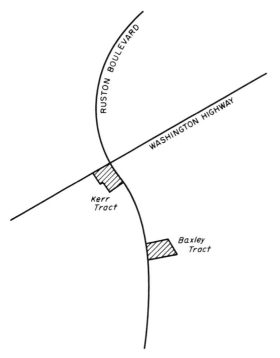

Figure 6-1 Hollyford's zoning problem with a shopping center.

No one bothered to consult Miss Bessie Kerr about the new zoning on her property. If anyone had, Miss Kerr would have made it known quite definitely that she had been born and reared on the property and that she intended to continue to live there until she died. She had absolutely no interest in selling or leasing the land for a shopping center. Miss Kerr was seventy-two years old, and her family was noted for its longevity. Several close relatives had lived past age ninety-five. Every developer who approached Miss Kerr was turned down—politely but firmly.

Meanwhile, Sanford Baxley, a shopping center developer, got an option to buy an 110-acre tract on the east side of Ruston Boulevard about one mile south of the Kerr tract. The property was zoned for single-family use, but Baxley went ahead and obtained lease commitments from three department stores and a mortgage loan commitment from a large life insurance company. He then applied for a rezoning to allow the commercial use. The planning board and council were in a quandary. The area zoned for a shopping center was not available for development, while another area not so zoned needed only a zoning change in order for development to begin. If they gave Baxley what he wanted, they would be departing from the plan and perhaps engaging in *spot zoning*. Owners of other land in the vicinity might clamor for similar treatment. If, on the other hand, they denied Baxley's request, a needed shopping center might not be built in Hollyford. It might even be built outside of Hollyford with a resulting loss of additional tax base.

The Hollyford council's problem was fairly simple compared to what it might have been. Miss Kerr stated plainly that she would not sell. In other locations, the lucky landowners with the commercial zoning might have been willing to sell—but only at unreasonably high prices. What is "unreasonable" is not easily established.

The *floating-zone* device could have taken Hollyford's council off the hook. If such a district for planned shopping centers had been put in the text of the ordinance, then the Kerr tract need not have been zoned as commercial. Designation of a specific site for a shopping center would have been left off the map until a developer came forward with an acceptable plan. Presumably, the first developer to do so would have won the race for approval, and no one else would have been able to muster the prime tenants or the financial commitments necessary for any additional centers. A major shopping center would have been built when needed and close to (but not necessarily identical to) the location indicated on the comprehensive land-use plan. If the members of the council had wanted to make sure that the location would be to their liking, then they might have drawn on the zoning map a circle with a one-mile radius around the intersection of Ruston Boulevard and Washington Highway, indicating that only sites within the circle would be considered for a *floating-zone* approval.

Floating zones have been a great help in many situations. The developer of a large site has much more flexibility in the arrangement of structures and uses than would be possible on a small site. (The text of the ordinance normally specifies a minimum size before a site may be considered for approval.) The added flexibility allows for the kind of traffic circulation, drainage, landscaping, and buffering that can minimize harmful external effects on surrounding properties. Overall, the concept must be termed a success.

Depite their usefulness, floating zones are not without problems. With respect to shopping centers (the most common subject of floating zones), there is no guarantee that only one application will be submitted for the same general location. Two developers might apply almost simultaneously, each having strong financial backing and each having major lease commitments. Each would be able to produce an impressive report from an economic consultant showing the feasibility of the proposed project. Each report might have been made without regard to the other, oblivious of the possibility that *two* centers might be built. Would two centers in the same general location be feasible? If not, then which should be given approval? Should a local council or board of commissioners get involved in trying to decide? These are tough questions. Perhaps it would be wiser just to leave the answers to market forces. On the other hand, if both centers are built, or if one is fully built and the other partly built, it is conceivable that one will fail. An abandoned shopping center, especially one that has not been completed, can present health and safety problems. It can also be an eyesore. New owners of the derelict project will likely press for zoning changes to allow them a profitable combination of uses. Fortunately, abandonments are not common occurrences. They do, however, demonstrate the point that floating zones do not represent an infallible technique.

In addition to the problem of site selection, floating zones present enforcement problems similar to those of conditional uses. Landscaping must be watched to see that it is maintained, and inspectors must apply a different set of restrictions to each site. The latter problem is not so serious with floating zones, however, as the sites are generally fewer in number than they are with conditional uses.

Planned-Unit Developments (PUDs)

Depending upon how it is described in a particular ordinance, a *planned-unit development* (also called Community Unit Plan, or CUP, and Planned Area Development, or PAD) is either a *floating zone* or a *conditional use*. If treated as a floating zone, then any site approved for a planned-unit development (PUD for short) receives a special designation as such on the zoning map. If treated as a conditional use, then a change in the map is not required. In either case, there must be an approved site plan and the plan, together with the conditions attached to it, constitutes additional restrictions on the property owner over and above the regulations stated in the text of the ordinance.

The conditional-use approval sought by developer Dan Carter for the Brady Estate is actually a request for a planned-unit development. You will recall that Dan is seeking "R-5 Single-Family" zoning for the tract, but that he wants to develop it with townhouses and condominiums. Overall, Dan will build no more units on the tract than would be permitted if he built conventional, single-family, detached houses on 6000-square-foot lots. The difference is that the townhouses and condominiums, instead of being spread evenly over the tract as the conventional houses would be, will be concentrated in clusters. The space immediately adjacent to each unit will be smaller, but the saving in individual space will permit Dan to provide several acres of common space for tennis courts, a swimming pool, and a private park for the residents. There will also be a saving in the area and pavement devoted to streets. This saving will benefit both Dan and the city.

Dan's proposal is only one example of a planned-unit development. Figure 6-2a illustrates how a tract might be developed in a conventional manner, and Figure 6-2b shows how the same tract might be developed for detached homes clustered on smaller-than-normal lots. Under some ordinances, a PUD will be approved only for a development that is overwhelmingly residential in use. Any commercial uses are limited to shops serving the residents of the project. Other ordinances permit greater mixtures of uses.

The kind of PUD depicted in Figure 6-2b is sometimes referred to as "cluster development." In addition to the advantages of having a smaller land area in streets, and a lesser number of linear feet in street pavement and utility lines, *cluster development* allows the site planner to designate only the most suitable areas of a tract for buildings and to reserve rock outcrops, tree clumps, flood-plains, ponds, historical sites, and other sensitive areas for common open space. Cluster development is often more energy-efficient and less harmful to the environment as well as providing for more aesthetic design and large open spaces.

The approval of a cluster development usually involves coordination be-

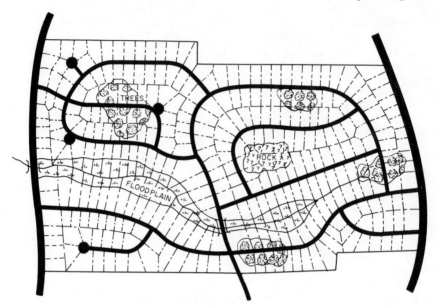

Figure 6-2a Conventional subdivision.

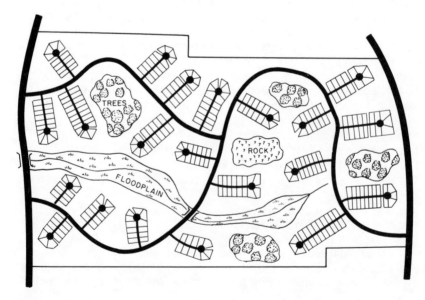

Figure 6-2b Cluster development of same tract.

tween zoning and another set of controls called *subdivision regulations*. Most communities having zoning ordinances also have subdivision regulations. The main purpose of subdivision regulations is to guide the layout of new streets and the creation of new building lots. These regulations usually include minimum standards for the area, width, and frontage of lots. Sometimes they also include requirements for building lines to be shown on a *recorded plat* (the *plat* shows the layout of the development and is recorded similarly to a deed). The zoning administrator is not ordinarily involved in the administration of subdivision regulations except to make sure that any permit issued for a new building is either for a lot shown on an approved and recorded subdivision plat or else for a *lot-of-record* that was recorded prior to the adoption of the regulations. The professional planning staff, the planning commission, and the city council, on the other hand, are involved with the approval of subdivisions, and when they approve a PUD for a cluster development under the zoning ordinance, they are simultaneously approving a subdivision plat.

In theory at least, *cluster developments* make a lot of sense. The developer achieves a more efficient use of land and cost savings in the provision of streets and utilities. The city experiences cost savings in the maintenance of streets and utilities. The general public benefits from the preservation of open space and special scenic or historic features. The neighbors also benefit presumably from their proximity to the open space. People who move into the PUD can enjoy some of the advantages of home ownership but with less direct responsibility for maintenance. Those who like to play tennis have courts almost in their backyards. Swimmers have a pool, but avoid the headaches of having to clean it out individually (people living in cluster developments normally join an association having responsibility for the maintenance of common areas). Those who love variety live in a neighborhood with a mixture of housing types.

Who can be against something that makes so much sense? Many people can, especially the neighboring owners of detached, single-family homes on conventional lots. They have been known to show up 300-strong at a public hearing to vent their indignation and demand to know who was responsible for inserting such an irresponsible thing as PUD in the text of the ordinance. The typical owners of single-family residences view any departure from conventional subdividing with suspicion and hostility. They are uncertain as to what kinds of people the PUD will bring into their neighborhood and as to what effects the proposed development might have on the resale value of their homes.

Consider *townhouses*, for example. Townhouses, a variety of what is sometimes called "zero-lot-line development," are modern successors to the old-fashioned rowhouse. They may look something like two-story garden apartments, because there are no side yards. Every townhouse, unless it is at the end of a row, is attached to houses on either side of it. Each townhouse, unlike each unit in an apartment building, is owned separately and sits on a separate, platted lot. Because no side yards will be needed, the lot for a townhouse is narrower than is normally allowed by subdivision regulations. You can imagine the reaction of nearby owners of homes on 100-foot lots when they hear that an application has been filed for a PUD to include townhouses on lots only 30 feet wide. At one stormy hearing, during the course of which an objector strongly suggested the need for a grand jury investigation, the angry opponents were asked why they had not objected to a nearby apartment development that was similar to the proposed townhouse project. After all, the apartments were occupied by renters, while the townhouses would mean more home-owners in the neighborhood. "That's just the point," said one of the objectors, "We can understand the renters, but what kind of a kook would want to *buy* an apartment? We don't want any nuts like that in our neighborhood."

In addition to the objections from the neighbors, cluster developments can meet with objections from public officials. They may fear that the common open space will some day become a governmental responsibility if the owners default in the upkeep of it. If a development is approved as a PUD, the approval will probably be conditioned upon a fairly tight agreement providing for automatic levies against all property in the PUD to guarantee maintenance of the common areas.

The cluster development is the most common kind of PUD, but it is not the only kind. Some ordinances have PUD provisions that permit a fairly wide mixture of uses on a single tract. The conditions attached to such developments can be quite elaborate, even going so far as to provide for different uses on different floors of a multistory building. Mixed-use PUD is found primarily in urban renewal areas and on very large tracts on the periphery of metropolitan areas.[1]

Contract Zoning

Contract zoning is a loosely used term that implies an agreement between the developer and local government to restrict usage or height, or to provide additional setbacks or buffers, over and above what is required by the text of the ordinance. In a sense, most flexible zoning is a kind of contract zoning, because all conditions are not specified in advance in the text or on the map of the zoning ordinance. Approval of a *conditional-use* or a *floating zone,* for example, may be contingent upon additional restrictions to which the developer must agree if he or she is to develop. These conditions are indicated in the official minutes of boards, commissions, or councils, or on site plans referred to in the minutes; or they are found in the form of recorded covenants to which neighboring property owners may or may not be parties.

Often, however, the term *contract zoning* is applied only to illegal or extra-legal restrictions. For example, neighbors might oppose the rezoning of a wooded tract for commercial development on the grounds that traffic would be increased on their street and glare from the commercial parking would shine in their windows at night. At the city council meeting at which the zoning amendment is being considered, a member of the council might suggest that the rezoning be approved only if the developer would agree to record a *re-strictive covenant* binding the developer and all successive owners of the

---

[1] The reader who would like to know more about PUDs, and especially about the large, mixed-use variety, should read the following book: Robert W. Burchell, *Planned Unit Development, New Communities American Style,* New Brunswick, N.J.: Center for Urban Policy Research, 1972.

project to the erection and maintenance of a barrier preventing the unwanted traffic movement.

Such a covenant might be reassuring to the objectors, but in many states the courts would not uphold such a covenant as enforceable. Unfortunately, some local governing bodies placate the opposition by agreeing to covenants while knowing full well that they are not enforceable in their state. The authors know of a case in which the county commissioners agreed to a covenant providing for a buffer of trees to shield a commercial development and then, a few months later and without notice to the objectors, rescinded the agreement. The first that the neighbors learned of it was when the bulldozers arrived.

Covenants for the purpose of protecting neighboring property owners are more likely to stand up in court if they are made prior to any public hearing, so that the possibility of coercion is diminished. They are more likely to be effective if the property owners themselves are made parties to the covenant.

Covenants are not the only conditions that can be involved in contract zoning. Sometimes the local government will suggest to the developer that approval could be withheld unless the developer agrees to dedicate a strip of land for a street widening or straightening. A binding agreement on such a matter could be difficult to reach. If the rezoning were granted before the dedication, then the developer might be able to back out of the commitment to dedicate. If the dedication were made first, then the government might be able to default on its commitment. Contract zoning is, to put it mildly, not something to be entered into lightly.

Incentive Zoning

Acme Limited Partnership is about to develop a site for an office building on prestigious Floral Boulevard. The site is in an "O & I (Office and Institutional)" district. The maximum floor/area ratio (F.A.R.) permitted is 8.0. As we explained in Chapter 4, this means that the total floor area in the building must not be more than eight times the total site area. If it were not for other controls on setbacks and lot coverage, Acme could cover the entire site with an eight-story building. Even with the other controls, seventy percent of the site could be covered with an eleven-story structure, and most of the ground area not covered could be used for surface parking.

Acme is not going to cover the ground level with parking, because the Metro City zoning ordinance contains some special features that encourage them to do otherwise. For example, for each 500 square feet of landscaped plaza that Acme provides at ground level, it may add 0.1 to the permitted F.A.R. up to a maximum of 1.5. Acme plans to have 7,500 square feet of plaza, so it will be able to use the full bonus, building to a maximum F.A.R. of 9.5. But that is not all. If Acme puts all of its parking in a structure that does not project more than three feet above the front grade, and if it covers the top of the parking structure with landscaping, then none of the floor space inside the structure will be counted in applying the floor/area ratio, and the ground area covered by the structure will not be counted as part of the lot coverage. Thus, all of the plaza that Acme plans to build can be on the roof of the parking structure. Furthermore, any ground-floor area of the office tower that is not enclosed by walls will not be counted as floor space either, and the space thus saved can be added on at the top of the building. Office space on upper floors is in greater demand than ground-level space, and the O & I district does not allow retail uses, so Acme can gain from this feature.

Thus, as a trade-off for putting parking undergound, constructing a land-scaped plaza, and not enclosing much of the ground floor of its office building, Acme will be permitted a taller building with more leasable floor area. A trade-off of this sort goes under the name of "incentive" zoning, because it makes use of bonuses or premiums rather than coercion.

The following calculations illustrate incentives that Acme can take advantage of:

Incentive	FAR	Lot Coverage	Number of Stories	Site Size (sq. ft.)	Floor Area (sq. ft.)
1. None	8.0	70%	11	40,000	308,000*
2. Provide 7500 sq. ft. landscaped plaza on top of parking structure	9.5	70%	13	40,000	364,000*
3. Unenclosed ground floor	9.5	70%	14	40,000	364,000 plus 28,000 open underneath building at grade

*Maximum floor area at specified height. A smaller "penthouse" suite could be added to up the maximums of 320,000 square feet and 380,000 square feet, respectively.

Traditional zoning is coercive. Owners of property are forbidden to develop or use their holdings in ways contrary to the zoning ordinance. Violators can be punished, and the threat of punishment will presumably deter any would-be violators. By this means, zoning prevents the worst from happening. But this is all that traditional zoning can do. It can stop the bad, but it cannot assure the good. Traditional zoning is valuable only as a restraint. For years, planners, architects, and others familiar with zoning have bemoaned its negative aspect while longing for a way to make it a more positive force in community development. Gradually this concern has been made effective, resulting in alterations to ordinances so as to reward the builders for doing things deemed beneficial to the community.

Incentives can be given for a variety of actions. Street widenings, provision of unobstructed views (as, for example, along a shore line), inclusion of theaters and retail space in office buildings, provision of walkways for public use (as, for example, a pedestrian bridge over a busy street), and preservation or creation of open space are a few examples. In mentioning this term "open space," we need to run up a caution flag. It is a term to which both planners and architects are greatly endeared and consequently has found its way into many zoning ordinances. It does not, however, have a universally accepted meaning. To the uninitiated it might seem that "open space" would be any space not covered by a roof. Not so! Parking lots and driveways are seldom included in the definition. To planners and architects, open space must either be aesthetically pleasing or usable for recreation in order to be worthy of the designation. Under some ordinances, the space must exceed a minimum area before it qualifies as open space. Rooftop space in excess of the minimum is sometimes included.

Not only does the term "open space" *exclude* some space that is open, but it frequently *includes* some space inside a building or otherwise under roof. In the example of the Acme Limited Partnership just cited, building area not enclosed by walls on the ground floor was not counted as part of the total floor area. Some ordinances count such area as open space. Other ordinances go further and include unenclosed area on upper floors or even special recreation rooms as open space.

Just as *open space* is probably the most common subject of incentives in zoning, so the *F.A.R. premium* is probably the most common kind of incentive, but it is not the only kind. In the example of Acme Limited Partnership, *additional height* was permitted in return for unenclosed space on the ground floor. In some ordinances, additional height is permitted in return for added setbacks at the base of the building. This might also be the incentive used for preservation of an unobstructed view. Another kind of incentive is *higher density*. For example, a PUD that preserves a significant natural feature, or an architectural or historical landmark, might be given a bonus of so many residential units per acre. Preservation may also be encouraged by allowing an *open-space credit* for keeping the landmark. For example, the preservation of a landmark building might permit a developer to count all of the floor area of the landmark as part of the *required open space*, even though the space is inside a structure.

Incentive zoning is sometimes used in conjunction with tax incentives. A developer is advised to explore various possibilities with local planners to determine the various incentives available in a particular locality.

Incentive zoning is still fairly new as a technique. New York City has probably had more experience with it than any other place, having incorporated the concept in its ordinance in 1961. We suggest that anyone who wishes to know more about the New York experience read a book by Jonathan Barnett entitled *Urban Design As Public Policy*.[2]

Incentive zoning does seem to have freed imaginative architects and builders from what has been termed indignantly the "strait jacket of zoning," but, in common with zoning generally, it has not assured good design from the unimaginative. Perhaps no zoning can ever do that. If somehow it could be made to prevent the worst without penalizing the innovative, it might be doing as well as we could have any right to expect. Incentive zoning may help us to accomplish this objective, but communities will probably be cautious in their approach to it. Many good ideas have turned out to have unexpected flaws.[3]

[2]Jonathan Barnett, *Urban Design As Public Policy*, New York, Architectural Record, 1974.

[3]For a discussion of some potential flaws in incentive zoning, see Daniel Mandelker, "The Basic Philosophy of Zoning: Incentive or Restraint" in David Listokin (ed.), *Land Use Controls: Present Problems and Future Reform*, pp. 203–211, New Brunswick, N.J.: Center for Urban Policy Research, 1974.

Map Amendment with Reverter Clause

As we pointed out in the discussion of *floating zones*, some land that is rezoned under traditional zoning goes unused because it is unavailable or priced unreasonably high, thereby forcing developers who wish to build to acquire or option tracts that are not properly zoned. Part of the reason for this state of things is that some applicants for zoning changes are not sincere in their stated intentions to develop; they are seeking rezonings only to raise the value of land for speculative purposes. Authentic developers often cannot afford the prices asked by the speculators, so they buy land not properly zoned at lower prices and make their own requests for rezoning. Opponents naturally point to all the properly zoned tracts that have not been used and question the need for any more such zoning. As a way out of the problems thus posed, some suburban governments have begun to make the rezonings contingent upon a genuine start of construction within a time period of, say, two years. Failure to start would cause the zoning to revert to what it was before. This might be called the "use it or lose it" approach to rezoning. It is a comparatively new technique and would seem to have some merit, but it certainly departs drastically from the goal of certainty in zoning. Even a bona fide developer could run into unexpected problems in getting a new project underway, and such a device would increase risks in an already risky business. Reverter clauses may also be questionable on legal grounds.

Flexible Zoning and the Developer

As we stated near the beginning of this chapter, flexible zoning bears mixed blessings for the developer. It permits things that would not otherwise be permitted but at a cost of added uncertainty. It can also cause higher initial outlays of capital and greater *time costs*. Time costs include interest and property taxes that the developer must pay while waiting for the project to be approved, while constructing it, and while selling or leasing it. *Time costs* also include the money that might have been made if time and effort had been concentrated on some other opportunity instead of on the project in question.

To appreciate what greater uncertainty, higher capital outlay, and greater time costs mean to a developer, let's look at Dan Carter's operation. Dan has been in the building business for twenty years. He started by building one or two houses at a time, gradually increased this number, and then moved into larger-scale residential and nonresidential development. His operations today are fairly large by the standards of the building industry. His net personal income is up in the six-figure category, and his credit is as good as any developer's, but he is just as highly "leveraged" as he was in the days of two houses at a time. By "leveraged," we mean that he operates on very little of his own money. He borrows heavily and constantly.

Whenever possible Dan avoids tying up money in direct purchases of land, preferring instead to pay a small amount for an option to purchase later when he is certain that he can begin construction. If a tract is large, and Dan intends to develop it in stages over several years, he might get a two-year option for part of it, a five-year option for part of it, and an eight-year option for the remainder. When he does buy, he may make a small down payment and sign a note for the remainder, to be paid off as the project is sold or rented. For construction money, Dan goes to a regular commercial bank. The bank charges Dan an interest rate that fluctuates according to the "prime rate" that the big banks in New York charge their best customers. Lately, Dan has been paying a rate $3\frac{1}{2}$ points above the prime rate, which means that, if the prime rate is 7 percent, Dan pays $10\frac{1}{2}$ percent. If the prime rate moves up to $7\frac{1}{2}$ percent, then Dan must come up with an additional $\frac{1}{2}$ percent for a total of 11 percent. Paying interest on time is one of Dan's single biggest headaches. Scraping up additional money on short notice when the prime rate rises is a continuing challenge.

If Dan were developing the Brady Estate in a conventional manner, he might construct a 500-foot length of street in the first year, install utilities along it, create lots, and build perhaps ten or fifteen houses (if the zoning could be changed to permit that density). Each year he would extend the street and utilities further and build a few more houses until the entire tract had been developed and sold. Construction outlays and the need for borrowing would be staggered. If the market should sag, he could cut back or postpone construction.

With PUD development, Dan still has an opportunity to stage his outlays, but not to the extent that he has with conventional development. His overall outlays for streets and utilities will be less in the PUD, but he will probably have to make more of the outlays initially. (Dan calls the initial outlays "front-end costs.") The initial outlays will have to be financed through borrowing, and the resulting annual interest payments could eventually exceed any savings made possible by the lesser lengths of streets and utilities in the PUD plan. Thus, after making the high "front-end" outlays, Dan will have little flexibility in the remaining construction schedule. He will need to complete the townhouses and condominiums as fast as possible in order to realize a positive flow of cash from the project and to cover his hefty interest requirements.

The Brady Estate is rather small as PUDs go. For the larger ones, there can be substantial predevelopment costs in the form of planning, environmental, and engineering studies. The higher these costs are, the greater the stake in approval of the PUD and the more risk there is in the possibility of failure to get approval.

All forms of flexible zoning do not have the same impact upon front-end costs and time costs as do PUDs, but all increase the amount of uncertainty and, thus, the risk in an undertaking. If flexible zoning continues to grow in popularity, then one result may be the gradual elimination of smaller developers who cannot take the risk, let alone put together large amounts of capital.

Flexible Zoning and Neighbors

Unlike Dan Carter, Mary Trigg does not have any problems with flexible zoning; for her, it can produce only benefits by allowing her to make pottery in a residential district. For her neighbors, however, flexible zoning does pose some problems, even though they are unaware of them. It also poses problems for the neighbors of the Brady Estate, but they are quite aware of them. Led by

Fred and Hilda Potts, these neighbors have been discussing the problems for some time at meetings of the Maplewood Homeowners Club. What both sets of neighbors have in common is *uncertainty*.

If Mary Trigg is successful in getting the ordinance amended to permit pottery making as a conditional use, then *anyone* may apply for such a use in that district. If Mary should sell her home and move away, then the new owner could continue the pottery making. The neighbors have confidence in Mary, but what confidence can they place in others whom they have neither met nor even thought of? At the moment they are interested only in helping Mary. Only later will they discover the uncertainty that they have helped to create for themselves.

Members of the Maplewood Homeowners Club have been uncertain about the future of Brady Estate for many years, but their uncertainty has been limited by their knowledge of what could be done by a developer under the "R-1" zoning. The minimum size for a lot in an "R-1" district is 30,000 square feet, and only single-family, detached homes are permitted. The longer the tract remains undeveloped, the greater the risk of a rezoning to allow higher density. The neighbors are not happy about the possibility of a change to "R-5" zoning, even without considering the possible effects of the conditional-use clause in "R-5" that permits PUDs. The "R-5" district permits lots as small as 6000 square feet, a size not in keeping with existing patterns of development in the neighborhood. On the other hand, they can see that a rezoning to "R-5" might not be all bad. If the Brady Estate were to be developed for single-family homes, even on 6000-square-foot lots, at least they would know what to expect.

The possibility of PUD introduces unknown factors. What can they expect? What kind of neighbors will it bring? What additional traffic will it generate? What will it do to their property values? Will it set off a chain reaction inducing other changes in the neighborhood?

Fortunately, the members of Maplewood Homeowners Club are able to discuss these questions rationally. Dan Carter has been in touch with them for several months, meeting with small groups in various homes to explain his proposal and answer questions. The neighbors still oppose Dan's project but concede that it might have some merit. The project will have tennis courts and a swimming pool, and Dan has offered the neighbors user privileges for both facilities, free for the first year and at a reasonable fee thereafter. The project will also have a large recreational room that could be made available to the Maplewood Homeowners Club for their meetings. Furthermore, Dan has proposed to the club that it approve the architectural controls for his buildings, so that their design will harmonize with the design of existing homes in the neighborhood. The neighbors have decided that they will oppose the application for rezoning to "R-5" but that, if they lose, they will seriously consider supporting the request for the PUD approval.

Flexible Zoning and Zoning Officials

Not only does flexible zoning open up new opportunities and problems for developers and neighbors, it also presents new questions for those officials who have to handle it. To begin with, the adoption of flexible procedures that are both workable and enforceable is an intricate and involved procedure. Planners and other officials who devise and vote to incorporate the techniques must ask: "What kind of problem will be solved by permitting more flexibility?" "Will the specific technique proposed be adequate to do the job?" "Will developers and others affected by it respond by using it properly and not abusing it?" "Can it be adequately enforced?" "Does it undermine any current regulations that have proven useful?" Only after such plaguing questions have been thoroughly settled and accepted by developers and property owners can the added flexibility be truly effective.

After adoption of flexible provisions, planners, planning board members, city council members, and enforcement officials find themselves with new discretionary powers that they have not had to exercise in the past under traditional zoning. Exercise of legislative and administrative discretion can always be challenged, and officials frequently become defensive about their actions. Iron-clad rules are always easier for officials to deal with than are open-ended techniques that require judgment, technical precision, and expertise (and perhaps liability). Indeed, if officials are not thoroughly qualified and competent to administer flexible techniques properly, then the cure for the "strait jacket" is worse than the disease itself.

In addition to the problems of discretionary power, there is also the possibility that flexible techniques can be used to accomplish questionable objectives. For instance, if a PUD is the only method of getting approval for apartments and other forms of higher-density housing, it is conceivable that the developers, officials, and citizens involved in each project may inadvertently (or covertly) set development standards so high that lower- and moderate-income groups would be unable to reside anywhere in the community. Such "exclusionary tactics" and other issues will be discussed in later chapters.

Conclusion

Flexible zoning has certain advantages and disadvantages for developers, neighbors, planners, and public officials. When properly used, the devices discussed in this chapter add to more rational and desirable development of land. When improperly used, these devices add unnecessary costs to development and actually are detrimental to sound planning and development.

The preceding chapters provided the reader with the tools and vocabulary of the zoning process. The subsequent chapters of this book deal with the application of these concepts. Winning at zoning requires careful preparation and understanding on the part of the participants. The next chapter deals with the nature of public hearings and how to present a successful case.

7
Public Hearings

The critical hour is now approaching for both Mary Trigg and Dan Carter. Public hearings are about to be held on their requests for amendments and conditional uses. Mary's preparation has been informal; she has made a point of talking with all of her neighbors within a radius of several blocks and has encountered no opposition. Dan's efforts have been more painstaking. He views a public hearing as a battle and prepares accordingly. As Dan sees it, to engage in a battle is to risk defeat, but to avoid one is to forgo a possible gain. Dan wants the gain, so he takes the risk, but he does everything possible to minimize the chance of defeat. He also knows that even in victory there may be casualties, so he does not enter into battle blithely. Before risking a public hearing, he explores all other legal possibilities for getting approval. If he opts for the hearing, he sets aside plenty of time for preparation, sometimes spending as many as one hundred hours to get ready for a one-hour discussion before a planning board or a city council. He also readies himself psychologically, knowing well that all of the other preparation can go up in smoke if he makes a serious slip in presenting his case.

It is well that Dan knows what to do, because he has formidable opponents. Fred and Hilda Potts and the other activists in the Maplewood Homeowners Club have also been busy. They do not have the financial resources that Dan has, but they make up for that deficiency by using an impressive array of volunteer talent from their own neighborhood. They too began their preparations well in advance of the date for the hearing.

If all parties to public hearings were as well prepared as our fictional characters, the typical hearing would proceed far more smoothly than it normally does. Many applicants, for example, are more like a broker/developer named Dick Smith in their approaches to hearings than they are like either Mary Trigg or Dan Carter. Dick Smith's saga may be somewhat exaggerated, but not greatly. Although Dick was not a novice like Mary, he had not learned much from prior experience.

Dick bought a two-acre parcel in his home town of Elmwood, got it rezoned, erected a building, and leased it to the Pizza Pizzazz chain for twenty years. (Even duffers like Dick win rezonings on occasion.) Two years later, Dick sold the property to an investor at a nice profit. Pizza Pizzazz liked the location and deal, so they approached Dick about a similar arrangement in another town, Mulberry, fifteen miles away. Dick found an ideal location, a 2.3-acre parcel located on Central Avenue, a main artery. An old, vacant two-story house owned by Mrs. L. B. Brown was on the parcel. Mrs. Brown had moved to Spain to live with her married daughter and wanted to sell the property. It was zoned "C-1," and restaurants were permitted in "C-1." The price seemed right, so Dick bought it. When Dick's contractor went to get the building permit, an inspector noted the indication of a serving bar on the plans and reminded the contractor that the sale of alcohol was not allowed in the "C-1" district. A "C-2" zoning would be required. As all Pizza Pizzazzes served beer and wine, Dick had a problem. He wasn't worried, however, because he had been able to get several zoning changes in Elmwood. He assumed that approval of this one in Mulberry would be perfunctory. He was wrong.

Comment

Dick has made two serious mistakes already. First, he has purchased the property outright without being certain of having the proper zoning. An option or a conditional sales contract contingent upon proper zoning would have been more prudent alternatives. The second mistake was in assuming that zoning in Mulberry would be like zoning in Elmwood with respect to the sale of wine. As we shall see, Dick continued to make unwarranted assumptions about zoning in Mulberry.

Dick was in a hurry to get his zoning application on the next agenda of the Mulberry Planning Board because he had another big deal cooking, so he sent his nephew Tom over to Mulberry to take care of all the details involved in submitting the application. Tom had just dropped out of college two months earlier to learn the real estate business. Tom came back from Mulberry with an application form that he filled out for his Uncle Dick to sign. He told his uncle that Mulberry required an applicant to contact personally all property owners within a 275-foot radius of the parcel under consideration and to get their signatures as being either opposed or unopposed to the proposed change. If more than twenty percent objected, then the planning board could not approve it by a simple majority vote; they would need a two-third's majority. Tom also showed Dick a sign that had to be posted on the property giving notice of what was proposed and when the hearing would take place. Dick thought that was odd, because in Elmwood the zoning officer put up the signs. He told Tom to post the sign and contact the owners of nearby property. It was late in the day, so Tom put the sign in the corner next to his desk and went to play tennis.

The next morning, Tom drove to Mulberry and began contacting the property owners. After arriving, he discovered that he had forgotten the sign. He had good luck in getting signatures, but many of them were from objectors. The next day, Friday, it was raining, so he stayed at the office. On Saturday he traveled directly from home to Mulberry and again discovered that he did not have the sign with him. He got more signatures, including that of Harold B. Morley. Finally, on Monday, he posted the sign. By Tuesday evening, he had all of the signatures needed. He was relieved to find that less than twenty percent were opposed. It was close, though. One more objector would have put him over the line.

Comment

Contacting the neighboring property owners is far too critical a matter to be delegated to an inexperienced subordinate. Getting the signatures should not be treated as a perfunctory task. Rather it should be looked upon as an opportunity to meet with the neighbors, explain the proposal, learn what objections they might have, and attempt to win their support. Dick is going to regret his mishandling of this matter.

On Wednesday, Dick was reminded by a note on his desk calendar that the hearing was to be on the following Monday at 11 a.m. It occurred to him that he ought to have an illustration of the proposed Pizza Pizzazz to show the people in Mulberry. He remembered one that he had used at the earlier hearing in Elmwood. What had he done with it? Maybe he had given it back to Pizza Pizzazz. He called Bill Ashby at the regional Pizza Pizzazz office. Bill did have it and promised to get it to him by Friday. Bill also had some slides of their various locations. Would Dick like to use them? Sure. They would also be delivered by Friday.

On Thursday, Dick spent all day at a condemnation trial involving property that he owned in the path of a highway project. On Friday morning he went to the closing on a commercial transaction that he had engineered. He had lunch with the seller and then drove out into the country to look at a 300-acre farm that the owner wanted to sell. This took longer than he expected, so he called Tom at the office to make sure that Bill Ashby had sent the material he promised. He had.

On Saturday, while playing golf, Dick decided that he ought to take along a traffic engineer to the public hearing. Before starting on the back nine, he called Ted Bailey, who had made several traffic studies for him. Ted said that he could not help without first studying the particular site and that he didn't have time for that before Monday afternoon. Dick played the back nine and forgot about traffic engineers.

Comment

It should be evident by now that Dick is being much too casual about the process. The strategy and tactics to be used should be decided in an orderly manner in a meeting between Dick, Tom, and any consultants that he might wish to use. It takes time to make studies and to prepare visual aids, and the people who are going to make them need ample notice. Furthermore, if a consultant is going to be asked to present material in person, them the time for the appearance needs to be reserved on the consultant's calendar. Chapter 9 will describe some of the supporting studies that are necessary for a strong case in a zoning hearing and later, if necessary, in the courts.

Dick went to church on Sunday and then he and his family spent the rest of the day with some friends at their weekend cottage. On Monday morning he went to a breakfast meeting of his personal development club and got to the office about nine o'clock. At ten, he and Tom loaded their materials in the car and drove to Mulberry. They were delayed by road construction en route. On arriving, they had trouble finding a parking space. Finally Tom took the wheel and let Dick out at the entrance to the town hall. Dick rushed panting into the meeting room with materials in each hand. He found a seat just in time to hear the eleven o'clock item announced. It was not his property! The item that was heard was routine. Then there was a fifteen-minute recess. Dick rushed up to the clerk to find out what was wrong. "You didn't put the sign up ten days in advance. It was only up a week. Now you will have to wait at least until the middle of the month."

"What do you mean, 'at least the middle of the month'?"

"Well, that's when our next meeting is, but the zoning ordinance says that notice of a proposed amendment must be advertised in the newspaper at least ten days in advance of the hearing. I was on vacation when you made your application, and somebody forgot to tell you. Sorry! Our local paper only comes out on Thursdays and I doubt that you can make the deadline for this week's edition."

Dick checked with the Mulberry Clarion. The clerk was right. The notice was arranged, and the hearing was rescheduled for the following month on a Monday. Dick and Tom drove home. He called Ted Bailey and asked him to study the location. Then he got busy with other matters and forgot all about the Pizza Pizzazz project.

Comment

Procedure can be as important as substance. The requirement for advertising in a newspaper is widespread, and Dick should have made a point of asking earlier if it was necessary to do so. He should not have relied solely on what a clerk said that he should do, especially considering the fact that he was using his nephew to relay the information. Dick also should have made periodic checks with the clerk to find out if everything was proceeding properly. A phone call on the morning of the meeting could have saved an unnecessary trip.

About two weeks later, Dick received a letter from the Mulberry town clerk saying that his item would be on the agenda at 2 p.m. On the next day, Ted Bailey called to say that he had studied the impact of the proposed Pizza Pizzazz on traffic flow and that, in his opinion, it would present no problems. Dick told him of the time set for the hearing and asked him if he could be there to answer questions. Ted said sure, but he had to be back in Elmwood by six to meet with an important client from out of town. Dick told him that the hearing shouldn't last more than an hour. Dick again put the hearing out of his mind.

On the day of the hearing, Dick and Tom left for Mulberry earlier than before and arrived in plenty of time to find a parking spot. They went into the meeting room and sat down. The hearing was in recess, so Dick began thinking about his presentation. It dawned on him that he had brought no projector for the slides. He sought out the clerk. "Yeah, we have one. It's over in that corner, but I don't know how you are going to display that fancy rendering. We had an easel, but it broke this morning."

Dick got the projector and tried to insert his tray of slides. Alas, the projector and the tray were incompatible. Frustrated, he gave up and went back to his seat. Ted Bailey came in and sat next to him. Dick felt reassured. Then he noticed numerous people arriving. Most of them wore blue blazers with emblems labeled "Briar Hills Civic Association."

The planning board members returned from the recess. Joan Baxter rapped with the gavel. She called the meeting back to order. "Before proceeding," she announced, "I want to say for the benefit of those who just came in, that we are running about two hours behind schedule because of the large number of people who spoke on three of the items that we heard this morning. As many of you know, we do not limit the number of property owners who may speak. The next item is the application of Virgil Jones for a special use permit for. . . ." Dick led the other two out of the room in search of a coffee shop.

Comment

Dick should have visited the hearing room at least a week in advance of the hearing to find out what equipment was available to help him in his presentation. If he had also visited a previous hearing, he might have learned that they often ran late, and he would have gained insights from observing their procedures.

At fifteen minutes till four, Dick, Ted, and Tom paid for their coffee and headed back to the meeting room for the fourth time. Now the meeting was running almost three hours late. Ted said he was sorry but he had to return to Elmwood. Tom and Dick went out for more coffee. At 4:30, they walked into the meeting again just in time to hear Dick's item called. Two applications scheduled before Dick's had been withdrawn at the last moment.

"Is the applicant present?" asked Joan Baxter.

"Yes, my name is Richard R. Smith. I am the owner of the property and I am requesting . . ."

"Just a moment, Mr. Smith. Before you proceed, let me explain that you are allotted ten minutes to make your presentation. Every other property owner present who wishes to speak will also be allowed ten minutes. Then you will have ten minutes for rebuttal. Now please continue. No, just a moment. I see someone standing at the other mike. Do you have a question?'

"Yes, I most certainly do. My name is Frances Morley. I live at 2243 Avalon Terrace, directly behind the Brown property. My house is on Lot 34, Block 6, Camelot Hills Subdivision. I have been out of town, and I was shocked to come back yesterday morning and find that my husband, Harold Morley, had signed a petition agreeing to the rezoning. My husband had no right to sign that petition. The property is in my name only! And I have a copy of the deed to prove it!"

Joan Baxter sighed and thumped her pencil several times.

"Mr. Smith," she said hesitantly, "this raises a problem. Mr. Carl Brand over there is our town attorney, and I am going to ask him what he thinks about this. Carl?"

"Well, it's pretty clear that it's the applicant's responsibility to get the names of the actual property owners. The ordinance requires that if twenty percent or more of the property owners within 275 feet object, then the planning board can make a favorable recommendation only by a two-third's majority. And that means six out of the nine members, regardless of how many are actually present."

Joan spoke slowly and deliberately.

"Mr. Smith, you may not be aware of it, but our ordinance also requires a two-third's vote of the Town Council to override an unfavorable recommendation by the planning board. Two of our members are absent this afternoon, so you are going to need at least six yes votes from the seven people here. Otherwise, you will need a two-third's yes vote from the Town Council. As a matter of courtesy, we always let an applicant postpone a hearing if a two-third's majority is required and the full board is not present. Do you wish to postpone this matter to the next meeting?"

Comment

By not informing himself regarding procedures in Mulberry, Dick has put himself in a bind. He also should have called Mulberry on the morning of the hearing to find out who would not be present. This move would have removed at least one last-minute surprise.

"Mr. Smith," repeated Joan Baxter, "Do you wish to postpone this matter to the next meeting?"

"I guess I don't have any choice. My lease agreement will expire if I wait any longer. I will have to go ahead with it today. Now what I am proposing is really very simple. This rendering I have here is a typical Pizza Pizzazz installation. As you can see, it is an attractive contemporary building which uses a lot of redwood. There is also a lot of glass. The premises are neat and well lighted. We have tried to minimize the area where weeds might grow. On the sides and rear, we have an ornamental fence made of precast concrete slabs with a buff-tinted surface of crushed sandstone. The only reason we need the zoning change is that Pizza Pizzazz serves some of the lighter wines, and, because of a technicality, wine cannot be sold in the 'C-1' zone. The old Brown residence is beginning to deteriorate, and certainly no one could afford to keep pouring money into it when the highest and best use of the property is obviously for commercial purposes. I think you will all agree that my proposal would represent a vast improvement for the property and help the neighborhood. I was going to show you some slides of Pizza Pizzazz in other towns, but . . ."

"Mr. Smith, would you please bring that drawing closer? I can't make out the details from here. Have you checked those signs against our sign control ordinance?"

"Well no, but please understand that this is simply a typical Pizza Pizzazz. The one in Mulberry wouldn't necessarily be exactly like this."

(By this time numerous people in the audience had left their seats and crowded around the front, trying to get a look at the rendering.)

"Will the meeting please come to order? If you will all return to your seats, I will ask Mr. Smith to turn the drawing around so that you can view it."

"WE CAN'T SEE IT FROM WAY BACK HERE!"

Comment

If Dick had checked out the meeting room well in advance of the hearing, he would have known that the rendering could not be seen easily. He should have known that most potential objectors are skeptical of renderings. He should have had visual aids that dealt specifically with the site at hand supplemented by examples of what was actually built elsewhere.

Joan Baxter's tone got firmer.

"Please return to your seats. Joe Grant wants to speak."

"Yes, I have been a member of this planning board for five years. We used to have several of these renderings at every meeting and we had so much trouble with them that, about three years ago, I thought we changed our rules not to allow them. This one may be perfectly all right, but I haven't had a chance to study it. Back when Pat Willard was on the board—Pat was a commercial artist you know—back when she was on the board, we found that some of the so-called perspectives were faked. I remember one for a high-rise apartment building that had a distorted view of the setbacks. I don't have anything against this particular one, but I just don't think we should be swayed by any of them, period!"

"Well it's already been done. This is something we can discuss further after the hearing. We are running way late, and we need to move on. Mr. Smith, your time is up, and we will now hear from anyone else who wishes to speak for not more than ten minutes. Will those wishing to speak please line up behind the other microphone?"

All of the people with the blue blazers labeled "Briar Hills Civic Association,' stood up and got in line. Joan Baxter groaned. "Everyone who wants to speak will be given a chance, but we ask that you not repeat what someone else has said before you. It would greatly help the progress of the hearing if you could select a few people to present your basic objections."

Dick had never seen any of these people before. He scrutinized them intently, trying to assess what they might do to his case. He wasn't encouraged. The first person in line looked like an outfielder and clean-up hitter for the Cincinnati Redlegs. His basso delivery had authority behind it.

"My name is John F. Pulaski. I live at 2223 Avalon Terrace. That's Lot 27, Block 6. My family and I moved there in 1955, and we now own it free and clear of any mortage. We have brought up three children in that house and we hope to live there for many more years. Now I don't oppose the rezoning per se; Central Avenue has already gone mostly commercial. What bothers me is the storm drainage—or lack of it. I don't live directly behind the Brown property, but I get the water from it. It flows along the back lot lines until it gets to my backyard. Then it turns and goes right back down my driveway. The more business development we get along Central Avenue, the more water I get. Every time it rains hard, my lot is a mess. It's not just the water either. There's a lot of trash that comes down with it—paper, tin cans, cigar butts, even a little garbage now and then. I have complained and complained. And nothing gets done. I happen to be a civil engineer, and I can tell you right now that there's going to be a lot more water running down my driveway if that Pizza Pizzazz is built. At present, some of the rainfall soaks into the ground, but once the whole property is either covered by a building or paved over like that illustration shows, we're going to have one hundred percent runoff. I object strongly to any development of that property until something is done about the drainage! Thank you."

John Pulaski was replaced at the mike by an attractive, soft-spoken, but forceful woman in her 40s.

"My name is Rachael Jacobs—Mrs. Irving B. Jacobs. My husband and I own Lot 25, Block 6, Camelot Hills. The address is 2119 Avalon Terrace. We moved there in 1961, because it was a quiet and pleasant neighborhood and we wanted to get away from the horrible strip commercial junk that was absolutely despoiling Benton Boulevard. Now it seems that a movement is underway to turn Central Avenue into another Benton Boulevard. The Brown property is already zoned 'C-1.' I suppose we can't do anything about that, but I am alarmed over some of the uses that are allowed in the 'C-2' district, and I feel very strongly that the line ought to be drawn and any further changes to commercial stopped. Last week I came down here to the zoning office and bought a copy of the zoning ordinance. Let me just read you some of the uses that can be put on this lot under 'C-2' zoning: Automobile dealers (new), appliance sales and repair, bakeries, bars, bowling lanes, dance studios, drive-in restaurants, service stations, and . . . *massage parlors*! How can we be sure that the Brown property is not going to be put to any of these uses? Mr. Smith may have perfectly good intentions, but suppose the Pizza Pizzazz closes? What then? Once it's zoned 'C-2,' then we have no more control over what happens. Mr. Smith says that Central Avenue is already zoned 'C-2' out as far as the lot next door and that all he wants to do is extend it another 200 feet. Well I say that we've got to draw the line somewhere. Otherwise this strip development will never stop. And one more thing. Mr. Smith says that it's only the technicality of serving wine that makes the 'C-2' zoning necessary. Let me point out that 'drive-in' restaurants are not permitted in 'C-1,' so even if he were not going to serve wine, he couldn't do this with the 'C-1' zoning that he has now."

Comment

If Dick had met with these objectors well before the meeting, he could have anticipated most of their complaints and had answers ready. He might even have eliminated some of them. For example, he might have offered a specific proposal to correct the drainage problem on the Pulaski lot.

"Excuse me. . . ."

"The chair recognizes Nat Greene, our zoning administrator."

"Yes, I simply want to correct a misimpression that many people have about the meaning of 'drive-in' restaurants in our ordinance. The way it's defined in our ordinance, this means serving people while they sit in their cars. We used to have quite a few of these around town back fifteen or twenty years ago. Now, though, the practice is for people to get out of their cars and go inside to eat. That's the way it would be at the proposed Pizza Pizzazz. Under the ordinance, therefore, this would not be a 'drive-in' use."

"Thank you, Nat. Now who's next?"

It was a short wiry man wearing gold-rimmed eyeglasses. His few strands of solid gray hair were parted on the far left, about an inch above his ear. He looked like a troublemaker to Dick.

"My name is Charles B. Stuart—'S-T-U-A-R-T.' " I have lived at 2248 Central Avenue for thirty-six years. My property is right next door to the Brown property. I am absolutely, unequivocally, and unalterably opposed to the sale of liquor next door to my house! I do not allow any alcohol inside my home, and I feel that having it sold openly and notoriously next door would be an unwarranted intrusion on my privacy. When I bought my home, it was zoned 'residential.' I didn't ask for the zoning to be changed to 'C-1.' It was done without my knowledge while I was out of the country. I have consistently objected to any further changes. And I am getting tired of having to come down here time after time to fight the same kinds of attacks on my neighborhood. Why stop with the Brown property? If you are going to zone it 'C-2,' then the only fair thing to do is to change my zoning too, so I can sell my property and move away from this constant harassment."

Next, in Dick's chauvinistic way of thinking, was another busybody.

"My name is Suzanne Edwards. My husband and I are co-presidents of the Briar Hills Civic Association. Our membership is made up of homeowners in the four subdivisions of Briar Hills, Camelot Hills, Avondale, and Springwood. At our regular monthly meeting last Tuesday night, we voted unanimously to oppose this requested change of zoning. Unfortunately, all of our members couldn't be here today because of other day commitments. So we only have eighty-six present, but I can assure you that there will be a much bigger turnout when this matter goes before the town council. In the past two years, we have fought five attempts to break down the zoning along this one-block stretch of Central Avenue: three changes in zoning, one application for a conditional-use permit, and one variance. We beat back every one of these attacks. We had to go to court to defeat the variance, but we won. We have a lawyer on retainer, and we will fight this one in court if we have to. We are sick of having to defend our neighborhood from assault after assault on its residential character. Now it's proposed that we have more strip zoning for a fast-foods franchise. Has anybody noticed how many vacant fast-food buildings there are on the west side? What happens to them when they are vacant? I'll tell you. They become hangouts for teenagers. They park their cars and motorcycles there at all hours of the night and drink beer and take drugs and create a general disturbance. If you don't believe me, just drive out Oakwood Avenue some night. There are four of those places that are closed. I have a friend who lives right behind one. They make noise all night and throw beer cans into her backyard. She's called the police, but they can't seem to stop it. We implore the members of this planning board not to let yourselves be swayed by Mr. Smith's argument that the present zoning doesn't permit the property to be put to it's 'highest and best' use. We have heard that term many times before. Mr. Smith should have known about the zoning when he bought the property. If he's made a bad investment, that's his fault. Don't bail him out at the expense of our homes and neighborhood. Thank you for your courtesy in listening to us."

The meeting went on in a similar way for another half hour. Frances Morley spoke again, complaining that there would be nothing to block the glare from the headlights of cars entering and leaving the parking lot. She said the lights would shine right in her bedroom windows and destroy the privacy of outdoor living in her backyard. Other people objected to the lack of trees and living shrubs in the landscaping shown on the rendering. Some objected to the building design, saying that it wasn't in keeping with traditional Mulberry architecture. Finally, Dick was given an opportunity for rebuttal.

Poor Dick was almost speechless! He had not anticipated any of the objections and did not know how to answer them. He stumbled and bumbled. He did manage to point out that Pizza Pizzazz was *not* a franchise operation . . . that the company directly managed every one of their establishments. He reminded those present that the rendering was simply an illustration of a typical site. He offered to execute covenants with the town to restrict the use of the property so as not to allow the things that Rachael Jacobs had objected to, but the town attorney interjected with an opinion that this would constitute something called "contract zoning" and would not be enforceable. Dick promised that, if the board would go ahead and approve his proposal, he would meet with the neighbors and try to work out the other problems. He would be happy to provide more landscaping and a shield from the glare. He was sure that Pizza Pizzazz would be amenable to modifying the design. The response was low-keyed jeers from the audience. Joan Baxter rapped the gavel. Dick got agitated. He pointed out to the board that it had an obligation to ignore the hysterical reactions of a mob. And he threatened to go to court if his zoning request were denied.

Comment

Losing one's cool seldom helps, and it often makes enemies who can do harm later. Even if Dick lost his case before the planning board, he still had an opportunity to win at a subsequent meeting of the town council. He might yet have been able to meet with the neighbors and overcome their major objections, but now he has alienated them by his ridiculous outburst.

To Dick's surprise, the board discussed his application briefly and *openly* and voted by roll call. (In Elmwood, all discussion by the planning board and all voting was deferred until the end of the day after all items had been heard. The board then closed the meeting to the public. Dick had not expected that the Mulberry board would vote openly right in front of all of the opposition.) The vote was six to one against Dick.

"Mr. Smith, the planning board has recommended to the town council that your application be denied. You will be notified by the clerk when the item will appear on the council's agenda."

Dick Smith may have blundered into a trap, but it was largely of his own making. He would do well to seek some advice from Dan Carter. Dan might make a few little mistakes now and then, and a big one on rare occasions, but his preparation for a hearing is so thorough that he can nearly always recover from them on the spot. As we pointed out early in this chapter, Dan begins his preparation well before the date of the hearing—even before he acquires the property. Prior to buying any building or parcel, he takes a good look at how it is zoned and what the zoning permits. He also looks into the zoning classification of neighboring property, because that may influence the chances of getting his rezoned. If a public hearing seems to be necessary in order to get the right zoning, Dan always estimates the odds on success before signing any contract to purchase. He often insists that the closing of the transaction be contingent on the zoning approval that he wants. Then, if he loses at the hearing, he can back out of the contract. As an alternative, he will often acquire only an option to purchase, as he did on the Brady Estate.

If the odds for zoning approval do not look promising to Dan, then he usually looks at an alternative site. If only one site seems to fit his needs, however, and getting the right zoning on it is going to require a public hearing, then Dan analyzes, *before* purchase, what else he might do with it if the hearing should go the wrong way. In general, Dan tries to stick to the following rules:

1. Select the right property that meets your needs for an economic development.
2. Consider alternative sites to buy if it is impossible or not feasible to rezone the first choice.
3. Study the zoning restrictions before signing a binding contract.
4. If the property must be purchased, minimize risks by making sure that the property can be put to some other use, or sold without a major economic loss, it the rezoning is not won.
5. Study the local procedures for rezoning in the ordinance. Ask the clerk or other appropriate knowledgeable person as to procedures and local customs that may not be written down. Consider the possibility of hiring a local attorney who is expert on these matters.
6. Consult local planners and zoning officials to determine possible problems in seeking a zoning change.
7. Consider if it is possible to accomplish the development objective without seeking a rezoning (as, for example, a modification of the proposed project to comply with a liberal interpretation of the rules by the zoning administrator).
8. Talk to neighbors and neighborhood civic organizations to determine support of, or opposition to, the proposal. It may be possible to achieve some compromise in advance of a hearing.
9. Estimate the odds of winning a rezoning at the public hearing on the basis of inputs from the planners and neighbors with whom the proposal has been discussed.
10. Prepare a well-researched and locally supported presentation for the hearing. Co-ordinate the presentation with appropriate experts who have been hired. Make sure that all exhibits are clear and that presentation equipment has been tested in advance of the hearing.

Testing the Wind

Even if Dan already owns outright a property that he wants to rezone, he finds it a good idea to estimate the odds before going through with a public hearing. The process could take many months of calendar time and consume many hours of effort. It might also require a sizable expenditure of money for expert help. Furthermore, he will probably have to pay a substantial fee when the formal application is submitted. Much can be done, however, short of making a formal application. Dan has found that informal inquiries to test which way the wind is blowing can often prevent troubles later on.

Dan builds in several different governmental jurisdictions in his metropolitan area, some more sophisticated than others. In testing the wind, he has found that a good place to start is at the city, town, or county office building. The zoning administrator and the professional planner (if there is one) can provide valuable insights. They might even be willing to support the proposal if it can be modified in certain respects. These public employees can be sounded out as to the propriety of approaching individually the lay members of the planning commission and the council members, selectmen, or county commissioners (supervisors). In some localities such an approach is proper; in others it is viewed as unethical. The public employees may also be able to provide information on neighborhood organizations and leadership.

Meeting with the Neighbors

Few things are a greater help to Dan's cause at a public hearing than support from neighboring property owners. In many situations the attitudes of the neighbors are *the* deciding factor. In nearly all cases they are important. (In an examination of applications over a five-year period in Atlanta, one of the authors found that unopposed rezoning requests had a 70 percent chance of a favorable outcome, while an opposed one had only a 48 percent chance.) Therefore, Dan approaches the neighbors well in advance of the hearing. He makes a determined and well-planned effort to explain the proposal to them and to modify it to overcome their objections. Even if their approval cannot be obtained, then perhaps their opposition can be blunted. If they do not have strong objections, they might not even come to the public hearing. The less overt the opposition the better.

In some cases, a trade-off can be made. For example, an old dirt road across an applicant's property might be letting unwanted traffic through an adjacent neighborhood. Support for rezoning the property could be obtained by agreeing to closure of the road. Even where no trade-off is possible, opposition might be lessened by agreeing to the dedication of a buffer or the recording of covenants restricting the use of certain portions of the property. In Dick Smith's case, he might have been able to help solve the drainage problems.

Neighbors can be approached in several different ways: as individuals or families, as organized groups in formal meetings, or as small informal groups. Dan likes to arrange a number of small gatherings in homes in the neighborhood. He makes them social occasions by offering to buy refreshments for the host family to serve. He finds it easier to discuss what he proposes in such a context. Of course, Dan's approach might not be best for every developer. Each applicant will have to decide what approach or combination of approaches to follow in a given situation. Regardless of the approach used, one meeting will seldom be enough. Dan starts his meetings far enough in advance of the public hearing so that several repeated sessions with the same group can be scheduled if necessary.

In meeting with neighbors, Dan is candid and honest. He knows that they are probably veterans of numerous zoning battles. They may have good cause to be skeptical of fancy architectural renderings and vague promises. However unfair it might seem, Dan can suffer because of the bad faith shown by previous developers in the vicinity. He has no control over other developers, but he can look out for his own reputation. Support or opposition by neighbors in future zoning matters could well hinge upon how well Dan keeps the promises that he makes. The authors know of one developer who was completely taken by surprise at a public hearing on a minor addition to an existing shopping center. Several hundred neighbors were present with vociferous objections. As it turned out, they were not really objecting to the minor addition. What they were upset about was the developer's failure to maintain a landscaped buffer on two sides of the center. The grass was not kept mowed; trash was allowed to accumulate; and an ornamental fence was broken in numerous places. The neighbors held up approval of his addition until he could convince them that he would henceforth live up to his promises. Unrealistic promises should not be made. All promises should be honored unless they can be renegotiated.

Sometimes an objector's property is for sale. One supermarket chain was able to soften opposition to a new store by purchasing the two homes immediately adjacent to the proposed building. Instead of demolishing them, the company maintained them as a buffer of sorts and rented them to employees.

Checking on Pre-Hearing Procedures

Dick Smith did not follow the required procedures for giving notice of his hearing, and this failure cost him time and money. Because procedures vary from place to place, Dan Carter finds it an absolute necessity to check them out thoroughly several weeks ahead of time. If a legal notice must be placed in a weekly newspaper, then the newspaper's deadline must be considered, as well as the amount of advance notice required by law. If it is the applicant's responsibility to contact all property owners within a specified radius, then time needs to be allowed for responses from people not at home on the first try.

Dan makes a point of learning what time of day the hearing is to be held. In most communities, an evening meeting will draw more opponents than a daytime meeting. If the hearing overlaps both daytime and evening hours, and if Dan has any choice in the selection of a time, he will choose a morning or afternoon scheduling.

Dan also checks to find out what other items likely to be controversial are on the agenda, especially if those items involve locations in the vicinity of his application. Rather than risk an enlarged group of opponents who are present to object to the other items, he sometimes finds it advisable to delay for a couple of weeks.

Scouting the Hearing

Prior to a hearing, Dan Carter goes scouting for two kinds of information about the mechanics of the hearing. One kind of information has to do with the rules and procedures to be followed; the other has to do with physical facilities. The facilities are easier to deal with, so we will discuss them first. What Dan looks for ought to be obvious to any other applicant, but it is amazing to discover in actual hearings how many important steps have not been taken.

The first step taken by Dan in scouting is to visit the meeting room *well in advance* of the hearing. By "well in advance," we mean before any visual aids are prepared. He examines the arrangement of the room; the lighting; the availability of screens, projectors, and easels; the placement of electrical outlets; and the distance between the location of displays and the people viewing them. This last item is especially critical. The authors have experienced numerous presentations of visual material that could not be seen in detail by the decision makers, either because of poor lighting, or because the details were simply too small to be viewed from more than three feet away.

If at all possible, Dan visits the meeting room during an actual public hearing several weeks before the one at which his proposal is to be aired. Not only does this reconnaissance give Dan a chance to observe the facilities in actual use, but it also provides insights into the reactions of those present to different kinds of presentations.

In addition to checking out the physical facilities, Dan needs to know the rules and procedures to be followed. Some of these can be found in the text of the ordinance, but others might be learned only by asking local officials or by attending an actual hearing. Besides the formal rules, there may be more informal standards or customs that ought to be adhered to if the applicant expects to be successful. Procedures for voting, the time allotted for the applicant's presentation and rebuttal arguments, and the weight given to the opinions of nearby property owners can vary from place to place. Such procedures and customs may not be in writing. There is really no adequate substitute for observing rules and procedures in use at an actual hearing.

Some of the questions that Dan asks himself when scouting are:

1. Is the voting done openly or in executive session?

2. If the voting is in the "sunshine," is it done immediately after each item is heard, or is all voting put off until all applications have been heard?

3. How long do hearings generally last?

4. Is an item scheduled for 2 p.m. usually heard on time? Is it not heard until several hours later? What are the possibilities that it might be heard earlier than scheduled?

5. Are spectators permitted to applaud or to stand up as a group and be counted?

6. If chances of approval do not look good, can an item be postponed or withdrawn "without prejudice"?

7. If this is not possible, then how long will the applicant have to wait before reapplying?

8. Do applicants ordinarily speak for themselves, or do they have lawyers to speak for them? Which appears to be the more effective?

Final Preparations

Dan Carter's final preparations for the hearing include:

1. Making sure that experts such as traffic engineers can be present.

2. Deciding who is to say what.

3. Rehearsing the presentation so that it will be concise and within the time limits.

4. Anticipating questions and objections and deciding how they are to be answered.

Conduct at the Hearing

The public hearing is often the climax of Dan's efforts. We say "often" rather than "always," because two public hearings are frequently necessary—one before the planning advisory board (or commission) and the other before the council (or elected board of commissioners). If two hearings are required, then Dan avoids blowing all of the ammunition on the first one. He always has something in reserve to throw in at the eleventh hour.

If preparation for the hearing has been as thorough as Dan's, then an applicant should be able to approach it with confidence. Dan likes for all present to take notice of his confidence; he thinks that it gives him a psychological advantage. He takes care, however, that the confidence does not come across as cockiness. The exact demeanor that Dan assumes depends, to some extent, upon what he has observed at the meetings that he scouted. In general, however, his bearing is one of quiet forcefulness combined with courtesy. Dan always has in the back of his mind the thought that an appearance at a particular hearing may not be his last one before the same group of people. He knows that it might be necessary to alienate some of the opposition in order to win, but he makes sure that it is necessary before doing it. Enemies should not be made lightly. Dan might win this time only to be confronted on another occasion by someone he offended in the process. Some objectors might be only mildly opposed to his proposal. Arrogance or sarcasm on his part could turn them into bitter antagonists. On the positive side, objectors might be won over, or at least neutralized, by calm, reasoned, and polite responses to their questions.

Dan begins the hearing with an open mind and a willingness to compromise. This does not necessarily mean that there must be compromise, but the possibility must be recognized. Dan must be able to sense *when* and *if* it is necessary, so that too much is not given away too soon—or that too little is not conceded too late.

Justifying the Application

In order to win a hearing, Dan ordinarily has to do one of three things:

1. Convince the hearing board that what is proposed is harmless to the community; or
2. Convince them that the proposal is so desirable to the community that the public interest outweighs any negative effects; or
3. Convince them that a denial would deprive him of basic legal or constitutional rights.

Exactly how he goes about making these points will depend upon previous observations made from scouting hearings. Different boards will react in different ways to similar arguments. Dan's tactics also vary according to the strength of the opposition. If there is no opposition, or only token opposition, many boards would be inclined to approve a proposal without close scrutiny. CAUTION: Although the neighbors' opposition might be weak, professional planners or other public officials might be strongly opposed.

Dan's first step in a presentation is to explain what is proposed. If there is no opposition apparent, then he keeps this explanation fairly general. If, on the other hand, there is strong opposition, he is prepared to go into considerable detail. Dan believes it important to establish firmly at the beginning that the proposal is for a definite use and not just for speculative purposes. Most people present will be thinking in terms of the specific use proposed rather than in terms of all of the other uses that might be put on the site if zoning approval is granted. If Dan once permits any doubts to arise about the certainty of what is to be done, then the hearing could easily get out of control. Dan is careful to avoid misrepresentation of facts, either intentional or unintentional. Besides being dishonest, it could backfire when exposed by later questioning.

After explaining what is proposed and what is to be done, the next step is to justify the proposal. There are various approaches to doing this. Some of the more common ones used by Dan Carter and other applicants are as follows:

1. *Emphasize the weakness of the opposition*. This approach can be especially effective if the opponents are few in number or lukewarm in their objections. A lone vociferous objector might be embarrassed by being forced into admitting that he had offered his property for sale to the applicant. Where the opposition is more numerous, Dan will sometimes be able to blunt the objections by calm, reasoned, respectful arguments to the effect that the opponents are not fully informed and that their fears are unjustified. If Dan has been able to negotiate successfully with neighbors prior to the hearing, then the climax of the entire presentation can be the presence of several neighbors who speak *for* the proposal instead of *against* it. Upon a show of unanimous support from surrounding property owners, some city councils will approve almost anything.

2. *Demonstrate that the original zoning was a mistake*. For example, it might be argued that a zoning boundary was originally drawn without adequate consideration for the direction in which the property faced, or in disregard of unusual problems of terrain. Evidence might be presented to show that a nonconforming commercial or industrial use next door has continually rendered the property unfit for the uses permitted.

3. *Show evidence that changing circumstances have made changes in use necessary*. This approach is often buttressed by maps, statistics, and photographs that suggest trends in the surrounding area involving change in land use or population or both. For example, the change might be in the form of increasing vacancies in an older retail district following the opening of a newer, planned shopping center a short distance away. In this case, Dan would argue that the older area was no longer suitable for the retail shops permitted and should be zoned for something else.

4. *Arouse the board's sympathy*. Dan is not in a good position to use this argument, but Mary Trigg might try it in her case. This can be done by mentioning a personal hardship of the property owner. It might be a chronic illness, widowhood, old age, or a faulty investment decision. None of these factors is properly a consideration, but few hearing boards will be completely unmoved by them. Another approach is to argue that the property owner made a wrong decision on the property as a result of a mistaken interpretation by a zoning official, or simply as a result of a misunderstanding in dealing with the official. A third argument is that the property owner is the victim of a street widening, expressway wall, or some other public project that has detracted from the value of the property.

5. *Remind the board of the exemplary record of the applicant*: the high quality of previous developments, the reputation for living up to commitments, the deep roots and continuing strong stake in the community. Dan uses this argument frequently.

6. *Argue that denial of the application would deprive the owner of the "highest and best use" of the property* and therefore would constitute a "taking" of a portion of the property's value without just compensation. This is a legalistic argument that may or may not impress a board comprised mainly of non-lawyers. It will not necessarily impress lawyer-members either. Sometimes when Dan uses this argument, he will

be represented by an attorney at the hearing, and a court reporter will be conspicuously present. The implication is that the applicant is prepared to appeal to the courts if necessary.

7. *Point out that the existing zoning would actually permit one or more uses worse than the one proposed.* For example, if Dan is seeking a change from apartment zoning to office zoning, he might bring out the fact that the apartment district would permit such high densities that far more auto traffic could be generated by apartments than by the proposed office building (which, unlike the apartments, would not involve nightime traffic to and from parties). It might be shown also that the setback requirements for the office building would be greater than those in the apartment district. In taking such an approach, Dan carefully avoids the appearance of threatening to do any of the undesirable things already permitted, but the possibility would not be denied.

8. *Demonstrate that the proposal would improve the surrounding area.* This approach is most effective if the proposed development is to replace an eyesore or a hangout for undesirable elements in what is otherwise a respectable neighborhood. It can also be effective if the proposal is for the first new building in an older area that has been declining for many years.

9. *Describe how the proposal will benefit the general welfare.* It might be argued that the development would provide needed retail facilities, jobs, or additions to the community tax base. This approach can also be used in a negative fashion. For example, it might be said that the denial of a requested rezoning for business or industry would mean that the potential user would leave the community and move to another one, taking along a portion of the tax base.

10. *Cite principles of good community planning.* There are two alternatives to this approach. One is to claim that the proposal is in keeping with the community's comprehensive plan. The other is to argue that, although the proposal is not specifically spelled out in the plan, it would not conflict with it and might even further the plan's objectives.

11. *Allay fears that the proposal would have adverse effects.* This approach generally requires opinions and supporting evidence from consultants that the development would not significantly affect traffic or overburden schools or other public facilities. It often includes a description of all steps that will be taken by the developer to minimize external effects. For example, Dan might present a civil engineer who then explains how a retention basin will trap water from a heavy rain and release it gradually so as to keep down drainage problems in the surrounding area.

Using Visual Aids

Dan Carter has found that visual aids, such as plans, diagrams, photographs, slides, and charts, can be very effective in generating interest and response in a zoning presentation. The old axiom that a picture can take the place of a thousand words holds true for almost any visual aids used in a presentation, especially in the highly emotional environment of a zoning hearing. A well-conceived and well-prepared visual aid is clear evidence that the speaker has carefully planned what to say and how to say it and carries with it the implication that the applicant's proposal is also well founded.

Unfortunately, applicants can sometimes be trapped by their own visual aids. A major oil company, for example, displayed at a hearing a beautiful pictorial view of a proposed service station. The conditional use for the station was approved, but the city manager insisted that the illustration be incorporated in the record as part of the site plan. His sharp eye had noted the fact that the signs shown in the pictorial view were smaller than normal. The oil company was forced to comply with the smaller signs.

Dan Carter uses visual aids but with discretion. He uses them only when he wishes to make a point forcefully, so that their effectiveness is not diluted through overuse. He works closely with the person preparing the aids so that they convey exactly his intent and nothing that is extraneous. Dan keeps a checklist of the following DON'TS:

1. Don't forget how far away from the aid the audience is going to be.

2. Don't try to show too much detail on a small map or illustration.

3. Don't be overly general on a large map or illustration.

4. Don't use colors or lines that are too weak to be contrasted from each other from more than a few inches away.

5. Don't use an aid at the wrong time in a presentation. Plan carefully exactly when it is to be used and integrate it into the oral remarks.

Using Experts

Dan does not hesitate to make use of outside experts to help in his presentations. He frequently consults his attorney, a land planner, a traffic engineer, and an architect, and sometimes appraisers, feasibility analysts, civil engineers, and others. Prior to a hearing, Dan decides which of these might be needed at the hearing and makes sure that those needed are available on call. He might even take some with him. Generally, however, he makes as much of the presentation as possible by himself, preferring to keep the experts in reserve. He wants to impress those present at the hearing with the fact that he, personally, understands the issues thoroughly. Furthermore, if he relies upon the experts too freely, there is always the risk that one of them will say too much and open up issues that Dan had rather not discuss.

Countering the Opposition

Because Dan Carter prepares thoroughly for a hearing, there are few surprises for him when the opponents have their say. Objections can be countered, and questions answered, in a pleasant but firm manner by himself or by an expert whom Dan has brought with him in anticipation of particular questions or objections. Surprises can occur, however, and they must be dealt with on the spot. If a surprise dims the chances for approval, then Dan has several options:

1. *Persuasion*. Show that the surprise argument or objection is not important or that the objection was not raised in good faith. Dan may stress that he has been careful to consult planners and neighbors and explain the proposal to them in advance of the meeting. Every step was taken to answer objections and respond to suggestions of people in the community. Dan may be able to argue that the objection is unfair, unreasonable, or a misrepresentation of facts. In doing so, he tries to remain calm and reasonable himself.

2. *Bulldoze*. Try to overpower the objections. This technique is most effective if the proposal would result in a substantial increase in the community's employment or tax base (or if it would avert a loss of jobs or taxes). It might also work if the proposal is for a use that fills a social need, such as housing for the elderly. It will nearly always make enemies, however, and should not be used lightly.

3. *Compromise*. Agree to reduce the extent of the request; agree to the attachment of conditions to the approval; or agree to enter into private convenants with the objectors. The last two techniques may encounter the objection of "contract zoning," so Dan has to be prepared in advance to handle such a possibility.

4. *Delay*. Ask that a decision on the application be postponed until a later meeting, by which time further study should produce an answer to difficult questions or a solution to major objections. Some communities use the term "withdraw without prejudice" as a synonym for "postpone," meaning that the request may be resubmitted at any time without going through the waiting period of twelve to eighteen months that is often required when an application is denied. Some applicants use repeated postponements as a tactic for wearing down the opposition. Usually there are fewer opponents present each time an item is reheard. If an application can be put off until the middle of the summer, then many objectors might fail to show up because of vacations.

The choice of an option can be affected by the procedure used for voting. At some hearings, the voting on each item is done on the spot. After applicant and opponents have had their say, the board discusses the issues openly and votes openly. If the objectors are numerous and vocal, then the board can easily be intimidated by them. At other hearings the discussion and voting is conducted openly but only after *all* items on the agenda have been heard. If this does not happen until several hours after a controversial application has been heard, then the board may not feel intimidated, especially if most of the objectors have drifted away. In states that have not yet passed "sunshine" laws requiring open meetings, hearing boards often withhold their discussion and their voting until all items have been heard and then go into "executive session," meaning that neither applicant nor objectors may be present. This practice can reduce the intimidating power of opponents considerably. Unless the vote is by roll call, the opposition will not know for certain who voted how.

Tactics for the Opposition

In the case of Dick Smith and his Pizza Pizzazz, the objecting neighbors were overwhelmingly victorious because:

1. They were informed.

2. They were prepared.

3. They were organized.

4. Dick Smith bungled his preparation and botched his presentation.

Defeating an inept applicant is easy, but it can lead to overconfidence. Hilda and Fred Potts, co-presidents of the Maplewood Homeowners Club, have no illusions about Dan Carter's ability as an opponent. Their first rule for defending their property and neighborhood is: *never become complacent!* Their second rule is: *never underestimate the potential effectiveness of persistent, forceful attacks on existing zoning by skilled applicants*. A successful zoning defense must be designed to discourage or defeat not just one assault but a continuing series of them. Winning these battles demands vigilance and perseverance. It also requires information, preparation, and organization.

Keeping Informed

Everyone affected by a proposal on the agenda at a zoning hearing has a right to be heard. This right cannot be exercised, however, unless the person affected is aware of the proposal and knows the time and place of the hearing. A brief description of the proposal, along with notification of the time and place of the hearing, is often brought to the attention of a property owner without being sought. It might be by official letter, a sign on the applicant's property, a public notice or article in a newspaper, word of mouth from neighbors, or a direct contact by the applicant.

None of these sources is fail-safe. Not all communities send out letters to individual property owners. Those that do must necessarily limit them to owners within a certain radius of the applicant's property—say 250 to 350 feet. Some letters may go astray. Others may arrive when the recipients are out of town. Signs can be overlooked. If the proposal is for an amendment to the *text* of the ordinance, then no specific parcel of property will be singled out; there will be *no* sign and *no* letter. Instead, general notice will be given to all property owners in the community. News articles are not written about every zoning proposal, and legal notices in a newspaper are sometimes tucked away in inconspicuous locations. Such notices might even be in a paper that the average person does not read. Some localities advertise in specialized news-papers for the legal profession. Others rely on local weeklies that might not be read by absentee owners living in nearby communities. Unless the property owner is part of a well-organized neighborhood group, reliance on word-of-mouth notice is risky. Dependence on notification by the applicant is also risky. In summary, no property owner should rely on some passive way of getting notified. Instead, the owner ought to take the initiative and actively seek to be informed.

To avoid missing out on an important zoning application, Hilda and Fred Potts check regularly with the office where applications are made. Like some other organizations of property owners (and like some single owners of large holdings) the Maplewood Homeowners Club is on the planning commission's mailing list to receive copies of meeting agendas on a regular basis. The mailing list is not a substitute for personal visits, however. Hilda and Fred want to learn of new proposals well before the agendas are mailed out in order to have plenty of time to study the details of the application and to prepare a defense. A personal visit to the zoning office provides an opportunity to examine the file on the application and to ask questions of the staff.

Even if these suggestions are followed, a property owner who is away for an extended period can miss out on an important application. There are three possible ways of avoiding such an occurrence. One is for the owner to head a firm large enough to permit the assignment of a staff member to keep up with zoning matters. Another is for the owner of investment property to retain a property manager with the resources for staying abreast. A third way, and the only way for most property owners, is to form an association of owners of property in a particular neighborhood or commercial area and to appoint a committee of reliable members to inform themselves and relay promptly any news of concern. This is what the members of the Maplewood Homeowners have done.

Organizing

An organization of property owners can be far more effective in dealing with zoning problems than the owners would be individually. This is especially true if the organization is one that is on-going. The Maplewood Homeowners Club has a dependable "Alert Committee" for actively scouting out what proposals are in the wind and for disseminating such knowledge to the entire membership. The members of the "Alert Committee" have clearly assigned responsibilities for the scouting and reporting. If one of them is planning to be out of town for a while, the others are aware of the fact.

An on-going association will be able to draw on expert help easily. The Maplewood Homeowners Club has a lawyer on retainer. Specialists of various kinds, such as traffic engineers and city planners, are among the membership. Where such skills are not represented, Hilda and Fred will know where to find them quickly. The association always has sufficient funds on hand to pay for at least a day or two of a consultant's time, or it will know where the services may be obtained inexpensively from an umbrella organization.

Meeting with the Applicant

The Maplewood Homeowners Club has no objection to meeting with an ap- plicant prior to a hearing. Furthermore, they have no objection to Dan Carter's tactic of meeting informally with small groups. They feel that this method gives everyone a better chance to become acquainted thoroughly with the proposal. They do, however, hold one or more subsequent meetings without the applicant present in order to work out common stands to take on the issues involved. They make sure that an applicant does not use "whip-saw" tactics to divide and conquer the opponents. If an applicant offers any sort of agreement as a trade-off for their support, they make use of their lawyer to obtain an agreement that is a binding one.

Meeting with Professional Planners and Politicians

Hilda and Fred consult the professional planning staff in city hall about every zoning item that affects Maplewood. They not only are seeking information, but they also are bringing to the planners' attention the objections of the neighbors. Although the planners are usually considered impartial, they have many items to evaluate, and they might pay more attention to some of the factors involved in a particular case if they are made aware that the objectors are going to bring up those factors at the public hearing.

The Maplewooders consult their council members on each item affecting their neighborhood, but they also cultivate these elected officials the year around by inviting them to their club meetings, especially those meetings that are likely to be well attended. At these meetings, the council members, and sometimes the mayor, are publicly thanked for their help to the neighborhood. The officials cannot help but be impressed by both the large attendance (all voters) and the enthusiasm. Consequently, when a Maplewood contingent shows up before the council at a public hearing, the council knows who they are and the strength that they represent. It is not absolutely necessary to have a large turnout at every hearing if the council is convinced that those who are present represent considerable voting power. Whenever possible, however, a big turnout should be generated as a reminder of that power.

Preparation for the Hearing

Hilda and Fred have several meetings with their zoning committee well in advance of a hearing to decide on strategy, tactics, and the use of experts and visual aids. They select carefully the members who are going to speak at the hearing, and they make sure that they are well rehearsed. They don't mind having some speakers repeat points made by others as a technique of emphasizing the most important objections, but they try to avoid thoughtless repetition, as that merely bores the people conducting the hearing. In general, they give the same meticulous attention to getting ready as does Dan Carter.

One of the tools that the Maplewood Homeowners Club uses is publicity in the newspaper, radio, and television media. Even before the hearing, the media are often contacted and advised of the club's official position on a particular matter. Several times in the past, the publicity generated by an effective television news-story, or by an article in the local newspaper, helped contribute to a massive public outcry that influenced the zoning decision makers to favor the club's position even before the public hearing.

The Maplewood Homeowners Club members have gathered signatures for petitions, have written personal letters to council members and planning commissioners, and have personally telephoned or visited their representatives on the council and the planning commission before rezoning hearings. The club members have learned that personal contact is generally more effective than impersonal form letters or petitions. Individual club members have worked on the political campaigns of several local politicians. Because the club uses such a broad arsenal of persuasive tools, it has been very successful in defeating nearly every rezoning request that it has opposed in the past.

Conduct at the Hearing

The Maplewood group is a little more subtle than the Briar Hills Civic Association; they don't wear blue blazers. They do, however, sit as a group and stand as a group. They try to make a good impression by refraining from applauding, cheering, or booing, but they will all raise their hands or stand as a body in response to a question from Hilda or Fred. This is not supposed to be done, but by the time the chair tells them not to do it, the impression of solidarity has already been made.

Here are some of the arguments that Maplewood members have been known to make in opposition to proposals:

1. *Making claims that procedural rules have been violated.* Fred and Hilda check each application closely to see if the applicant has met all requirements for filing deadlines and giving notice. If they can find any procedural violations, they bring them up at the hearing, thus putting the applicant on the defensive. They may be able to wear the applicant down through postponement of the item, perhaps thereby causing the applicant to miss a deadline for exercising an option or executing a lease. Of course, they must be careful not to wear down their own troops by their delaying tactics.

2. *Pointing out that approval of the application would lead to a violation of private deed restrictions.* Logically this argument is not a relevant one, because zoning is not supposed to be used to enforce private agreements, but practically speaking, it often impresses the decision makers.

3. *Bringing up the past record of the applicant,* showing failure to live up to past promises. Strictly speaking, this is not relevant either. Zoning is supposed to deal with property—not with particular property owners. In actuality it can be quite effective.

4. *Citing conflict with the comprehensive plan.* The Maplewooders are thoroughly familiar with the comprehensive plan and its application to Maplewood. When an application seems to conflict with the plan, they side strongly with the need for rational planning; when no conflict is apparent, they ignore the subject.

5. *Arguing that the proposal would overload public facilities.* Members of the civic club have files of current information on the capacity of water lines, sewer lines, storm drainage, schools, and streets. After learning the details of any new zoning proposal, they descend on city hall to ask the professionals there pointed questions about the impact that the proposal is likely to have. The answers given them are used to develop arguments against the proposal.

6. *Showing that the application would be detrimental to the public health or safety.* This argument makes use of alleged air pollution, noise, traffic conflicts (especially those involving pedestrian hazards), and dangers from hazardous materials that might be present on the site.

7. *Claiming probable adverse effects on surrounding property.* This is what the Briar Hills group did at the hearing of Dick Smith's proposal. They cited drainage problems, for example, and glare from headlights.

8. *Demonstrating lack of need for proposed use.* The Maplewood zoning committee drives around the city looking for similar uses and for similarly zoned sites that have not been developed. They present the details of what they find at the hearing, arguing that there is an abundance both of the uses and of the land properly zoned to accommodate them.

9. *Arousing concern for adverse impact on the natural environment.* They cite the need for preserving woods and for reducing runoff and erosion.

10. *Threatening retaliation against office holders.* This tactic can backfire, so the Maplewooders don't use it much. If threatened, the officials will sometimes hold tenaciously to their positions. On the other hand, the tactic if used sparingly can be very effective. Three years ago, the Maplewood members threatened to retaliate against two members of the city council. They formed a coalition with several other neighborhood groups and succeeded in turning the officials out of office. It hasn't been necessary to use the threat since then. Everyone is aware of their power.

11. *Attacking the applicant's exhibits*. We have already pointed out some weaknesses in exhibits, such as signs made unintentionally small or perspectives deliberately faked. The Maplewood group looks for such discrepancies and makes full use of any that they find.

12. *Responding to the applicant's use of experts*. Hilda and Fred try to anticipate what kinds of experts the applicant might use, so that they can have their own there to provide counter opinions.

13. *Suggesting alternatives*. The Maplewood Civic Club seeks to persuade those conducting the hearing that they are not against the use of the property in question. They simply oppose the particular application being heard. To reinforce their claim of a positive attitude, they often suggest alternative courses of action. For example, they may recommend public acquisition of the property for a park, or they may raise the possibility of a new kind of zoning district that does not permit as great a range of uses as does the one sought in the application.

Maintaining Flexibility

Like the applicant, the opponents must maintain enough flexibility to enable them to compromise if and when it seems desirable. The decision to compromise is not one that can be made easily by a large group during a hearing. If compromise is thought to be a possibility, then the general framework has to be agreed upon by the membership in advance of the hearing, and the leaders of the group need to be given the authorization to act when and if they deem it in the group's interest. The Maplewood Civic Club, for example, has agreed that Hilda and Fred will oppose flatly both the rezoning and the conditional use sought by Dan Carter. If, however, the city council should approve the zoning change, then Hilda and Fred are to negotiate to seek more concessions from Dan on the conditional use. In such event (and providing they are successful in extracting concessions from Dan), they would consider supporting the conditional-use request.

After the Hearings

Readers who have been championing the cause of Mary Trigg will be pleased to learn that she made a clean sweep of the hearings. Her neighbors rallied to her side and she was able to obtain an amendment to the text of the ordinance to allow pottery making as a conditional use in the R-3 district. She was then able to get specific approval of the conditional use on her property. Finally, she appeared before the board of adjustment and asked for the variance from the rear-yard requirement. No one was there to object, and the board didn't even bother to look for a hardship to justify their action. They simply granted the variance.

Mary is quite happy about the outcome, and her neighbors are not displeased. Without being aware of it, however, they may have set the stage for some future problems. They would do well to organize like Maplewood because:

1. They have helped to set a precedent for future variances without showing of hardship.

2. They have consented to a use that could last way beyond Mary's ownership and occupancy of the property. What happens in the future if the business is so successful that it needs to expand?

Dan Carter won the endorsement of the planning commission, but when his proposal got to the city council for the second public hearing, it was turned down by a vote of five to four. The issue has not been finally decided, however. Although zoning is in some respects like a game of sport, there are important differences. In zoning, unlike baseball, for example, it is possible for both sides to win or for both sides to lose. It is also possible for the game to resume at any time. Dan is supposed to wait eighteen months before submitting another application for rezoning the same property, but meanwhile he can appeal the denial to the courts. He could also exercise his option and make the objectors uncomfortable with his use of the property. For example, the authors know of one developer who rented the old house on a five-acre tract to a hippie family who (a) seldom cut the grass, (b) broke windows that they didn't replace, (c) parked a red, white, and blue (and very rusty) school bus in the front yard, and (d) had many late-night parties, during the course of which they threw beer cans all over the lawn. After an eighteen-month wait, the neighbors supported the developer's application for conditional use for condominiums. On the other hand, we know of another developer who tried a similar tactic, thereby making the neighbors so angry that they held up his proposal for five years.

Dan Carter does not engage in such tactics, and fortunately both for Dan and for the Maplewood residents, the two contending parties ended their battle respecting each other and still on speaking terms. They may yet be able to reach an agreement. Here are some reasons why the Maplewooders might be willing to bargain.

1. It is probably unrealistic to expect a conventional subdividing of the Brady Estate into 30,000-square-foot lots.

2. The Brady Estate could deteriorate and cause problems while the outcome remained in limbo.

3. The board of adjustment (not subject to election) could grant a variance unsatisfactory to the neighbors. They might be able to overturn the variance in court, but the process would take time and money.

4. They personally trust Dan, although they are aware that Dan could die or sell the property. The successor to Dan might not be as ethical or trustworthy.

5. They would like to settle the future of the Brady Estate once and for all in order to preserve the stability of their neighborhood.

Conclusion

This chapter has provided the reader with a basic framework for understanding the process of the zoning hearing. With careful preparation and understanding of local procedures, both proponents and opponents of zoning can make effective and convincing presentations. The reader is cautioned that each case is unique and requires careful study and evaluation. Not all rezonings are bad. In many cases a proposed use will enhance property values and stabilize a community. Each case should be considered on its own merits.

A decision at a zoning hearing is not the final disposition of a problem. As for Dan Carter, he has several alternatives open to him. He may go back to the neighbors and work out differences and resubmit his application. There is a required waiting period before the same application can be submitted, but Dan may be able to get a waiver of this requirement. Alternatively, he may seek a different use that requires no rezoning or find a different use that requires a lesser, and more acceptable, rezoning. Because Dan intends to continue working in the community, he should take care to develop a project in good faith and consistent with any promises that he may have made at the zoning hearing and to neighbors. Many developers, once they achieve a favorable rezoning, ignore the promises that led to the favorable decision because they were not legally binding. This makes it more difficult to achieve a rezoning in the future.

Dan may consider appeal of the decision to the courts. If Dan had won his case, the neighbors could also go to court to attempt to prevent the rezoning on legal grounds. Chapter 8 discusses the considerations and problems of appealing to the courts and Chapter 9 deals with supporting studies that are useful, and in many cases essential, to a case in a zoning hearing or in court.

8
Appeals
to the Courts

Appeals to the courts are involved in only a small percentage of the zoning matters decided at public hearings. The possibility for such an appeal is always present, however, and a property owner who expects to win at zoning should have at least an elementary understanding of what such litigation might involve.

Zoning cases are usually won or lost long before the time of the trial. Consider the contrasting situations of Dan Carter and Dick Smith. Before Dan acquired the option to purchase the nineteen-acre Brady Estate, he consulted his attorney for advice. Dan believes in practicing preventive law. Preventive law is much like preventive medicine. In medicine it is usually easier to keep a patient well if he or she exercises, eats properly, and takes other health precautions. In law it is usually easier to accomplish what a client wishes if appropriate steps are taken in advance to ensure that all legal rights are protected. Dan knows that there are occasions when it might be necessary to appeal a zoning decision to the courts. By developing a strong record of the case in advance, the chances of winning in the courts are significantly enhanced. A record is built by introducing appropriate evidence at the hearing to develop a *prima facie* case that the rezoning is justified. A *prima facie* case is one that contains all of the elements of proof necessary to justify a legal conclusion.

While Dan speaks for himself at the zoning hearing, his attorney is present to give him advice and to make sure that the facts and expert testimony are properly presented for the record. Building the record is critical in many states where courts review zoning cases by *writ of certiorari*. A *writ of certiorari* examines the record of the zoning board's hearing and decision to determine whether any errors of law have been made. Ordinarily no new evidence is permitted. In states where the courts review by *writ of certiorari*, Dan Carter has an excellent chance of reversing the unfavorable rezoning decision. Dick Smith, on the other hand, has virtually no chance, because he built a very weak case at the hearing. His failure to introduce evidence to build a strong record at the hearing would make an overturn of the denial very unlikely.

In some states the courts have *de novo* hearings in rezoning cases. A *de novo* hearing permits each party to present evidence and expert testimony in a new hearing. Even in states which permit a *de novo* hearing, well-prepared litigants like Dan Carter are in a position superior to those like Dick Smith who do not think ahead to the next potential step.

Zoning cases are complex and normally take a great deal of time to prepare and assemble. The problem rests primarily in collecting sufficient facts to support a legal conclusion. These facts include, among other things, a detailed description of the land-use pattern surrounding the subject site, traffic counts, the relationship of the proposed rezoning to the community's comprehensive plan, the adequacy of the comprehensive plan, value estimates on the subject property before and after the proposed rezoning, and impact of the rezoning on surrounding land uses.

The complexity of the evidence is different with each zoning case. Dan Carter has already assembled his case. Dick Smith will have to hire an attorney to collect the necessary evidence, hire experts, and research the law. Because this is time-consuming, the legal fee that Dick will be charged will ordinarily have to reflect this effort. By practicing preventive law, Dan Carter saves legal fees in the long run.

Selecting an Attorney

While theoretically a person does not require an attorney to litigate a case in court, it is almost always advisable to do so. There is a maxim which states: "A person who represents himself has a fool for a client." An attorney brings to the court an objective viewpoint and is usually able to detach the case from emotionalism. Judges are seldom impressed with amateur would-be lawyers who are unfamiliar with the law and with local procedures.

Dick Smith has no intention of representing himself. After losing his request for rezoning, he called his golfing friend, Jerry Healey. Jerry graduated from a local night law school two years previously and has developed a large divorce case practice. Jerry has every appearance of success. He leases a new Cadillac, belongs to a country club, and maintains an elegant office that is filled with leased antique furniture. On several occasions, Jerry has been successful in having traffic tickets dismissed for Dick. While Jerry has never handled a zoning case before, he is interested in expanding his practice and is willing to accept the case.

Comment

Dick has used the wrong criteria to select an attorney in this case. While Jerry may be an excellent lawyer, Dick has no real way of knowing this. Success in one area of law does not necessarily imply competency in other areas. The symbols of success such as a new car or a fancy law office do not necessarily mean that a lawyer is capable.

Dan Carter's attorney is Susan Brown. She has been practicing law for several years and has specialized in land-use litigation and local-government law. Her hourly fees are slightly higher than Jerry Healey's, but in the long run the overall cost is lower. Jerry Healey will have to spend a great deal of time familiarizing himself with zoning cases that were previously decided in the state and with other aspects of the law. The time that Jerry spends educating himself will be charged to Dick Smith's account.

How did Dan Carter find an attorney who specialized in zoning law? Like medicine, the law has become so complicated that many attorneys have begun to specialize in narrow areas. Numerous states give recognition to this specialization by permitting attorneys to hold themselves out as specialists. Some local bar associations run lawyer-referral services, which seek to match a specialist in a particular area with the client's needs. A degree of caution should be exercised, though, because a referral service does not necessarily certify that the suggested attorney or attorneys have any real expertise in a subject area. Often the attorney has only indicated preferences. Dan Carter did not rely solely on a lawyer-referral service. He began his search for an attorney by talking with people who themselves were very familiar with the real estate field. He talked to mortgage lenders, appraisers, architects, real estate brokers, and an officer of a title insurance company. Several of these people mentioned that they were impressed with Susan Brown as being a very competent lawyer. Dan also talked to his tax attorney for suggestions. His tax attorney said that Susan was considered to be a tough, but fair, opponent by members of the local bar association. Dan looked up Susan in a national law directory to determine her education and background. He was reassured with what he found.

Dan made an appointment to talk to Susan to determine whether he would engage her services. During the initial appointment, Dan asked her how many zoning cases she had handled and what the outcomes had been. He also inquired as to the professional organizations of which she was a member. He discovered that she had published in current law journals and had appeared on continuing-education programs for lawyers. Early in their discussion, Dan Carter and Susan Brown discussed legal-fee arrangements and the scope of services to be performed. While Dan was interested in assuring himself that the fee was reasonable, he was more concerned with the experience and expertise of the attorney. As Dan dealt with large projects that would potentially earn him many thousands of dollars in expected profits, he realized that shopping around for the lowest hourly price was a false economy. Professionals tend to set their fees on the basis of what their services are worth. Dan has discovered that over the years, Susan has saved him over a hundred times her legal fees.

Unlike Dan Carter and Dick Smith, Mary Trigg will become involved in the court system in a different way. Both Dan and Dick are considering appeals of their cases, and in legal terminology they will be known as "plaintiffs." Mary Trigg will become involved in the judicial system as a "defendant." Ruth Cramer, who has been in Florida for the winter, has returned to town. Ruth is Mary's next-door neighbor and is jealous of Mary's self-sufficiency. Ruth's husband died several years ago and her only child was killed at war in Southeast Asia. As a result, Ruth became embittered. When Ruth discovered that Mary had received approval to expand her home occupation, Ruth decided to file a suit to prevent this. While her motivation may have been based on a psychological disorder, this ordinarily would not be the subject of court inquiry. The court would consider the legal basis of a suit. Ruth's legal reasons are reasonably sound. Mary has been storing broken pottery outdoors and has thereby created a breeding ground for mosquitos. Ruth has filed a case to abate a *nuisance*. A *nuisance* is any activity on a person's land which damages an adjoining land owner. Mary has a trusted family attorney who is a member of a large law firm. The firm has a specialist in real estate law who will be handling Mary's case.

Dan Carter, Dick Smith, Mary Trigg, and Ruth Cramer will all become participants in the judicial process. As our society is becoming more litigious, it is useful to understand how the judicial system can be an extension of the zoning process. By understanding the purpose of the courts and how they operate, a person increases the chances of winning at zoning.

The Court System and Jurisdictional Requirements

A person who is dissatisfied with a zoning decision may, under certain circumstances, have a choice of seeking appeal in one of two separate court systems: *state* and *federal*. Because access to the federal courts is narrowly defined by subject matter, or by diversity of citizenship and other technical requirements, a litigant is usually confined to the state court system. The subject matters which come under the jurisdiction of the federal courts are called "federal questions." For the purpose of simplification, *federal questions* arise under the U.S. Constitution and under federal statutes or treaties passed pursuant to the powers delegated under the Constitution. (Constitutional issues will be discussed in a subsequent section of this chapter.)

When access to the federal courts is feasible, an attorney will need to determine which forum (state or federal) is more advantageous to the client. Considerations in deciding which court to use include:

1. *Jurisdiction.* Can the court resolve the entire controversy? A court must have jurisdiction in order to hear a case. Courts receive power to hear a case either from a constitution or from legislative enactment. Jurisdiction may depend upon the subject matter involved, whether a person may be served with process, and where the property is located. If a court determines that another court may more properly resolve the issues to be litigated, the court may refuse jurisdiction. Zoning cases are ordinarily decided by state courts. A zoning case would be heard in the district or circuit in which the land in question is located.

2. *Remedies Available.* Are the remedies adequate? Consideration must be given to the remedies that the court is able to give. Remedies include such things as money damages for loss sustained, injunction, which is a court order not to do something, and other actions by the court.

3. *Time.* Speed with which a case may be litigated and resolved in a particular court can be a critical concern. Many court calendars are so crowded that it could take several years to litigate the issues fully.

4. *Procedure.* An advantage may exist in one court system in procedural rules and in *discovery*. Discovery relates to the legal techniques that a party to a suit may use to collect facts about the case. Through discovery, the opposition may have to produce evidence and answer questions or face contempt-of-court charges. Broad discovery is designed to reveal the full extent of either party's case and is supposed to encourage settlement out of court. Discovery procedures in the federal courts tend to be more liberally construed than those in state courts. Specific discovery techniques will be discussed later in this chapter.

5. *Precedents*. Consideration is given to precedents which may be favorable or unfavorable to a client's cause. Our judicial decisions are influenced by a legal doctrine
called *stare decisis*. This doctrine requires courts to follow past precedents decided
by the same courts or by higher appellate courts.

   In order to decide a case differently from past cases, the court must show a good
reason or changing conditions. For example, it was formerly held by the courts that a
person owning a tract of land also owned all air rights as far as the human eye could see
and all subsurface rights to the center of the earth. This would form an inverted pyramid
as illustrated in Figure 8-1. With the invention of the airplane, and the necessity of
overflight, the courts reinterpreted this right of ownership. The rule became that a person
owned only that airspace which could reasonably be used. Past a certain point, airspace
could be used by the public for aircraft without the aircraft operator's being held liable in
trespass to the property owner. Once it had been decided that the public might use the
airspace, this decision became binding on future cases.

Each state has developed its own procedural and jurisdictional rules defining
how appeals may be taken to the courts. A distinction is often made between
appeals from (*a*) decisions rendered by zoning boards of adjustment (boards
of appeals) and (*b*) decisions rendered by legislative bodies. Appeals from
decisions rendered by a zoning board of adjustment are more likely to be
controlled by the state's *administrative procedures act*. A board of adjustment
is normally required to base its finding on facts that are permitted to be used
by statutory standards. One who objects to a board's decision must base an
appeal to a court on the record created at the hearing level. An inadequate
record is usually fatal to a successful appeal.

A person seeking review under a state administrative procedures act must
ordinarily show *standing*. Standing is a requirement that prevents persons with

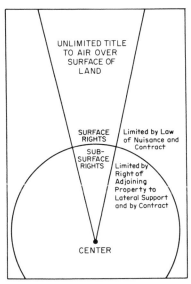

PROPERTY RIGHTS AFTER REVOLUTION
AND BREAK FROM ENGLAND

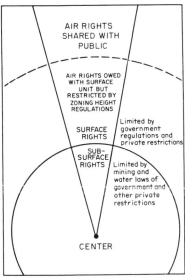

PROPERTY RIGHTS IN THE PRESENT

Figure 8-1

only an incidental interest in a decision from taking up the valuable time of the court. *Standing* may be shown by any person who is "aggrieved" by a decision. This normally means that a person must show (*a*) some way in which he or she has been damaged by a decision of a local board or (*b*) some legitimate interest that is recognized by law. Zoning ordinances often give special standing to neighbors who live within a specified number of feet from the zoned property and to officers, departments, boards, or bureaus of a local government. Any person who has a property interest in the real estate (such as an optionee) can normally show standing without any difficulty. Some state laws give any taxpayer standing under certain specified circumstances, as, for example, if a rezoning is likely to have an ecological impact that is adverse to the environment. The administrative procedures act may require that an appeal be filed within a certain number of days or be permanently barred. (This time period is normally thirty or thirty-five days after the decision.)

Where a zoning decision is construed as a legislative act (such as a rezoning) rather than an administrative one, the administrative procedures act might not apply. *Standing*, however, must be demonstrated in order for a person to file an appeal to the state trial court of general jurisdiction. In addition, many states require the *exhaustion of administrative remedies*. First, an appellant must seek to determine if adequate remedies are available within the administrative structure, or if there are administrative appeals that have not been tried. An appellant is not required to exhaust administrative remedies if it can be shown that the remedies are inadequate or that the effort would be futile. An "appellant" is a person who disagrees with a lower court decision or a decision of an administrative board, and who seeks a reversal by a higher judicial tribunal.

An aggrieved person has several alternative approaches to seeking judicial relief. The first approach is to seek reversal of a lower decision either by a *writ of certiorari* or trial *de novo*. Other approaches include: (1) *injunction*, (2) *writ of mandamus*, and (3) *declaratory judgment*.

An *injunction* may be sought to halt or limit the enforcement of the zoning regulations. If it can be shown that irreparable injury will result from enforcement of an invalid ordinance, or an invalid application of an ordinance, a property owner or other appropriate party may seek to challenge the constitutionality of the action by injunction. Likewise, neighboring property owners may seek an injunction to prevent a nuisance, despite the fact that the land use or activity is consistent with the zoning regulations. This is the approach that Ruth Cramer is taking against Mary Trigg. An injunction may be temporary, or it may be permanent, depending on the circumstances of the fact situation.

Normally an injunction that is an *equitable* remedy may not be used if there is an adequate remedy *at law*. Under English common law, courts had either power *in equity* or power *at law*. Power "at law" refers to a court's authority to apply rules or principles developed by legislation or by previous court cases. Power "in equity" refers to the authority to decide a case on the basis of fairness and justice. The courts of equity originally developed from the Old English court of Chancery. The court of Chancery was under the King's Chancellor, who was a high-ranking church official. The court of Chancery was used to administer the King's mercy or justice. Today there has been a fusion of these powers with powers "at law" under a single court. The distinction, however, is important because *equity* involves broader discretion on the part of the court and no jury is usually involved. Equitable relief is not proper if other relief is adequate. For instance, if a suit for damages would correct the situation, an injunction would not be issued.

For example, suppose a city decided to excavate a ditch cutting all access from a particular convenience store. The store owner might seek injunctive relief to prevent this action if the ditch would remain open for an unreasonably long time and if no provisions were planned to give access to the store by a bridge or detour.

A *writ of mandamus* may be sought to require a public official to act in a certain way. This writ will not be issued if the public official is entitled to act at his or her discretion. A legislative act, such as a rezoning, would be considered discretionary, and thus a mandamus would not be proper. If the act is *ministerial*, this writ is appropriate. An act is ministerial if it involves a mechanical action by a public official upon the showing that certain requirements, such as payment of fees, have been met. If a person can show that all requirements of a zoning ordinance have been met and that there is no other legal bar, a building inspector might be required by mandamus to issue a building or occupancy permit.

A *declaratory judgment* is an opinion by the court as to the legality or constitutionality of a particular fact situation. It is more than an advisory opinion. For example, in order to give a court jurisdiction in a zoning case, a person must show how he or she is being damaged by the application of the zoning regulations. The person could challenge the ordinance indirectly by creating a use in violation of the ordinance and daring the local government to seek an injunction or criminal sanctions. Rather than exposing a person to this kind of risk, a court is empowered to render a *declaratory judgment* without requiring a citizen to violate the law in order to adjudicate an issue.

Once a judicial decision has been reached in a zoning case, it applies only to the case in question (that is, it doesn't become a precedent) unless it deals with fundamental constitutional or legal issues. Most law cases other than zoning are controlled by the doctrine of *res judicata*. This doctrine states that once a case has been decided it may not be relitigated. In zoning cases, however, the doctrine is only applied in a limited sense. Most ordinances allow a new application for rezoning to be filed within eighteen or twenty-four months of the first filing. If the new application is turned down, a new appeal may be made to the courts. Some ordinances have no waiting period.

A previous decision by a court regarding a particular property may or may not be a controlling precedent, depending on changes in circumstances and the discretion of the court. If a zoning ordinance is declared unconstitutional as it applies to a particular property, there is little that can prevent the local government from passing a new ordinance that is almost as strict as the old one. For example, in one case, a property owner challenged the application of a minimum 4-acre lot-size requirement for his residential property. After several years of litigation, that owner was able to have a court decide that the 4-acre minimum was unreasonable. After the decision of the court, the local government changed the minimum requirement to 3.9 acres. In another case, a municipality was required to permit one of four lots at an intersection to be used as a service station. When another property owner sought a similar rezoning on the basis of the precedent set, he was advised that the precedent did not apply to his property, and that if he wished a zoning change, he too would have to litigate. These cases indicate that a judicial remedy may not always be adequate or advisable. This is especially true if the litigant manages to anger the local officials. Winning a law case is sometimes more trouble than it is worth.

If a party loses at the trial court level, state procedure determines whether an appeal will go to some intermediate court or directly to the state supreme court. The trial court determines questions both of facts and of applicable law. Appellate courts, such as a state supreme court, only consider matters of law. If the state supreme court renders a decision that is contrary to the U.S. Constitution, appeal may be taken to the U.S. Supreme Court. The U.S. Supreme Court will rarely agree to review a zoning case. In a few instances, where fundamental constitutional cases of a national impact are brought to the Court's attention, a case may be heard. The U.S. Supreme Court has generally considered zoning to be a state or local matter and is reluctant to disturb decisions reached by state supreme courts (see Figure 8-2).

Developing the Legal Theory of the Case

Before a party seeking judicial relief may appeal successfully, a sound legal justification must exist. A zoning decision by a legislative body (such as a town council or county commission) is presumed valid. This means that a person challenging a zoning decision has the *burden of proof* to show convincingly to the court why the decision is wrong. If the issue is fairly debatable, the issue is resolved by the courts in favor of the local government in most states. The attitude of the courts tends to require that the private citizen seeking to challenge an action by the legislative body (city council or county commission) must overcome presumption of validity by convincing proof that the local

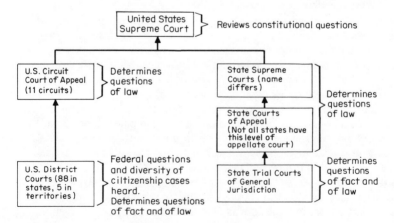

Figure 8-2

government acted unreasonably or unconstitutionally. This burden of proof is greater than the burden of proof in most civil cases. In most civil cases, a party must show a preponderance of evidence. However, the burden of proof is not as great as in criminal cases, where the state must prove its case beyond a reasonable doubt.

Attitudes of courts change over time, often swinging like pendulums. In Georgia, for example, the Georgia Supreme Court wrote in a 1960 case that:

... the Constitution respected and held inviolate private property ... But the people by their votes amended or changed this constitutional guardianship of private property to protect it ... By the constitutional change the people voluntarily subjected their property to unlimited control and regulation of legislative departments.[1]

A nationally prominent commentator, in discussing this opinion, wrote that the Georgia Supreme Court ruled that it had no power to question the validity of any zoning regulation.[2]

Under this case, the Georgia Court abdicated any responsibility to overrule the legislative decision of municipalities. This seemed to make local zoning decisions absolute in Georgia. By 1975, however, the court had swung to the other extreme. In a case the court wrote:

As the individual's right to the unfettered use of his property confronts the police power under which zoning is done, the balance the law strikes is that a zoning classification may be justified if it bears a substantial relation to the public health, safety, morality, or general welfare. Lacking such justification, the zoning may be set aside as arbitrary or unreasonable. [Footnotes omitted][3]

The court, in effect, shifted the burden of proof to the local government once the private citizen was able to demonstrate harm by the denial of a rezoning application. Most states' courts do not require a "substantial relation" to the police power; the local government is merely required to show a "reasonable" relationship. Once the private citizen is able to overcome the presumption of validity, however, the local government then has the burden of justifying the validity of the zoning ordinance or validity of official actions.

After a legal theory of the case has been developed, a party must introduce appropriate evidence to support the theory. A legal theory is based on some principle of law supported by the facts that, if accepted by the court, will permit a favorable decision. How this may be done will be described in the next section. Legal theories may be categorized as:

1. Procedural denials of due process.

2. Technical challenges to jurisdiction, standing, or other such factors.

3. Challenges to the authority of local government to act.

4. Substantive challenges relating to a denial of due process or equal protection as a zoning ordinance is applied to a particular property.

[1]*Vulcan Materials Company v. Griffith*, 215 Ga. 811, 814 (1960).
[2]Richard F. Babcock, *The Zoning Game*, Madison, Wis.: The University of Wisconsin Press, 1966, p. 103.
[3]*Barrett v. Hamby*, 235 Ga. 262 (1975).

5. Substantive challenges that the application of the ordinance has no relation or insufficient relation to the police power.

6. Other constitutional attacks on the ordinance which are based on various grounds of public policy.

A discussion of these various theories will be useful in helping the reader understand the various arguments that have been used to defeat a zoning ordinance or a particular application of a zoning ordinance. It should be noted that states will differ on the validity of these arguments. It is important to research the law in each state, since each jurisdiction has its own unique blend of precedents and applications. Also, as noted in the Georgia example, courts are often willing to change their attitudes and reasoning if a compelling case can be set forth.

The function of the courts is to apply principles of the law to factual situations that have been presented. A legal theory without facts to support it is not very useful. If facts are not properly introduced into evidence, this also is fatal to a case. A lawyer therefore has a threefold job. The first part of the job is to determine the facts. The next part of the job is to develop a theory which will justify a decision in a client's favor and which is consistent with the fact situation. The third part of the job is to introduce the facts into the record, and to convince the court that the theory and facts justify a decision in favor of the client.

Procedural Denials of Due Process

Under the Fifth and Fourteenth Amendments of the U.S. Constitution, each citizen of this country is entitled to *due process*. The courts have interpreted this term as involving both *procedural* and *substantive* due process and as applying to actions on the part of federal, state, and local governments. There are several *procedural due process* arguments that may be raised. Procedural due process deals with the right to notice and to a fair hearing. A citizen has the legal right to be notified of any action that may affect his or her property or personal rights. In addition, a citizen is entitled to an opportunity to be heard before a governmental decision affecting his or her interests is reached. In rezoning cases, the notice requirement is usually fulfilled by advertisement in a local newspaper, the posting of a sign, or the sending of letters. Actual notice is not essential in many instances so long as a citizen reasonably could have found out about the pending action by reading the advertisements. This is what is referred to as *constructive notice*. Under certain circumstances *actual notice* through service of process is required. These circumstances involve a direct action by some instrument of government to life, liberty, or property. Only *constructive notice* is given in the case of a neighbor of a property for which rezoning is sought. In the case of Ruth Cramer's suing Mary Trigg to abate a nuisance, *actual notice* is required.

If a person is not given a fair hearing, there are grounds for a suit on the basis of a denial of *procedural due process*. For example, assume that Dan Carter's application was turned down because one of the members of the zoning board was attempting to purchase the Brady estate herself. This is a conflict of interest which should have caused voluntary disqualification of the board member from voting. Some state courts will not accept this improper interest as being fatal to the board's decision, because of a *separation-of-powers* argument. *Separation of powers* means that courts will not interfere with actions of a board that are clearly legislative in nature. The basis of our federal system requires separate and equal branches of government. This is illustrated in Figure 8-3. The court may also reason that the motivation of a single individual is not sufficient to disallow the legislative action of an entire board, unless the vote was the deciding vote.

Another problem occurs when there is *ex parte* contact with the decision makers outside the formal hearing in an attempt to present evidence or otherwise influence the decision of the case. *Ex parte* contact is any contact outside the formal hearing structure without appropriate notice to other parties to a case. Depending upon the seriousness of the *ex parte* contact, a decision maker may have to refrain voluntarily from the voting. One reason that judges refuse to comment on cases pending before their court is this rule against *ex parte* contact. Because zoning is part of the political process, the rules on *ex parte* contact are somewhat flexible. The closer a zoning board's function is to a judicial or quasijudicial function, the more the rule against *ex parte* contact will be applied. Several states, including Oregon, Washington, and Colorado, have begun to define rezoning hearings as quasijudicial proceedings.

Technical Challenges

Judges may use several procedural or technical grounds to dismiss a case. One such ground is *mootness*. Mootness deals with the notion that, even if the case is resolved in the favor of the plaintiff, no legal advantage will accrue because of a change in circumstances that makes the litigation irrelevant. One such situation would exist if the local government passed a new comprehensive zoning ordinance that permitted the use that the plaintiff was seeking under the prior ordinance. In such a case, further litigation to change the zoning would be irrelevant. For example, assume that the town of Mulberry changed the text of the zoning ordinance so as to permit the sale of alcohol in the "C-1" district. As Dick Smith was attempting to rezone property to a "C-2" district in order to allow the sale of alcohol in the proposed Pizza Pizzazz restaurant, further litigation would be moot with the change of the "C-1" restrictions.

Other technical grounds include challenges to *jurisdiction*, *standing* of the

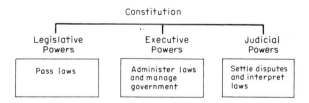

Figure 8-3

opposing parties, the passage of time under the state's *statute of limitations*, and *laches*. Challenges to *jurisdiction* may occur when there has been improper notice of the trial to indispensable parties to the litigation or if the plaintiff has failed to exhaust administrative remedies. A challenge on the basis of *standing* would occur if one of the parties did not have an appropriate property interest in the subject matter of the litigation. For example, Dan Carter would not be entitled to appeal the decision of the zoning board if his option on the Brady Estate had expired. If a party has failed to appeal a decision within the time specified in the ordinance or in the state enabling legislation, a suit might be barred by the passage of time. This time requirement is called the *statute of limitations*. If the party is seeking equitable relief, such as an injunction, and waits too long, the court may refuse to issue the remedy because of *laches*. Laches is similar to the running of the statute of limitations except that it is a court-imposed doctrine, while the *statute of limitations* is passed by a legislative body.

If it can be shown that one of the parties is improperly using the judicial system to harass another party and not for the real purpose of litigating the issues before the court, a judge may dismiss the suit on the grounds that the suit is an *abuse of process*. For example, if it can be shown that Ruth Cramer has filed her suit against Mary Trigg for the purposes of carrying out a personal vendetta, the judge might dismiss her action.

Another reason that a suit might be dismissed is an agreement by both parties to withdraw the action due to an out-of-court settlement. Often the parties may agree out of court and ask the judge to issue a court order which settles the suit in such a manner that it will be enforced by the court in the future. A violation of a court order is considered to be contempt of court unless good cause can be shown why the order could not be obeyed.

Challenges to the Legal Authority of Local Government

A local government can only exercise those powers which have been delegated to it by the state constitution, by enabling legislation, or by a charter given it by the state. In addition, the government may exercise those powers that are inherent to government or those which are necessarily and logically implied from the delegated powers. The right to zoning has been litigated many times and is ordinarily an accepted power of government. However, if the exercise of the zoning power requires certain prior actions, such as the adoption of a master plan, the review by a planning commission, or a local referendum, the local government is not authorized to exercise the zoning power until the specified prior actions have been accomplished. Further, if the power to zone has not been properly delegated to the local government by the state, the locality might not have the power. Some state courts would rule that zoning is a natural outgrowth of the police power, while other courts would rule that the zoning power must be specifically delegated. An action by local government that exceeds its authority is called an *ultra vires* action.

Although the zoning power generally has been accepted in most jurisdictions in this country, everything done under the name of zoning is not necessarily acceptable. Many local governments are experimenting with innovative techniques of land-use regulation. A discussion of some of these innovations is contained in Chapter 11, Current Issues and Emerging Concepts. Where a local government engages in experimentation of this nature, it must demonstrate that this is within its legal authority. Fruitful results from litigation may occur when such actions by local governments are challenged as being *ultra vires*.

Substantive Constitutional Challenges

Substantive constitutional challenges may be classified into three general types: (1) denials of substantive due process, (2) denials of equal protection, and (3) a taking of property by the public without just compensation.

Unlike procedural due process, *substantive due process* deals not with the manner in which decisions affecting a person's individual and property rights are made, but rather with the inherent reasonableness and fairness of the regulations. If there is relatively little public gain from the regulation as compared to the hardship imposed upon a property owner, or if the regulation is unsuitable to the nature of the property, courts may disallow the application of the regulation on the basis of substantive due process. This type of argument is very similar to an argument in equity under common law. *Substantive due process* is a very broad argument and is constantly evolving.

A denial of *equal protection* may be argued when it can be shown that the zoning ordinance discriminates between property users without logical basis. For example, if a zoning ordinance permits sorority houses in one district but disallows fraternity houses, this would be deemed a denial of equal protection. However, some groupings have been upheld. For example, a city has been permitted to zone a certain area for the exclusive use of housing for the elderly. The reason for this is that the elderly may require special medical attention and other special needs that a concentration of such uses would permit. If the zoning restriction on a particular property is inconsistent with surrounding land uses, a party might be able to argue successfully a denial of equal protection. For example, if Dick Smith's property, which was zoned "C-1," were totally surrounded by "C-2" uses or "C-2" zoning, he might have the "C-1" restrictions overturned.

The purpose of the *due process* and *equal protection* clauses in the Fourteenth Amendment of the U.S. Constitution is to shelter the citizen against excessive or unfair government power. Thus, any zoning ordinance that is arbitrary or capricious as it applies to a particular property may be a denial of due process or equal protection.

The power to zone is justified on the basis of the *police power*. The police power is the inherent right of the state to enact and enforce regulation without compensation to the parties being regulated. The regulation must be justified on the basis of public health, safety, morality, or welfare. One important restraint on the government's police power to regulate is the extent to which the regulation may go before the government exceeds the police power and must compensate the property owner under its *power of eminent domain*. In the Fifth Amendment to the U.S. Constitution is a clause: ". . . nor shall private property be taken for public use without just compensation." In the landmark U.S. Supreme Court case, *Pennsylvania Coal Company v. Mahon*, Mr. Justice Oliver Wendell Holmes stated, "The general rule is that while property may be regulated to a certain extent, if the regulation goes too far it will be recognized as a taking."[4]

Prominent legal scholars have discussed this test, which is known as "the balancing test," in a book entitled *The Taking Issue*.[5] They suggest three major considerations in applying the test. First, the objective of the regulation is considered. For example, if the land regulation seeks to abate a common law nuisance, the regulation will probably be upheld. On the other hand, if the benefit will accrue to a narrow segment of the population rather than to the community as a whole, then the ordinance might be invalidated. Thus, provisions restricting polluting industries from residential neighborhoods are generally upheld, but, for example, zoning enacted to prevent a shopping center from being constructed next to an existing center in order to prevent competition would not be valid. The courts are likely to disapprove of a scheme that enriches the government in its proprietary capacity at the expense of the individual land owner. For example, zoning a property so that it loses value for the purpose of acquiring it later at a lower price by condemnation is invalid. Likewise, the courts look askance at a regulation that is meant to accomplish the acquisition of rights or property for the public benefit rather than to protect the public interest. Protecting the public from harm is valid, but refusal to grant a rezoning because the city wishes to use a person's land for a park without compensation is invalid.

The second consideration in applying the "balancing test" is the suitability of the regulation to the nature of the property. For example, the court looks to determine if the regulation permits the land to be used in a manner similar to uses of surrounding or nearby land. The court also seeks to determine if the regulation is rational. Does the regulation promote the public welfare, and how does the regulation help to implement the comprehensive plan?

The third consideration is the extent of loss in land value. The test is stated as follows: ". . . whether a regulation so restricts the owner's land as to deprive it of all present economic productivity. Any regulation that makes a private right essentially worthless is a taking for which compensation must be paid."[6]

The extent of loss that would lead a court to construe the regulation as a taking differs from state to state. Certain land, such as that which is located in environmentally sensitive areas, may be more highly regulated than less-sensitive land located in a commercial or industrial area.

Challenges that the Regulation Has Little Relation to the Police Power

A zoning regulation will be disallowed if it bears little or no relation to the police power. In order to make a case on this type of argument, it is critical for the

[4]*Pennsylvania Coal Co. v. Mahon*, 260 U.S. 393 (1922).
[5]Fred Bosselman, David Callies, and John Banta, *The Taking Issue*, Washington, D.C.: Superintendent of Documents, U.S. Government Printing Office, 1973.
[6]*Ibid.*, p. 209.

attorney to examine the comprehensive plan and other appropriate planning studies. We have noted that the police power is based on the idea of promoting the health, safety, morality, and welfare of the community. If the zoning ordinance is contrary to these objectives, the courts may disallow the regulations. For example, an ordinance limiting nursing homes to locations in heavy industrial districts probably could not be justified.

Sometimes a zoning ordinance is contrary to community needs and the community plan. By examining the underlying planning documentation, an attorney may find inconsistencies between the comprehensive plan and the ordinance. A careful examination should be made of the text of the plan. Often there are criteria that a proposed rezoning fails to fulfill. This failure strengthens the case of opponents to a zoning change. If a zoning change has no rational connection to a plan, courts may often disallow an amendment to an ordinance. One example of this kind of argument is that the zoning change is a *spot zoning*. Spot zoning, as we noted in Chapter 3, is a zoning of a small parcel of land for uses incompatible with the surrounding district. The nineteen-acre Brady Estate that Dan Carter asked to be rezoned is small compared to adjacent zoned areas; an opponent might use the argument that Dan is seeking a spot zoning. Spot zoning is also disallowed on grounds of equal protection, because it gives the property owner preferential treatment over the owners of surrounding land uses.

An argument might be made that there is a mistake in the original zoning ordinance or plan. Alternatively, a person may point out that due to changed circumstances, such as the widening of a road or the construction of nearby incompatible uses, neither the original plan nor the zoning ordinance is any longer valid. Some changes in the surrounding environment are not sufficient to justify the argument that a rezoning is proper. For example, residential growth that occurs and provides an adequate market for a convenience store is not sufficient justification by itself for a rezoning to permit the construction of the store.

A party may argue that the regulatory objective is improper and thus cannot be justified on the basis of the police power. Examples of an improper regulatory objective are attempts to limit commercial competition or attempts to drive down prices of land in contemplation of future acquisition by the local government. A party may also argue that the regulatory object is proper but that it is beyond the scope of the police power. For example, although jurisdictions differ, in many cases a zoning ordinance designed solely to promote aesthetics or to create open space may not be sustained on the basis of the zoning power.

Other Challenges

After Mary Trigg was able to receive a "conditional use" to expand her home occupation, she immediately began construction of the addition to her house. Ruth Cramer talked to one of the city council members at her garden club and was able to convince her that the amendment to the text of the ordinance permitting such a conditional use was a major mistake. At the next meeting of the city council, a motion was passed to cancel the original amendment.

Ruth Cramer then sought to enjoin Mary Trigg from finishing the construction of her addition. Mary's attorney successfully argued that Mary's rights to the conditional use had *vested*. Vesting refers to the idea that a person's legal rights have become permanent property rights that cannot be arbitrarily removed. Mary's conditional use will be treated as a nonconforming use and will be entitled to all of the legal rights associated with this type of use. If a zoning ordinance is passed after a person has undertaken expenditures of a significant magnitude on the basis of reasonable reliance on the previous zoning, that person's rights may have vested and she or he may be permitted to complete the project. During this trial, Mary's attorney was able to consolidate both the suit by Ruth Cramer to abate the nuisance and the suit to stop her from completing construction. It was shown that Mary was making reasonable use of the property and that it was not a nuisance. Ruth Cramer's action was dismissed.

Other challenges may be developed on innovative legal theories. An attorney should search current law journals to discover new directions that are being taken by the courts and new ideas proposed by legal scholars. Arguments have been developed that a zoning ordinance tends to exclude low-income or minority groups and thus is a denial of equal protection. Innovative lawyers have also argued that some zoning or land-use regulations violate certain First Amendment rights such as the right to travel, free speech, or freedom of religion. (See Chapter 11, Current Issues and Emerging Concepts.) The arguments that are developed must be justified on each unique fact situation.

Bringing the Case to Trial

Once it has been determined that a legal theory exists that will assure a reasonable opportunity for success by appealing to the courts, a case normally goes through several different stages.

Initial Stage

The first step is to notify the court and opposing parties of the suit. Procedures differ slightly from state to state, and from state to federal courts. Several states have adopted in whole or in part the Federal Rules of Civil Procedure, which permits a simplified notice pleadings, while other states require the issues to be defined clearly by common law pleadings. The term "pleadings" refers to the way in which facts and legal issues are presented to the court and other parties. In the pleadings, the plaintiff, who is the party bringing the case, must show that the court has jurisdiction over the person and subject matter of the case. The suit is ordinarily begun when the plaintiff files a *complaint*, or petition, which contains a summary of the facts alleged in the case, a statement of the law, and a "prayer" or request for a remedy. The opposing party, or defendant, is given a copy of the complaint and is also usually given a summons for appearance at trial.

After the complaint is issued, the defendant has a specified number of days to make an answer. An *answer* might be in the form of a motion to dismiss because the plaintiff has failed to state a claim upon which relief can be granted, even if all of the alleged facts are true. At this time, challenges to the court's jurisdiction might be made. Usually, however, the answer will state the specific points of disagreement and state any counterclaims or crossclaims that might be appropriate. A *counterclaim* is any claim that a defendant has against the plaintiff. A *crossclaim* is any claim that one defendant has against another defendant stemming from the same set of facts in litigation. Any new facts for affirmative defenses must also be stated at this phase. An *affirmative defense* is any defense that the law requires to be raised, such as statute of limitations or bankruptcy, to bar the claim of the plantiff. If an affirmative defense is not raised, it is usually considered to be lost.

After the answer has been filed, the plaintiff may make a *reply*. If the defendant has made an affirmative defense, the plaintiff must show why it is not appropriate. The plaintiff may also deny any counterclaims. On occasion, amendments or supplemental pleadings might be made as the case develops. An amendment before the actual trial will customarily be allowed as a matter of course, but once the trial has begun an amendment will be allowed only upon the showing of good cause. The court may in its discretion accept or reject amendments. In some jurisdictions a pretrial conference may take place in order to give the parties an opportunity to settle out of court or to narrow the issues that are being disputed.

Discovery

After the complaint is filed, either party to the case may use various *discovery* devices to obtain facts, documents, testimony, and other evidence that is in the possession of various persons. *Discovery* is a powerful tool in determining the strengths and weaknesses of the opposition's case. It is also a tool for obtaining evidence that is within the possession of the opposition. In states which follow the Federal Rules of Civil Procedure rules, the scope of discovery is very broad. A party normally is not limited just to evidence that is admissible in court, but may seek evidence that may *lead* to admissible evidence. Discovery may not be used solely for "fishing expeditions" or as a means of harassing the opposition, nor may discovery be used to require the opposition to develop the case for the discovering party. A court order may be used to protect one party to an action from the abuse of this tool by the other. *Discovery* is used to prevent most surprises at trial. Because of the broad scope of this tool, it is virtually impossible to keep information hidden from the other side in a case.

In zoning cases, the opponent is usually the local government that has denied the zoning application. In a surprisingly large number of cases, the attorney working for the local government is overworked and understaffed. This often leads to the result that the local government has failed to develop an adequate defense because of a lack of time and manpower. Discovery may often lead to a determination of the various weaknesses of the local government's case. In many cases, a demonstration to the municipal attorney that the local government's case is weak can lead to out-of-court settlements and compromises. A party's bargaining position is significantly enhanced if it can be shown that one's own case is well researched and supported by strong facts. It is a question of tactics, however, as to whether one wishes to compromise or to seek all-out victory at trial. It should be noted that a victory at trial is not very helpful in the long run if it also succeeds in getting the local government angry or embarrassed.

The right to discovery differs in each state. In states where discovery rules are limited, information may still be acquired from public sources in those states which have passed "freedom-of-information" acts or public-record legislation. While a full description of discovery devices that are available in most states is beyond the scope of this book, the reader should at least be aware of some of the more important devices that are used. A brief description will be given of written interrogatories, depositions, motions to produce and inspect documents, and requests for admissions.

Written interrogatories. are a series of questions which must be answered in writing by the other party to the controversy. Under certain circumstances, a person who is not a party to a suit may, by stipulation of the opposition, answer interrogatories. This technique is a means of discovering general information. For example, this device may be used to discover all the relevant studies that have been commissioned by the opposition that might be relevant to the controversy. Written interrogatories may be used to establish a foundation for using other discovery devices. A set of interrogatories should be developed with the experts who have been hired by the party to assist in the case. Experts can assist in suggesting questions to ask, the proper terminology to use in seeking to identify various studies, and other information that would be helpful in sifting through relevant and irrelevant data.

Depositions are used to ask questions of witnesses under oath in the presence of opposing counsel for the purpose of making a record of the witnesses' testimony. This is a time-consuming technique but has the advantage of permitting immediate follow-up questions and of exploring subject areas in depth, something that is very difficult to do with written interrogatories. In addition, provision is made for cross-examination. Depositions may be used to determine the motivations of various parties to the controversy. Outside experts may be asked what kind of instructions they received from the other party to the controversy. Information can be obtained to ascertain if the local government had previously hired an expert who made findings adverse to the government's case.

One practice that is fortunately infrequent is to send out of town on business an expert witness who has arrived at a weak or adverse conclusion. The witness stays out of town for the period of the trial. This is an unethical practice that might conceivably be discovered through a deposition. Such information would be of particular interest to the disciplinary board of a local bar association if such a suggestion had been made by the opposing attorney. In any case, this information would be useful in showing bad faith on the part of the local government.

Depositions may be used to find contradictory positions of various public decision makers, a lack of support, or ignorance of reasons why certain decisions were made. This information would be useful in demonstrating the lack of connection with the decision and the police power or that the decision was arbitrary and capricious and a denial of substantive due process.

Motions to produce and inspect documents may be used to give access to various correspondence, planning studies, reports by consultants, minutes, and other data. Again, the expert may be used to check the relevancy and completeness of the information collected. A careful examination of the documents might lead to the discovery of the existence of other documents that are also subject to a motion to produce. Where a document cannot be moved physically, a photograph or other reproduction may be made. This reproduction can serve as insurance that the evidence will remain as part of the record. Public records often disappear mysteriously. The disappearance is usually due to a misfiling or careless mistake. In a study of one city's zoning dockets, one of the authors of this book discovered that some yearly files over a twenty-year period had as many as thirty percent of the dockets missing.

Requests for admissions are used to simplify the introduction of evidence and proof in a trial. Parties may be asked to concede the accuracy of evidence so that the dispute may focus only on those facts which are in disagreement.

Using Expert Witnesses

Proper use of expert witnesses will improve a person's chances of winning at zoning by appealing to the courts. In Chapter 9, Supporting Materials for Zoning Requests, we will discuss some of the experts and reports that can be used to develop a sound case in zoning litigation.

Attorneys who are inexperienced with the use of expert witnesses often make several fundamental mistakes that limit the effectiveness of these people. These mistakes include:

1. Not selecting an expert early enough. An expert should be selected early in a zoning case to permit the development of research and exhibits. An expert can be invaluable in developing a sound presentation at the hearing level.

2. Selecting an expert who makes a poor witness. Knowledge of subject matter does not guarantee that the expert witness will be convincing on the stand. Just as any witness, an expert witness may mumble, stutter, look shifty, answer questions vaguely, or freeze on the stand. Often expert witnesses use jargon and terminology that no one understands except another expert in the same field. An expert witness should be asked to answer questions in clear and simple English.

3. Failing to coordinate properly the testimony of the expert witness with other expert testimonies and with the legal theory of the case. The expert witness should be carefully briefed on the facts of the pending controversy. The criteria of the zoning ordinance should be explained from a legal perspective. The witness should be briefed on the expected testimony of other experts in the case. An assessment should be given to the strengths and weaknesses of both the plaintiff's and the defendant's cases in the controversy. The expert may be able to suggest new evidence that can be used to strengthen the client's case or to weaken the opponent's case.

4. Not advising an expert witness as to the proper dress code for the trial. Many witnesses lose credibility because of being overdressed or underdressed. Grooming and attire are part of body language, which is a means of communicating with the listener. Many attorneys have become skilled in such nonverbal communication devices.

5. Failing to run through the expert's testimony under mock trial conditions. The expert should be given a rehearsal of a vigorous cross-examination. Many witnesses try to

memorize their testimony in advance and break down under questions that are asked at cross-examination. A cross-examination strategy should be developed to protect the witness from "trick" questions. Such questions include: "How much have you been paid to reach your conclusion?" The witness should indicate that the pay was for the time involved and for the research, not for the specific conclusions. During this rehearsal, the expert might be able to suggest the wording of some of the questions that could be used on direct examination.

6. Not cautioning an expert witness to answer questions directly and to avoid arguing with the other attorney. If an expert does not know or remember the answer to a particular question, this should be admitted. Even in relatively narrow fields of study, no one can always know all of the information and literature which exists. It is usually easy to develop questions with the help of other experts to trap a witness who refuses to admit his or her own limitations.

7. Selecting experts who sound cocky or superior, act nervous, fail to answer questions directly, lose their temper when their credentials or opinions are challenged, and commit other mistakes which make them less effective. Witnesses like these should be avoided if possible.

8. Inadequately briefing the expert witness on local rules and procedures as to evidence and testimony that is admissible. Even an expert who has testified in other jurisdictions may be surprised at the variation of court rules. Some courts, for example, will not permit motion pictures or videotapes to be used as demonstrative evidence, while others will. Some courts will not permit the expert witness to give his or her opinion on the actual facts in the case, but will require questions to be framed into hypothetical situations.

9. Using a witness too broadly or too narrowly. If a witness is used too broadly, the testimony might be in areas in which the witness has limited knowledge or in which another expert would be more qualified and effective. For example, one attorney could have a land economist discuss the impacts of the zoning ordinance on the land-use pattern and the impacts on the value of a specific parcel of land. Another attorney, who is more experienced, would bring in a credentialed appraiser who had the MAI and SREA professional designations to discuss the impact of the zoning ordinance on the value of the specific parcel of land.

10. Failure by an attorney to understand thoroughly the testimony of his or her expert witness. Further, the expert witness might have written articles, in scholarly journals, that contradict the testimony that will be given at the trial. A competent opponent will read all of the articles that the other side's experts have written.

Proceedings at the Trial

If a controversy is not settled out of court, or if a motion to dismiss the case is not granted, the case will ultimately come to trial. Dan Carter and his attorney strive to settle a case out of court whenever possible. In some jurisdictions, a zoning case may be subject to a jury trial. However, because of the technical nature of the subject matter, often the trial is apt to be held before a judge without a jury or before a special master appointed to determine the facts. In cases where a jury is used, it is necessary to select and empanel a number of jurors. In civil cases the number may vary, and the vote of the jury does not have to be unanimous in many jurisdictions.

The trial begins with opening statements that define the arguments to be made and evidence to be presented. After the opening statements, the plaintiff will begin to present his or her case. The plaintiff has the burden of proof and thus must make a case which proves the facts alleged in the complaint. If the case is a challenge against the decision of the local government, the case must also overcome the strong presumption of legislative validity. After the plaintiff has presented the plaintiff's side of the case, the defense may make a motion for a directed verdict. If the plaintiff has failed to overcome the presumption, or has otherwise failed to make a case, the judge will decide that the defendant has won as a matter of the law. If a directed verdict is not granted, the defendant will then have an opportunity to make a case in defense.

Evidence that is permissible in a trial includes demonstrative evidence, documentary evidence, testimony by witnesses of observed facts, and opinions and statements of fact by expert witnesses. *Demonstrative evidence* includes graphs and charts, maps, photographs, models, and other such evidence. *Documentary evidence* includes various contracts, public records, and other printed material that is used to prove various aspects of a case. Documentary evidence must be authenticated and ruled admissible by the court. *Testimony* is entered into the record through direct examination. This involves a series of questions and answers between the examining attorney and the witness. The opposing attorney has opportunities to object to evidence that is improper or misleading. After direct examination, the opposing attorney may attempt to impeach the credibility of the witness, or of the witness' facts, or may seek to introduce other evidence that will strengthen the opposition's case.

Care must be used not to go too far in cross-examining the witness. Attorneys are normally advised not to ask questions unless they have a reasonably good idea of what the answer will be. The following story that most attorneys have heard is told in law schools: A young attorney was cross-examining a witness who had testified on direct examination that the attorney's client had bitten off the nose of another man. When asked if the witness had actually seen the client bite the nose off, the answer was "no." Rather than dropping the questioning after that satisfactory answer, the young attorney pressed on. He said, "Well if you didn't see my client bite off the nose, how do you know that he did?" The witness answered: "I saw him spit it out."

After evidence and testimony have been introduced, each side makes closing arguments. In jury trials, each side has an opportunity to submit "charges" that they would like the judge to make to the jury. A *charge* is a statement of how a law is applied in certain situations and general statements of the law that might be helpful in the jury's deliberation. The judge will then decide which charges, if any, to give to the jury. The purpose of the jury is to draw conclusions of fact. These conclusions of fact are rendered in the jury's verdict. The function of the judge is to draw conclusions of law. This is done by rendering a judgment. If a judge determines that the verdict by the jury is not supported by the law, he or she may issue a judgment not withstanding the verdict. After the judgment, a party may appeal errors of law to a higher appellate court. If the judgment is not appealed, it is considered final, and the winning party may then proceed to enforce the judgment.

Developing a Successful Legal Strategy

A successful legal strategy begins by preparing a case early and thoroughly. Preparation often begins before an option is acquired for the land that is to be developed. An early examination should be made of the local zoning ordinance, procedures for rezoning, and court decisions that have involved the zoning ordinance of the local jurisdiction. Many courts tend to be biased in favor of the local government, while others tend to favor land owners.

Care should be given in developing a clear record at the hearing level of the rezoning process. Evidence and facts should be marshalled and presented as if the application would ultimately be reviewed by a court. Experts should be consulted early in order to prepare the exhibits, do the necessary studies, and prepare the necessary supporting evidence. The facts of the case should be collected and carefully preserved so that they will be readily admissible at trial. If the case should have to be appealed, intelligent use of discovery devices will help strengthen one's case and expose the weaknesses of the opposition. Every effort should be made to settle the dispute out of court.

A sound legal theory must be developed and supported by the facts. Both the theory and facts must be effectively communicated to the court in order to increase the chances of a favorable decision. In developing the case at trial, care should be taken to show sound policy reasons why the rezoning would benefit the community at large. Although a trial is theoretically based on legal reasons, decisions are sometimes tailored to fit a result that is beneficial to the public at large. Many judges are political animals who may also run for election and thus are reluctant to reach decisions that are detrimental to the public good.

In the pleadings and during the trial, it is usually advisable to recognize that some local governments may seek to circumvent the decision of the court if it should prove adverse to the local government. The court should be asked to retain jurisdiction until the development is completed.

Finally, a party should assess the short-term and long-term costs. Care should always be taken to assure that the long-term relations of the developer with the local government will remain good. Court cases should be treated as business judgments that weigh gains and risks and should be stripped of emotionalism. Zoning is not just a game; it is part of daily living. Winning at zoning involves intelligent dealings with people. A successful legal strategy will always consider the human element.

9
Supporting Materials for Zoning Requests

Winning a zoning battle can depend upon the wise use of facts, technical studies, and expert opinions, as well as upon strategy and tactics. The side that can marshal the more impressive materials and the more persuasive experts is often the side that carries the day. Both sides need to know how to go about gathering information; what information should be gathered; what analysis, if any, should be made; when to use consultants and which ones to choose; what reactions to expect from other parties; and how to respond to materials presented by other parties. As we did in Chapter 7, we are going to discuss first the role of the applicant and then that of the opponents.

The applicant who wishes to use supporting materials properly must begin by considering the exact nature of the problems to be overcome. Different kinds of situations, and different kinds of people to be persuaded, call for the use of different kinds of materials. A request to rezone a large tract of land on the outskirts of a community, for example, will not require the same kind of supporting materials as a request to rezone a vacant warehouse in an older part of town. A request that is likely to be litigated before it is resolved may need a different kind of support from one that is going to be decided by a board of county commissioners (supervisors). Materials should be selected carefully to fit both the environmental conditions and the personalities to be faced.

Once the nature of the problem has been identified, the applicant has a wide array of possible materials that might be used. Some materials are simply available facts assembled in tables or charts or on maps. Other materials are the results of surveys made by, or on behalf of, the applicant. A third category consists of "studies" and "analyses" which contain conclusions, judgments, forecasts, expert opinions, and/or recommendations.

Simple Factual Information

An applicant may be able to find enough support from information already available to make a strong case without resorting to special surveys or studies.

Depending upon the particular environmental factors associated with the applicant's property, the factual information may be used to demonstrate basic assertions that (1) the existing environment is unsuitable for any use now permitted by the zoning ordinance; (2) the proposed use would be in keeping with the existing environment; and/or (3) the proposed use would at least not conflict significantly with the existing environment.

The information that is available has usually been prepared by governmental agencies and ordinarily can be presented as being both authentic and unbiased, but it should not be used without careful thought. The opponents can be expected to attack it. The applicant, therefore, needs to make certain that it is valid. Even if it was accurate when collected, it may be outdated. It must not be presented in such a way as to be misleading, either intentionally or unintentionally. Besides being dishonest, misleading presentations can backfire when the flaws are discovered. The applicant also must guard against the thoughtless inclusion of information that might provide ammunition for the opponents.

The kinds of factual information that applicants might possibly draw upon are almost infinite. We will limit ourselves to describing only a few of the more common varieties.

Land Use

Information on existing land use in the vicinity of the applicant's property can frequently be obtained from a local planning department. If up-to-date information on land use is not available locally, then a special survey might be made by the applicant. The information is normally presented in statistical form and/or on a map. Charts may also be used. The principal value of such data to the applicant is in demonstrating that (1) existing uses on surrounding properties are adverse to the use of applicant's property for anything permitted by the present zoning and/or (2) what the applicant proposes would be in keeping with what already exists in the vicinity.

The original information on land use is collected by a field survey. The field workers either walk or ride slowly down a street while noting the uses on each site. The information is recorded on a map that shows property lines. Frequently, much of this information is recorded on the map prior to the field survey by making use of aerial photographs, city directories, and other sources. The field survey is then used as a check.

After the basic information is collected, it is transferred to another set of maps by recording colors or other symbols on the individual parcels. All parcels designated by the same color or symbol can then be measured to ascertain the area covered by that particular category of use. In many communities, the land-use data are entered in a computer file that already contains an identification of each parcel and the area thereof. Thus the area devoted to each use can be calculated quickly.

In presenting information on land use, an applicant must decide how large an area of the community should be included. Too large an area would include extraneous information that could confuse the issue. Too small an area, on the other hand, could leave out important uses that might be supportive of the applicant's case.

Traffic Volumes

Traffic counts for streets and intersections close to the applicant's property are often available from a local department of traffic engineering or from the state highway department. Presented either on maps or in statistical tables, such data are sometimes used by applicants as evidence that traffic volumes on a street or at an intersection are so heavy as to be detrimental to the continued use of abutting property for single-family residences.

Most counts these days are made by automatic devices that are connected to rubber hoses stretched across roadways. Each time a vehicle crosses such a hose, the counter is tripped. The counters are moved around periodically, so that what is obtained at a particular location is only a sample of all volumes at that point during the course of a year. Fairly reliable conclusions can be drawn from the data collected, however, as to the average daily traffic and the average peak-hour traffic.

The information from automatic counters is sometimes supplemented by manual counts of turning movements and of specific kinds of vehicles (e.g., trucks).

Structural Quality

In some communities, the local planning agencies have information pertaining to the quality of housing and other structures on a parcel-by-parcel basis. This information, displayed on a map, can also be used in some situations by applicants to show the unsuitability of the environment for uses currently permitted by the zoning.

Most information on structural quality will have been collected from field surveys that involved on-the-spot evaluations by trained personnel based on exterior observations. In some communities, however, more detailed surveys, encompassing interior inspections, have been made. Regardless of how detailed the surveys may have been, many subjective judgments will have been made, and the applicant using such information must be prepared to deal with possible challenges to its validity.

Soils

The United States Soil Conservation Service, using samples gathered from field surveys, has prepared fairly detailed maps showing soil types for many counties. Accompanying the maps are reports describing the suitability of these different soils for various uses, including urban uses. With the assistance of such information, an applicant might be able to argue that the soils on a particular tract are so adverse to the kind of development permitted that only the change sought would justify the capital outlay required for development.

Other Factual Information

Other information that is commonly available and sometimes used to support zoning applications include facts relating to the location, size, and capacity of schools, other public facilities, utilities, and drainage. Such information can sometimes be used to back up assertions that a tract can support the desired intensity of development. Additional information on geology, hydrology, and topography can lend weight to claims that a tract is unsuitable for uses permitted under existing zoning or is suitable for the use proposed.

Much, and frequently all, of this information can be obtained from the local planning department, but sometimes it is necessary to visit the public works department and the school board. Information on topography and hydrology might be available only from the U.S. Geological Survey, or from its counterpart at the state level.

Surveys

In the absence of some existing information, an applicant might wish to make special surveys in order to obtain it. Mary Trigg, for example, made a special survey of all home occupations in her neighborhood and indicated their locations on a large map. She also collected information as to their nature (e.g., music instruction, dancing instruction, and accounting), in an effort to show that her activity was not a radical departure from what was already being done. Dan Carter has made *vacancy surveys* in older retail areas to emphasize his contention that the zoning was unrealistic. He has also had special *traffic surveys* made to provide detailed information on turning movements at intersections and volumes at peak hours. Sometimes he has called in specialists to survey the noise generated on properties adjacent to his. In brief, the possibilities for special surveys are endless, but the applicant should take care to see that any survey made is tailored to fit the problem at hand.

Studies and Analyses

Some zoning problems are sufficiently complex to justify doing more than simply presenting factual information. Complex problems require analysis by specialists, preferably by those who have images as "experts." It is not just the analysis itself that the applicant is presenting, but also the creditability of the analyst. There are many kinds of consultants who make studies related to zoning applications, and there are innumerable kinds of studies that theoretically could be made. We will describe a few of the more common studies and analyses (these two terms are sometimes used interchangeably) and then discuss the kinds of consultants often employed.

Neighborhood Analysis

Simple factual information may not provide enough support for an applicant's claim that the environment is unsuitable for any of the uses permitted. The objectors' response to such material might be that the applicant, and other property owners in the vicinity, are not seriously trying to make the existing zoning work. The objectors might point to similarly zoned areas in other parts of town that have few vacancies. In such an event, the applicant may wish to have made a *neighborhood analysis*, which, in addition to containing factual information, will include a description of the changes that have occurred in the vicinity of the property over a period of time and an interpretation of those changes as they affect land use and zoning.

What the applicant hopes to gain from a neighborhood analysis is a demonstration that changes occurring since the original zoning, or since the last comprehensive update, have made the zoning obsolete and no longer valid. The changes might be in the form of land uses, traffic patterns, incidence of crime, tax deliquencies, structural blight, zoning variances, or other occurrences.

A neighborhood analysis is probably most useful in areas that have been developed for twenty years or more, but newer areas can also be subjected to unexpected change. For example, the construction of a new freeway and its interchanges can have unplanned effects, including swelling traffic volumes on streets feeding the interchanges, diverting through traffic from established retail districts, and creating higher noise levels along each side of the right-of-way. In an area where such effects have occurred, a neighborhood analysis can demonstrate that vacancies, blight, and other adverse indicators have increased along with the growth of traffic and noise. The implication is that the traffic and noise are causes of the adverse symptoms.

Highest and Best Use Study

In trying to convince decision makers that the existing zoning is obsolete, an applicant might supplement a *neighborhood analysis* with an additional study purporting to demonstrate that existing zoning no longer permits the most economic use of the property in question. Evidence that zoning does not allow a site to be put to its "highest and best" economic use is especially important in some states where the courts tend to favor property owners.

"Highest and best use" is a term used by appraisers to denote the most profitable use to which a site might reasonably be put in the near future. A use cannot be "highest and best" unless it is legally permitted on the site, meaning, among other things, that the zoning must be right for the use. It is not unusual, however, for a client to ask an appraiser to ascertain what the "highest and best use" would be if zoning were not a constraint. The conclusion might then be construed as evidence that the zoning should be changed so as to conform to the realities of the market place. The argument is sometimes made that zoning should not be used to set the values of sites; it should be used to reflect the values established in the market. According to this way of thinking, zoning is needed only as a check on ill-informed property owners who might abuse a site by developing it for the wrong use, thereby depressing the value of surrounding properties and perhaps overloading public facilities.

An applicant will probably select an appraiser who believes in this philosophy of zoning and who can make a creditable presentation as an expert witness if the need should arise. In making the "highest and best use" study, the appraiser does not analyze in detail *all* possible uses of the site but only those few alternatives that seem to be the most appropriate, some of which may have been suggested by the client.

Marketability Analysis

A *marketability analysis* is a more thorough study of what seems to be "highest and best use" of a site to see if there is sufficient market demand for that use at that location. The results of a marketability analysis are sometimes used by zoning applicants as evidence that what they are proposing to do is likely to succeed. In making a marketability analysis, the analyst (1) studies the overall strength of demand in the metropolitan area for the uses contemplated, (2) identifies the particular segments of the market to which the proposed project might appeal (usually called "target market"), (3) estimates the share of the target market that the project might capture from the competition, and (4) calculates the rate at which the various kinds of space created can be absorbed by the market.

To the private sector, the analysis is critical in determining if the project will develop sufficient revenue to make it a worthwhile undertaking. To the public sector, a marketability study may show that there is a *demonstrated need* for the uses proposed. Such a demonstrated need is often accepted as a substantial justification for a zoning change, because it lessens the possibility that the applicant is acting in a speculative manner.

Feasibility Analysis

A *feasibility analysis* goes beyond a *marketability analysis* to consider the probable costs of development, operating expenses, financing terms, projected income, and the rate of return that a particular developer would receive from a project. As real estate is often used as a tax shelter, feasibility is usually concerned with the tax-free, or after-tax, cash flow and other financial benefits (such as capital preservation and appreciation) that the investor would receive. Its use in a zoning battle, however, is similar to the use of a marketability analysis, i.e., to provide assurance that the proposed project can be completed and operated as planned and to alleviate fears that the project might end up as an abandoned eyesore. It is also used to support an applicant's assertion that the zoning sought is not for speculative purposes but for bona fide development.

When Dan Carter presented the results of both marketability and feasibility analyses last year in seeking approval of a rezoning for a shopping center, he did not expect to change the minds of objectors, or even to convince anyone on the fence. All that he hoped to do was to give some support to the reasonableness of this position. The studies had to be made anyway in order to persuade potential lenders and investors of the financial soundness of the proposal. No additional expense was incurred in using them as evidence in the zoning hearings. Dan did take care to select an analyst for the studies who could be effective as an expert witness in the event that the rezoning became the subject of litigation.

Dan was realistic in not having high expectations for the impact of the two studies. Both neighbors and planners were skeptical. Questions were raised about the assumed extent of the trade area and about the share of the market that Dan's center could be expected to capture from the competition. One of the objectors was a building contractor who questioned the estimated costs contained in the feasibility analysis as being much too low. On the other hand, when the matter came before the city council for final determination, the council members who were already favorably inclined toward the proposal cited the studies as partial justification for approving it.

Dan has learned that, while many studies do not by themselves make or break the rezoning request, the strategy of providing well-documented information that proves the worthiness of the project allays many fears about the nature of its operation and why the developer is undertaking it. In addition, it may provide insights about the details that help to gain public and official approval of the project.

Site Analysis

The most effective study that Dan Carter has used to bolster a rezoning application is one called *site analysis*. Two years ago, he obtained an option to purchase a 1100-acre tract in outer suburbia. The tract obviously had some potential for development, because it was adjacent to one quadrant of an interchange on the beltline freeway and was also bounded by a railroad on one side. The site did present some problems, however. The topography was rugged in spots; there were outcroppings of rock; part of the tract was on the wrong side of a ridge from a trunk-line sewer; the soil was mucky in places; and for several hundred feet, the tract bordered a subdivision containing $90,000 homes, whose owners might object to any nonresidential uses on the tract. Dan retained a land planner to make a *site analysis* of the tract.

In making the site analysis, the land planner had to consider the interrelationships of many features of the site. In this case, the planner began by delineating the parts of the site that contained critical topographic problems, i.e., areas where slopes were so steep that roadways and structures were inadvisable. To develop the steep slopes would result in unjustifiable costs for earth-moving and possible environmental problems from erosion.

Next, the planner made a series of separate maps for soil characteristics, rock outcroppings, vegetation, water areas and floodplains, and miscellaneous natural features. The information was transferred to clear, acetate overlays, so that various combinations of information could be superimposed. Thus areas containing similar problems or potentials could be identified. After studying the information on the overlays, the planner came to the conclusion that about eight percent of the site could not be used for anything except open space.

In a second part of the analysis, the land planner studied some cultural and legal factors that, along with the natural features, seemed to limit or expand the site's capability for supporting various kinds of development. Items analyzed included the locations of existing structures on, and adjacent to, the site; the locations of railroads and highways (especially those providing access to employment centers and shopping areas); locations of any electric transmission lines and pipelines; the quality of land uses along the vehicular approaches to the site (a critical element in developing a marketing strategy); and the configuration of the site's boundaries. The configuration of the boundaries frequently dictates the kind of design necessary to give a project a unified feeling. It also helps to determine where and how street connections to adjacent sites must be made.

After analyzing the artificial components of the existing environment, the planner reviewed all of the pertinent elements contained in the community's comprehensive planning documents, as well as ideas that the public planners had not yet been able to incorporate into formal documents. Suggested sites for parks, schools, fire stations, and other public facilities were noted on the site analysis maps, so that they could be included in the site planning process. A careful distinction was made between those public facilities budgeted for construction in the near future and those not having a financial commitment. The generalized pattern of future land uses was excerpted from the Comprehensive Land Use Plan, and all zoning proposals under consideration by the public planners were also taken into account.

The site analysis was valuable to Dan because it helped him to determine which portions of the tract were most suitable for which kinds of uses. The site analysis was well received by the opponents, the public planners and county commissioners. They did not agree completely with all of the uses and densities that Dan proposed, but they at least had a common set of facts on which to base their respective judgments. A *site analysis* is much more readily understood by the uninitiated than either a marketability study or a feasibility analysis.

Applicant's Approach to Supporting Materials

If supporting materials are to be truly supportive of a zoning request, they must be assembled with a specific set of objectives in mind and must be tailored to fit those objectives. Before initiating a study, the applicant needs to consider carefully the exact nature of the problems to be overcome. For example, is the request for a rezoning of a site or building in a previously developed neighborhood that has been experiencing significant change? If so, then what are the objections that might be raised? Are the objections primarily ones having to do with the effects on nearby properties, or do they involve questions of the larger public interest? Who are the personalities to be convinced, reinforced, or overcome? Are they property owners, planners, elected officials, or representatives of "public interest" groups?

The next step is to select the appropriate study or studies. A *neighborhood analysis* would certainly be appropriate for the above-mentioned example, but it would probably be of little help in a situation like the Brady Estate, where a sizable tract is surrounded by a stable neighborhood.

The third step is for the applicant to assess the relative strengths and weaknesses of the request. This is a prerequisite to deciding who is going to make a particular study. If the arguments for the request seem weak, the applicant might seek out a consultant who has a reputation for producing impressive reports that favor the client's case. If the case seems strong, the applicant might select a consultant who has a reputation of independence from clients and of drawing objective conclusions. The applicant might even suggest that the study be made by or under the supervision of the local planning staff in order to demonstrate confidence in impartial analysis.

Consultants

The fourth step is to decide what consultants, if any, are to be used. Consultants often used in making supporting studies include architects, landscape architects, city planners, traffic engineers, economic analysts, environmental specialists, and real estate appraisers. Each kind of consultant has special talents, although there is some overlap. Often an applicant will select one of these as a master, or prime, consultant, who in turn will select and coordinate the other consultants. If the applicant has a competent technical staff, some or all of the analysis might be done by them in lieu of using consultants. (This practice will not necessarily save money, however. It might cost more.)

Selecting Consultants

What Dan Carter experienced in using consultants on one of his recent projects is typical of what many small- and medium-sized developers have been experiencing recently. Early in 1977, Dan decided to revive a proposal for a neighborhood shopping center that he had originally tried to put together in 1974. In reviving the proposal, he at first thought that he could update the earlier marketability study by himself. He quickly discovered, however, that conditions in 1977 were quite different from what they had been in 1974, and that there were few pieces of information readily available to him without a major research effort (which he really didn't have time to undertake). He decided to go back to R.I.C., Inc., the firm that had prepared the complete planning and market research package in 1974, because they had a large research, planning, and engineering staff and could do all his work under one roof (even though their fees were a little high).

To Dan's surprise, the sign on the office door no longer read "R.I.C., Inc."; it said simply "Glenn Rogers, Real Estate Consultant." When he entered there was another surprise—Glen Rogers was working at a desk surrounded by papers and files, and there was no one else (not even a secretary) in the office. Seeing the shock on his client's face, Glenn explained that he had had to let virtually all of his staff go in the past 2½ years, because the consulting business had dried up with the tight mortgage market, rapidly inflating costs, and ensuing depression in the real estate business. He had managed to survive by working on some independent appraisals, and he was not in the process of rebuilding his firm. For the time being, he could do only marketability and feasibility studies, but he could get a good "A and E" (architectural and engineering) firm to "joint venture" the contract with him, and still give Dan good service. If any other specialists were needed, Glenn had a long list of other potential partners for joint ventures. In addition, Dan could provide some services and information himself and thereby reduce consulting costs.

Dan decided to retain Glenn as prime consultant. Even though Glenn's staff capabilities were greatly diminished, his past work had always been done professionally and completed on schedule, and Dan had a great deal of faith in Glenn Rogers' insights about real estate markets. As prime consultant, Glenn would select, with Dan's approval, the architectural and engineering firm to analyze the site and prepare a plan for its development. For his part, Dan would provide information about development costs, overhead costs, raw-land costs, carrying costs, required return on investment, and other financial factors that Glenn would need in making a feasibility analysis.

By designating Glenn as prime consultant, Dan avoided some of the headaches of putting together a joint-venture consulting group and of coordinating their activities. He was sure that Glenn would choose a competent firm and that the joint effort would incorporate a unified approach to his problem.

Glenn's scope of services under the contract included the making of an initial marketability study, so that Dan would be able to start planning his marketing strategy and would have information to show to public planning officials to support his request for rezoning. Dan made sure that a deadline would be included in the contract to the architectural and engineering firm to ensure that a site analysis and preliminary plan of the development would be ready for him to use at the public hearing on the rezoning request, scheduled in two months. Dan also obtained two contingencies in the contract. First, the work would be reviewed upon completion of the marketability study, so that he could decide whether to continue with the remaining studies once the strength of current market forces and his probable market share had been identified. Secondly, Dan could revise or cancel the remainder of the contract if the rezoning request were denied or drastically changed. Glenn readily agreed. He knew that it would be useless to continue if either potential situation caused the project to go sour.

With respect to fees, Dan negotiated a firm price for the specific items, such as the marketability and feasibility studies and the planning documents, but the contract provided for a review-and-approval process to release contingency funds in the event that the consultants experienced cost overruns as a result of unforeseen circumstances. Glenn's fee for his coordinating role and prime consultant was a little tougher to establish. The two finally agreed that Glenn would bill on a "cost-plus" basis for this function; that is, he would send Dan a monthly statement which charged a hourly rate sufficient to cover his salary, profits, direct expenses, and overhead costs up to some maximum amount.

Selecting and negotiating with consultants can be a pretty complicated business. Like Dan, most developers who have frequent encounters with consultants usually develop good working relationships. There are, of course, pitfalls, especially when one is inexperienced or dealing with a particular consultant for the first time. A novice might do well to seek assistance from professional organizations, public agencies, and other groups that help to maintain ethical conduct and professional quality among various groups of practitioners.

There is always the question about whether or not a person should use a consultant or try to perform the job with in-house staff. Unfortunately, there is no clear-cut answer. Besides the obvious consideration of ascertaining if staff personnel have the specialized skills needed to get the job done, it is also important to analyze the costs of reassigning personnel to perform new tasks and the costs associated with delaying or omitting the work they are currently performing. It generally doesn't pay to acquire new staff unless the work is of a continuing nature and of a sufficient scale to justify the expenses involved. In the final analysis, the value or benefits derived from the work must outweigh all direct and indirect costs involved in completing the work. Even then, there are intangible factors to be considered. For example, consultants can often bring a more objective, "outside" point of view and a special area of expertise, as well as a respected professional reputation to bear on a problem. In addition, consultants can often be used as expert witnesses in court cases should the need arise. Whoever is responsible for a study, whether consultant or staffer, will be faced with the problem of finding and verifying the information to be used.

Problems with Supporting Studies

The problems for an applicant in using supporting studies are several. First of all, there is almost never enough information in the right form to support an unassailable conclusion. Knowledgeable opponents using the applicant's own data may make contrary conclusions seem just as plausible as those drawn by the applicant. Second, even the best of studies is going to be received with skepticism. Public officials and opposing property owners expect a study submitted by the applicant to be self-serving and are prepared to be suspicious of anything presented. The applicant must win credibility in the face of this suspicion—or at least enough credibility to enable those decision makers who support the request to the study as justification. Third, the materials and conclusions will be presented to a variety of individuals who will have different and sometimes conflicting reactions to what is presented.

Audiences for supporting materials might include public planners, owners of neighboring properties, lay planning board members, elected officials, and judges. A judge will supposedly view the supporting materials in terms of their relevancy as evidence in helping to resolve a question of law. Neighboring property owners will presumably respond according to what they perceive to be their self-interest, although they are likely to consider their self-interest as being the same as the "public interest" and to express it accordingly. Public planners, lay members of the planning board, and elected officials are all responsible for acting in the "public interest," but they are likely to have differing perceptions of just what the public interest is.

To illustrate how the different parties involved respond in different ways, let's look at what happened to the Buffington Property. The Buffington Property is a ten-acre parcel located on the east side of Weldon Boulevard in the section of Metro City known as Woodland Park. The parcel is now vacant, but it formerly was the site of the Buffington family residence which had been built in 1912. Large homes of similar design were constructed at about the same time along both sides of Weldon Boulevard on lots five to ten acres in size. In 1916, a trolley-car line was extended out to the southern edge of Woodland Park, and the entire area was then subdivided into lots averaging 8000 square feet in size. By 1929, approximately two-thirds of the lots had been developed with $2\frac{1}{2}$-story residences. The remaining lots were gradually built upon during the 1930s and finally developed completely in the late 1940s. (See Figure 9-1.)

During this entire time, the half-mile stretch of Weldon Boulevard through Woodland Park remained residential with two exceptions. In 1925, a 200-foot strip of small retail shops was developed on the west side, and in 1937, when the trolley-car line was abandoned, another set of small shops was built on the site of the former terminal on the east side.

Except for the two short commercial strips, which are zoned as "B-1 Neighborhood Business," all of Woodland Park is now zoned as a "R-1 Single-Family Residential." To the north and south of Woodland Park, however, there have been changes. In the 1950s, Weldon Boulevard became the principal axis of growth for Metro City. Churches, funeral homes, low-rise office buildings, and low-rise apartment buildings replaced many of the fine old homes that had lined it in former times. Woodland Park, though, held firm. No rezonings whatsoever took place along its half-mile section of Weldon Boulevard.

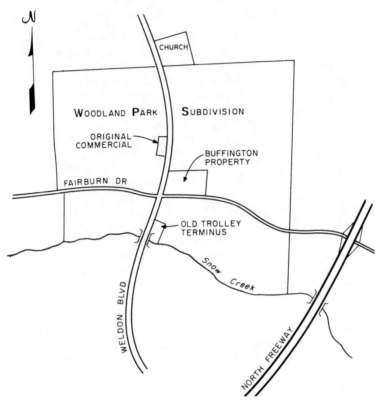

Figure 9-1

The solidarity of Woodland Park residents continued to hold until 1965. That was the year in which the North Freeway was completed. An interchange with Fairburn Drive, which traversed Woodland Park from east to west, introduced much more traffic to the neighborhood, and residents along Fairburn Drive began to put their homes up for sale. Between 1965 and 1970, the Metro City Board of Adjustment, which was very liberal during that period in giving use variances, granted four variances along Fairburn Drive for conversions of single-family residences to duplexes. They also granted variances on the east side of Weldon Boulevard to permit the use of two old homes as offices for charitable organizations. Finally, in late 1970, the ordinance was amended to prohibit use variances.

Three years ago, the Buffington Property was purchased by a speculator who had the home demolished and tried unsuccessfully to get the parcel rezoned for an office building. Six months ago, Helen Davis, a real estate broker, located a buyer for the Buffington Property, but the sale was contingent upon a rezoning to "RM-3 Multiple-Family/High Rise." Helen persuaded the seller to engage a consultant in city planning to make a *neighborhood analysis* and a real estate appraiser to make a *highest and best use study* and a *marketability analysis*.

The planning consultant drew on a variety of sources to collect information pertaining to changes in Woodland Park and along Weldon Boulevard over a fifteen-year period. Facts about land use were obtained from the city planning department, from aerial photographs, and from old city directories. Data regarding zoning variances, violations of housing, building, and zoning codes, and the number of applications for rezoning and conditional-use approvals were also assembled from the files of the planning department. Traffic volumes along Weldon Boulevard and Fairburn Drive on an annual basis were gleaned from the statistical reports of the city traffic engineer. Up-to-date data on population were harder to come by. The consultant was able to compare the population characteristics reported in the 1960 and 1970 censuses for the census tract in which Woodland Park was located, but for current information it was necessary to make do with the city directories and with information supplied by the home interviews (based on a five percent sample) that the metropolitan planning commission made three years ago for an *urban area transportation study*. The planning consultant also made a sample survey of families living along Weldon Boulevard and Fairburn Drive, interviewing them as to their satisfaction with the environment.

With the information obtained from these various sources, the consultant made a set of maps. There were four basic maps showing the land-use pattern at five-year intervals. Superimposed on each were clear overlays showing other indicators of change for the same years. The consultant also made charts that indicated, for each year, the traffic volumes, the number of violations of various codes and ordinances reported, and the number of variances and rezonings requested.

The planning consultant prepared a thirty-page report narrating and interpreting the changes that had taken place. The report concluded with a recommendation that the property zoned "R-1" along Weldon Boulevard be changed to "RM-3" and a further observation that property along Fairburn Drive should probably be changed to "RM-1 Multiple-Family/Low-Rise."

The real estate appraiser, in making the *highest and best use study*, sought to ascertain what that use would be if the zoning could be changed to reflect the findings of the study. There is more than one way to approach a study of "highest and best" use, but in this case the appraiser estimated the costs of development for each alternative use and the net operating income to be expected from each. In theory, part of this income is a return on and of the capital invested in the building and the remaining part of a return on the value of the site. The appraiser separated these two parts, estimating first the rate of return that an average investor would expect on and of the capital invested in the building. Applying this *capitalization rate* to the estimated cost of the building, the appraiser calculated what net income the building should produce. This net income attributable to the building was subtracted from the estimated total net operating income and the residual was assumed to be the income belonging to the site. The appraiser then *capitalized* the site income at an assumed rate to arrive at an estimated value for the site. The alternative use that seemed to produce the greatest value for the site was assumed to be the "highest and best" use. In this case, the answer turned out to be "high-rise apartment building."

The appraiser then engaged in a *marketability analysis* of the site for high-rise apartments in order to confirm the conclusion that this was indeed the "highest and best" use. In making the marketability analysis, the appraiser obtained reports and data from the metropolitan planning commission relating to trends in the local economy and population. In particular the appraiser was interested in getting forecasts of the rate of household formation, the size and composition of households, and the probable family incomes to be expected in the future. Information was also obtained from the planning commission on the volume of housing construction in recent years for different structural types (i.e., single-family, multiple-family high-rise, etc.). The appraiser was able to identify the principal apartment complexes built on the north side in recent years and, through interviews with knowledgeable parties, estimate the rent levels and vacancy rates in these existing structures. On the basis of these facts, the appraiser concluded that, over the next five years, there would be a continued strong demand for high-rise units of the kind and rental level proposed and that other competitive projects known to be in the planning stage would not be sufficient to meet that demand.

At the public hearing conducted by the planning board, Helen Davis' client, the would-be seller of the Buffington property, appeared in person to ask for the rezoning, explaining that the property had been on the market for several years to no avail. Now there was an opportunity to sell it, but the zoning needed to be changed to reflect reality in order for the sale to be consummated. The planning consultant and the appraiser were introduced by the client, and they briefly summarized their findings.

Before the objectors could be given their opportunity to speak, one member of the board asked that the professional planning staff explain orally the recommendations that they had made in writing to the board members. Briefly the planning director explained that the staff had made a *cost/benefit analysis* of high-rise apartments along Weldon Boulevard and low-rise apartments along Fairburn Drive. This analysis took into account the additional load that the higher densities would create for streets, utilities, and public facilities in the area, as well as the need for an additional aerial-ladder truck for the fire department. It involved estimates of the probable increase in annual city expenditures brought about by the apartment development and estimates of the probable annual tax revenue that the development would produce. The staff had concluded that development at the densities proposed would result in added expenditures in excess of the revenues to be produced.

The planning staff agreed that the property along the two streets in question was no longer entirely suitable for the uses permitted under the existing zoning, but the staff had a counterproposal that would be more in keeping with the other properties in Woodland Park and that would not require additional city outlays for sewer lines, drainage, street widenings, or fire trucks. The city planners proposed the creation of two new zoning districts to be applied initially in Woodland Park but eventually elsewhere in similar situations. Under this proposal, the Buffington Property, together with other property zoned "R-1" along both sides of Weldon Boulevard, would be rezoned to an "RO-2 Residential/Office" classification. This new district would permit single-family dwellings, two-family dwellings, apartments in buildings no taller than five stories, and certain kinds of business, professional, and institutional offices that would not be likely to generate visits by clients or customers. The office buildings would also be limited to five stories in height. The planners proposed that both sides of Fairburn Drive be rezoned to "RO-1 Residential/Office." The "RO-1" district would be similar to the "RO-2," the only important difference being that building heights in "RO-1" would be limited to two stories. In both "RO" districts, buildings would have to comply with the "R-1" requirements for yards. In the "RO-1" district, however, walls, fences, or hedges would be permitted along the front property line to shield residential uses from the effects of traffic.

The action of the city planners in making a counterproposal illustrates the fact that more than two parties are involved in making and interpreting special zoning studies. As we pointed out in Chapter 5, the role of the public planner can vary from community to community, but public planners often try to act, as they did in the Buffington case, as *mediators*, as *guardians of the public interest*, and as *impartial analysts of special problems*. They may also provide information to both applicants and opponents, coordinate input of other governmental expertise, bring to everyone's attention what the master plan has to say about a particular matter, and, where effective opposition appears absent, attempt to play the role of consumer advocates.

Opponents' Response to Applicant's Supporting Material

The single-family homeowners in Woodland Park (except those remaining along Fairburn Drive) were not impressed by the applicant's supporting materials. Helen Davis did not expect them to be. The opponents were out to save their neighborhood from nonresidential encroachments, and for the time being at least, they felt that a nonnegotiable stance would be the most effective one to take. As we pointed out in Chapter 7, objectors must be prepared to compromise at the right time, but knowing what is the "right time" is an art based upon experience. The Woodland Park residents did not sense that the right time had arrived. They reacted to the applicant's supporting material by attacking it and trying to discredit it.

The opponents' first step in their response was to demand copies of the applicant's studies in advance of the hearing. They threatened to seek a postponement of any action by the planning board unless these materials were made available to them. Once the Woodland Park residents had the reports, they made several copies for distribution to key leaders in their fight. These leaders read the material several times, looking for distortions and/or omissions. They made several trips to the city planning department to discuss the reports with the professional planners. They also visited an appraiser and a private planning consultant and obtained insights from them. From these private consultants, the objectors learned that some key conclusions in both the marketability study and the neighborhood analysis were based upon subjective judgments with which reasonable people could differ. For example, the applicant's planning consultant had assumed that a heavily travelled street was, per se, undesirable for single-family residences. The opponents' planning consultant cited examples right in Metro City where heavily travelled streets had retained their residential character. In particular, the consultant pointed to homes occupied by elderly people who liked to watch traffic and who found it convenient to be close to bus stops.

The opponents looked for weaknesses in the applicant's data. For example, they noted that the most recent information on structural quality was five years old. They were able to point to several major renovations that had taken place since the information was collected. They discussed the applicant's sample survey of residents with a statistician, who questioned the procedures used in selecting the sample.

At the public hearing, the opponents did not take at face value some charts and graphs that the applicant displayed. They had not seen these materials previously, but they knew what to look for and quickly noticed that there were some distortions. The objectors were taken by surprise by the counterproposal from the city's planners, but they stuck to their no-compromise stance, indicating that they would rather not have any change in the zoning.

In the Buffington case, the opponents confined their response to the proposals made by the applicants and the city's planners. In others situations, opponents may find it desirable to make counterstudies. Some neighborhood associations go so far as to hire consultants. Others use their own volunteer talent and labor. It is possible, for example, for a fairly effective neighborhood analysis to be conducted by an intelligent group of homeowners. Simple traffic surveys can be made by relying on manual counts taken during selected hours of the day. Information as to the existing capacity of utilities and public facilities can be obtained from city hall and compared with an applicant's proposal. If any utilities or facilities appear inadequate, the objectors are then in a position to make a counterproposal for a kind of zoning that would not produce an overload. Another kind of counterstudy that objectors might undertake themselves is one involving a survey of the external effects of existing uses similar to what the applicant is proposing. If, for example, the applicant wishes to build a fast-food restaurant, the opponents would do well to present objective evidence of the external effects around existing restaurants belonging to the same chain or having the same franchise. The opponents can gather facts about hours of operation, traffic volumes, left turns, accidents, noise, and glare. They can also take pictures of site conditions at the existing operations.

Opponents' countermaterials can be presented in various ways: in written reports, orally, or as displays. The opponents have just as much right to call in experts as the applicant does.

The Planning Board's Response

The lay planning board must react to the applicant's presentation, to the response by the professional staff, and to the response of the objectors. It is difficult for an applicant to gauge the probable response of a board unless something is known of the background and personality of the individuals making up the board. An architect on the board, for example, cannot be expected to react to a neighborhood analysis in exactly the same way as would a member of the clergy. An architect's response would likely be influenced by a concern for aesthetics combined with an understanding of some of the practical problems involved in development, while the response of a priest, minister, or rabbi would probably reflect concerns for morality, justice, and improved human relations. Members of a planning board can normally be expected to act in ways that, in their respective opinions, would be in the best interest of the community as a whole. Each of them, however, may have a different perception of what the public interest is. In the Buffington case, the board decided that the public interest required the preservation of older neighborhoods, but they were sympathetic to the applicant's plight. They recommended that the re-zoning be denied, but they also decided to initiate a public hearing at a later date to consider the counterproposal of the planning staff as an alternative.

When the request to rezone the Buffington property came before the city council, the individual members of the council responded to the supporting materials in an expedient manner. As politicians in the best sense, they were interested in resolving a conflict in a way that would maximize the satisfaction, or at least minimize the dissatisfaction, on both sides. Without being cynical, they tended to use the supporting materials as justification for whatever in-dividual shifts they made in attempting to resolve the conflicts. They finally persuaded the applicant to agree to a deferral for three months in order for the staff planners' counterproposal to be given official consideration.

Should the Buffington issue become a subject of litigation, then still another party—a judge—would reveal still another response. The judge's perception of the public interest will be based on the concepts of law and equity discussed in Chapter 8.

Both applicants and opponents will need to consider the varying perceptions of the public interest and consequently the differing reactions that can be expected to their supporting materials. Any strategy for winning must take into account the possibility that what is strongly supportive at one stage in the process may be less than supportive at another stage. It must also take into account the possibility that use of supporting materials at an early stage would give the other side more time to prepare an effective rebuttal.

10
Zoning as
a Game

As illustrated by some of the examples that we have described in previous chapters, a zoning conflict often generates strong emotions among the parties involved. Emotion, if controlled, can frequently help in winning at zoning, because strongly held, sincere feelings can impress decision makers. Emotion can also be a disadvantage when it interferes with the ability to view problems objectively. Property owners can become so wrought up that they are unable to perceive where their own best interests lie, let alone act to further them.

Games and battles (to which we have previously likened zoning) are also accompanied by strong emotions, and they too can be lost through failure to keep one's cool. They differ from zoning, however, in that both games and battles have been studied dispassionately by theorists. As a result, there is a considerable body of literature about both that can be read and reflected upon by participants during periods when they are not caught up in the heat of a contest. If the participants in a zoning contest could view an approaching decision with detachment as either a game or a pending battle, perhaps they would find it easier to identify issues and alternatives and thus heighten their prospects for winning.

If zoning is to be viewed as a game, then what kind of a game is it? The games that we are most familiar with are those played by either two persons or two teams which are competing against each other (e.g., tennis, football, bridge, and chess). Each side in one of these games has an interest completely opposed to that of the other side. Any gain by one side is automatically an equal loss for the other, and only one side can win. People who study the theory of games call such a contest a "zero-sum" game.[1]

Zoning is not necessarily a "zero-sum" game. It can be, but it doesn't have to be. Let's take, for example, the developer who has a thorough knowledge

[1]For the interested, but nonmathematically inclined, reader who wishes to know more about game theory, we suggest the following two books: Morton D. Davis, Game Theory: A Nontechnical Introduction, New York; Basic Books, Inc., 1970; and Anatol Rapoport, Fights, Games and Debates, Ann Arbor: The University of Michigan Press, 1960.

of the local zoning ordinance and who wishes to do something out of the ordinary (say, place a twelve-story building at a forty-degree angle to the adjoining streets on a corner lot). The developer's architect suggests that a variance might be needed, because the zoning provisions were not drawn up with such a situation in mind and do not clearly permit it. The developer notes that they do not clearly prohibit it either and makes a visit to the zoning administrator to seek agreement on a favorable interpretation. The developer and the administrator are not antagonists. If a favorable interpretation can be made, then each can "win," because each wants the building erected. The developer wants the building in order to make money; the administrator wants it in order to impress the city manager and council with the revenue from the permit fees and the added assessment to the property tax rolls. Thus, the developer's interests and the administrator's interests coincide, and either they both win or they both lose.

In actuality, zoning consists of many games—some similar to the example just described, some in the "zero-sum" category, and most somewhere in between. Some are "one-person" games, some "two-person" games, and some so-called "N-person" games involving many parties. To a considerable extent, the choice of the game to be played is up to the players. Recognition of the alternative games, or combinations thereof, that are available in a particular situation can be a key to winning, because the player who has picked the kind of game to be played has already gained an advantage—if the pick was made intelligently.

As illustrations of just a few of the many possible zoning games, consider the following:

1. *The cooperative game*, in which there are two or more parties who not only have no conflicting interests, but who have some common goals and therefore can gain by cooperating. In order to cooperate most effectively in this game, all parties should have some technical knowledge of the subject. In the example of the developer and the zoning administrator that we just cited, the zoning administrator gains by cooperating with the developer, but in doing so needs a good justification for the decision made in order to avoid being vulnerable to possible future criticism. The administrator might be able to find sufficient justification without any assistance, but the developer greatly enhances the chance of success by having a good knowledge of the regulations and a suggested basis for the favorable decision.

2. *The "solitaire" game* with no opposition and no interest in collaboration. For an example of such a "one-person game" consider a building owner who wishes to change the use of a building. Changing the use is permitted, but the key words permitting it are buried in a section of the ordinance where no reasonable person would expect them to be. The zoning administrator has no incentive to recall that such words exist, because merely changing the use would produce no significant revenue for the city. The burden of finding them is on the property owner, and success depends solely on the owner's knowledge of the ordinance. As in card solitaire, however, there is always the chance that the "cards won't fall right;" i.e., the right words won't be there. Once they are found, the change is clearly allowable, and permission is granted without argument.

3. *The one-person debate*. Like the one-person solitaire game, this game has no opposition. It differs from the solitaire zoning game, however, in that the decision maker does not automatically make a favorable response to the evidence presented. The

evidence must be accompanied by persuasion. For example, a property owner wishes to get property rezoned. The neighbors do not object (they might even give some support). At the public hearing, the city council must be convinced by the applicant that the zoning change should be made. The council members basically have no objection, but they have to look out for their image. In voting on a previous item on the same agenda, they might have made a questionable decision; in subsequent votes at the same meeting, they may lean over backwards and adopt a hard-nosed posture in an effort to offset somewhat the unfavorable image that they created for themselves earlier. In such an event, it is crucial for the applicant to be persuasive.

4. *The battle*. Most zoning battles take place at public hearings—usually at hearings on rezonings, but also at hearings on variances, conditional-use permits, and interpretations of the ordinance. Unlike a military battle, and unlike a game such as football and tennis, the zoning battle does not pit the antagonists directly against each other. A zoning battle is more like a debate, in which each side tries to convince the decision makers. At the same time, the opposing parties also try to convince each other, and they may even find it advisable to cooperate to some extent. Unlike a debate, however, the zoning battle may or may not be a "zero-sum" game.

In addition to the fact that zoning is not always a "zero-sum" game, it differs from games like football and chess in another important respect: there are more than two sides involved. In this respect, zoning is more like poker and Monopoly. Zoning differs from poker and Monopoly, however, in that poker and Monopoly are always "zero-sum" games. Furthermore, zoning often has "arbitrators" or "umpires" who are involved parties themselves. We are referring here to city councils and county boards of commissioners who stand to gain or lose future votes or campaign contributions according to how they vote on a given issue.

The various sides in zoning sometimes make multiple moves simultaneously by talking privately with council members, planning board members, or members of another side's coalition. Only at the public hearings do the various sides sometimes find out what the other has been doing—and not always then. Thus, zoning is not a completely open game like tennis. It is less open than football, which involves secret huddles and deceptive practices. In football, after an opponent has run a play it is apparent what play has been run and what the results are. In zoning, however, one side might run several plays, and the other side might counter with several defenses before either knows what the other has done.

In addition to being neither completely open or completely closed in terms of the information available to both sides, zoning is also a game of imperfect communication. In some games, like bridge, for example, the opponents do not communicate with each other, except indirectly in bidding and in the playing of certain cards, and the persons on the same side communicate only imperfectly by means of a code. In poker, the players communicate freely albeit deceptively. In a zoning game, free communication between opposing parties is possible theoretically, but emotion and distrust often interfere. A member of a coalition who communicates directly with the enemy risks suspicion or wrath from other members of the coalition. Communication directly with individual members of a planning board may be limited by law or protocol to public hearings.

When communication between sides is feasible in a zoning game, it is sometimes possible for both sides to win. Consider the following example: along one section of University Drive, there were five lots that backed up to an undeveloped eighty-acre tract zoned for apartments. Each of the five lots contained a single-family residence. The lots were 80 feet wide and 110 feet deep. The residents/owners of the lots lived in a constant state of uncertainty in regard to the future of the large tract. Their backyards were too shallow in depth to offer much visual protection from whatever was put on the tract.

The large tract was optioned by a developer who asked that it be rezoned for an office park. Prior to the scheduled public hearing, the developer and the neighbors negotiated. The developer offered to provide a landscaped buffer with a wall running along the 400-foot length of the rear lot lines. The buffer would be 20 feet wide. Thus, the developer would be, in effect, giving up a strip of land of 8000 square feet, or less than 0.2 acre out of the eighty-acre tract, an insignificant fraction of the whole. The neighbors worried about future maintenance of the buffer, so the developer offered to sell portions of the buffer to each of them: one dollar each for five strips of land only 80 feet long and 20 feet wide. Thus the insignificant subtraction from the developer's acreage would provide an addition of almost twenty percent to the area of each of the home lots, and the additions would come complete with wall and landscaping. In return for this, the developer would gain the support of the neighbors and be relieved from responsibility for maintaining the buffer. Besides gaining the additional landscaped area, the neighbors would also be relieved of the constant uncertainty regarding the future of the tract. Both sides could win!

The main reason that both sides could win is that the 20-foot strip had a different utility and value for each side, and the developer could easily afford to part with it as a payment for support. An added factor was, of course, the desire on the part of the neighbors to end the uncertainty.

Uncertainty and risk are important considerations in zoning games. Take the Misty Meadows Subdivision, for example. Misty Meadows is almost completely developed with single-family homes, and has been so for twenty years. The sole exception is a row of ten vacant lots fronting on Poplar Avenue, an arterial street. On the average of every two years, someone applies for a rezoning or a conditional-use permit for this property. Proposed uses have included apartments, a medical office, and a child-care center. At every public hearing, the neighborhood civic group has been able to defeat the application. The neighbors have adamantly refused to consider any use for the property except single-family homes built to the same height, yard, and density standards as those already existing.

Each time the game is played, the neighbors win. But each time they win, they can be sure that the game will be played again. It is clear that no one wants to build single-family homes on the ten vacant lots—at least not to the same standards as those already existing. As long as the issue is unresolved, the game will be repeated. Each time the neighbors win, they are rewarded with another two years of continued uncertainty. The uncertainty involves the risk that once, *just once*, they will not win, and they cannot afford even one loss. Unlike league baseball, in which the object is to achieve the most wins in a season of many games, a zoning game for the neighbors is a game of "sudden death"—sort of like Russian Roulette. The first time they lose, the game is over. (This is not always true for the developer. For example, the builder of a chain of fast-food restaurants who needs ten sites rezoned can continue playing until ten games have been won.)

The risk that Misty Meadows will lose is a composite of several factors. One is that their friends on the city council might be turned out of office at an election. Another is that Nora and Tim Williams will switch sides. Nora and Tim live on Poplar Avenue right next to the disputed lots and are the most seriously affected. They intend to retire in three years and move to the seacoast. What are the chances that they will drop their opposition and support a rezoning in the hope that their property, too, can be rezoned and bring a higher price when they sell it? Another component of the neighbors' risk is litigation. In some states, the denial of a request for rezoning can be contested successfully in the courts. If a developer is successful in litigation, what will the court decree?

The continued uncertainty, and the risk of a subsequent loss, that the neighbors face after each successful encounter are unsettling to their nerves. It would seem sensible for them to reach an agreement with the developer whereby in return for the approval of, say, townhouses, the uncertainty could be ended and the risk eliminated.

Such an agreement would not necessarily be easy to reach. Much would depend upon just how averse the neighbors are to taking the risk for another two years. The neighbors are a coalition of individuals having different levels of aversion to risk. For example, a family that moves every three or four years to a different city might have a very low aversion to the risk. They won't be around long enough to be risking much. On the other hand, they prefer not to have any change in zoning at all in the next two years. They wish to continue their quiet enjoyment of their neighborhood while they still live there. In contrast, a family intending to remain in Misty Meadows for another twenty years would probably have a high risk aversion and thus be more likely to go for the compromise.

To many people, the word "compromise" has undesirable connotations. It implies the giving up of something that one should not rightly have to give up, or at best, it conveys the idea of dividing an inadequate whole into less-than-satisfactory parts. For example, Jean and Bob both like cake. They are presented with a cake that either could eat alone. Neither will be completely happy with the division of the cake between them. Each will feel somewhat deprived, because any division will be on a "zero-sum" basis. Some zoning disagreements may be like this example, and in these cases, any compromise will result in less-than-satisfactory results for all concerned.

"Compromise" can also have another meaning, however. Let us suppose that Jean and Bob are given both a cake and a pie. Jean likes pie and cake equally; Bob has a much stronger preference for pie. In dividing the cake and pie, they will not simply divide each in half. They will negotiate, taking into account the differing preferences of each and the strengths of those preferences. Bob will probably end up with more than half of the pie, but he will likely find it necessary to give Jean much more than half of the cake in return, because Bob feels he has a much stronger preference for pie than Jean has for cake. In this transaction, both Jean and Bob may consider themselves "winners," because each has received more in terms of utility than would have been the case in an equal division. Used in this sense, "compromise" means "barter," a rudimentary form of business transaction and a respectable technique in many other kinds of negotiations. A zoning compromise can also take the form of barter.

Zoning As a Game of Diplomacy

As the Misty Meadows example indicates, zoning games are not necessarily limited to single encounters. In this respect, the Misty Meadows example bears some similarities to games played in international relations. There, too, the various parties form coalitions, maneuver, and negotiate, and there, too, members of coalitions sometimes switch sides. Other multi-encounter games of zoning that bear some resemblance to diplomacy include:

1. The owner/operator of a nonconforming use who persistently attempts to expand or alter the use in violation of the ordinance.
2. The large-scale developer who requires ten or fifteen years to complete a project. In the meanwhile, there are continuing conflicts with the purchasers and occupants of the portions already completed.
3. The successful business that is periodically in need of physical expansion.
4. The development originally approved as a conditional use or floating zone and which is the subject of frequent complaints from neighbors.

The first two of these examples might be likened to the kinds of conflicts that nations have over unassigned territory or territory not clearly assigned as to use, such as the ocean beds or the continent of Antarctica. The second two might be likened to conflicts along the borders between assigned territories. Of course, the analogy can be carried too far. In international relations, there is no mandatory and enforceable arbitration, such as a city council can provide in a zoning dispute. Not all zoning relations between neighbors, however, are easily, or even best, solved by arbitration. Sometimes the parties involved need to bargain or negotiate among themselves. Then, too, agreements or understandings between parties in a zoning controversy are not always enforceable in court. It might help, therefore, to view a neighborhood as a mini-nation and look at the neighborhood's continuing zoning encounters in that light.

Before looking at a particular zoning conflict as part of a game of diplomacy, it must be established clearly that the parties have some common interests. As Fred Charles Iklé points out in his book *How Nations Negotiate*,[2] two nations who have no interests in common simply have no basis for negotiation. The only common interest might be in avoiding a battle, but that is a very significant common interest and is ample justification for negotiating or bargaining. It should be recognized, however, that in some zoning conflicts there are no common interests. For example, a developer wants either rezoning to a certain classification or a refusal. If the request is granted, the developer will build; if denied, the option will not be exercised. Nothing in between would be satisfactory. In such a case, the only course of action is to do battle in a zero-sum game.

[2]Fred Charles Iklé. *How Nations Negotiate*, New York: Harper and Row, 1964.

If a zoning conflict can be looked at as a game of diplomacy, then some of the strategy and tactics of diplomacy might be adapted to the resolution of the conflict. Iklé describes two alternatives to war that nations use in resolving conflicts. One, "negotiation," involves the communication and discussion of formal proposals and often leads to signed agreements. The other, "tacit bargaining," may involve little or no communication but can result in informal understandings. For example, a nonconforming business backs up to a single-family neighborhood. The owner of the business maintains a thirty-foot strip in trees and grass along the boundary. This is not a required buffer; nor is there any formal agreement regarding it. The business owner, however, makes sure that the grass is cut regularly and the trash cleaned out. The neighborhood garden club is given oral approval to landscape the strip. The result is the sort of informal understanding that nations sometimes have regarding their territorial borders. The business owner can violate the nonconforming provisions to some extent without complaints from the neighbors. The precise extent is not defined but is more or less understood.

To some extent, a city council, or other local governing body, serves as a third-party mediator in zoning disputes, trying to help the antagonists in arriving at agreements and/or understandings. Such a role is not explicitly spelled out in the ordinance, however, and the mediation provided takes place in the setting of a formal meeting. Perhaps the antagonists might profit from using the diplomatic device of third-party mediators in less rigid settings than those provided by a public hearing. The authors are not aware of any use of such mediation in the resolution of zoning conflicts, but the practice seems to be growing in other areas of conflict along with the practice of voluntary arbitration. Mediation might be used to avert all-out battles at public hearings much as nations use it to avert war.

Viewed as a game of diplomacy, zoning is a state of peace that is continually being interrupted by war or threats of war in the form of contentious public hearings and/or litigation. The peace is interrupted by an aggressor who upsets the equilibrium of property owners who wish only to be left alone.

Just as perceptions can differ in diplomacy, however, so can they differ in zoning. Which party is the aggressor is a matter of opinion. In Chapter 1, for example, we related the experience of Ed and Frances Sousa, who bought a home that had a room with separate bath, a kitchen, and an outside entrance. When they innocently tried to rent out the extra room, they were cited for a zoning violation. To the Sousas, the neighbors who complained to the zoning administrator were the aggressors; to the neighbors, the Sousas were the aggressors. The differing perceptions can complicate negotiation and bargaining in zoning just as they do in international relations. They can also lead to misunderstandings over any agreements that are reached.

Tactics of intimidation and bluff are used in zoning just as they are in international relations. A developer who seeks a rezoning for an office building might warn that the existing apartment zoning would permit far greater generation of traffic and noise (especially during nighttime) than would the proposed office project. The developer might even threaten to create an undesirable, but legally permissible, use, if thwarted at rezoning.

Sometimes a developer will intimidate by actions rather than by words. For example, a developer wished to buy an old private school and redevelop the site for a commercial use. The school agreed to the sale contingent upon the developer's provision of a suitable new site close by. The developer found two five-acre lots side by side each occupied by a sixty-year-old residence. Surrounding the site were newer homes on much smaller lots. The zoning was single-family, but private schools were permitted as conditional uses. The neighbors were unanimous in opposing the approval, and the permission was denied. As we indicated in Chapter 7, the developer then leased one of the two homes to a hippie "family." The "family" did not cut the grass during the entire summer. They had lots of parties, which resulted in pushed-out screens and beer cans in the yard. They also parked an old, rusty school bus in the driveway. When the developer returned with another request—this time for a mini-PUD for townhouses—the neighbors were unanimous in their support of it.

In a similar happening in another city, the intimidation backfired. The neighbors were infuriated and went to court, which, in zoning, is a battleground.

Neighborhoods, like nations, may feel constrained to take particular actions in order to maintain their credibility in bargaining. For example, in Chapter 7, we also related the story of the owner of a shopping center who sought an amendment to the original floating-zone approval in order for a modest addition to be built. At the hearing, there were numerous neighbors in opposition. They were not opposing the addition itself; instead, they were seeking to force the developer to maintain the original buffer, which was in a deplorable state. The proceedings were delayed, and the developer reached an understanding with the neighbors. They then withdrew their objections, and the addition was approved. We did not relate the sequel to this story. The sequel is that the developer failed to live up to the promises made. As there had been no agreement that could be enforced in court, the neighbors could only bide their time. The next time the developer sought approval for an addition, the neighbors struck back. This time, they had no interest in bargaining; they simply wanted to establish a hard-nosed reputation with the developer and with the city council. They showed up at the hearing in such force and with such fervor that they killed the request.

Two other aspects of zoning as a game of diplomacy are:

1. *Constraints on the negotiators*. Neighborhood leaders, like the leaders of nations, are limited in the actions that they can take without renewed consultation with the members of their organizations. They must be careful not to raise suspicions that they are about to "sell out" their constituents.

2. *Shifting goals*. Neighborhoods, like nations, are capable of changing their policies to cope with changing circumstances. For example, a neighborhood consistently opposed the rezoning of a tract for commercial use over a period of several years. Upon the announcement that the tract was under consideration as a site for low-rent public housing, the neighborhood quickly revised its attitude and supported a conditional rezoning for commercial use. The commercial project fell through, and the proposal for public housing was dropped. The neighborhood then reassumed its earlier stance, opposing any further attempts at commercial development.

In discussing zoning as a game of diplomacy, we are not saying that the techniques of diplomacy should be applied literally to every zoning conflict. Indeed, there are other areas of conflict resolution, such as labor/management relations, that might also provide approaches worth considering in a zoning problem. The point in making the analogy to diplomacy is that voluntary negotiations and bargaining have important roles to play in the zoning process. War can be costly for all of the participating nations; a zoning battle can also be costly in both time and money for all parties involved. The game of diplomacy is a means of averting war. If zoning could be viewed from this perspective, perhaps more zoning battles could be avoided.

For the reader who wishes to explore more fully the subject of negotiation, we suggest the Iklé book, already mentioned, and a book on the subject of negotiation in general by Gerard I. Nierenberg.[3] For those interested in reading about bargaining in the framework of game theory, we suggest a book by Thomas C. Schelling.[4]

Zoning as a Game of War

As the game of diplomacy between nations sometimes turns into war, so does the game of zoning between property owners. Real war, especially twentieth-century versions, is an odious subject to discuss. Nevertheless, some comparisons of it with zoning conflicts may provide insights helpful to the participants in those conflicts. Zoning battles, in the form of hotly contested requests at public hearings and, perhaps, litigation, do not result in mangled bodies, or even the shedding of blood. They do, however, have the potential for undermining the financial and emotional investments that people have made in property. They can create severe personal anxiety and conceivably could lead to coronary failures and cerebral strokes. They are serious affairs.

War has always been a serious affair, even in its pre-twentieth-century versions. Throughout most of history, however, it has been viewed as an event to be expected periodically and, therefore, one to be prepared for. Carl von Clausewitz, the nineteenth-century military theorist, looked upon war as simply a form of diplomacy involving the substitution of fighting for words, a continuation of it "by other means," ". . . another kind of writing and language for political thoughts."[5]

Zoning fights might also be considered as occurrences to be expected from time to time. However unpleasant they might be, they should be prepared for. They might even be contemplated as deliberate expressions of policy.

Whether entered into deliberately, defensively, or accidentally, a zoning battle requires a knowledge of tactics somewhat similar to that required of a general. The zoning general must have an understanding of the terrain, psychological insights regarding opponents, and the ability to maintain high morale among one's own troops. Qualities of boldness, determination, perseverance, and flexibility in dealing with the unexpected are desirable. The importance

[3]Gerard I. Nierenberg, *Fundamentals of Negotiating*, New York: Hawthorn Books, Inc., 1973.

[4]Thomas C. Schelling, *The Strategy of Conflict*, Cambridge, Mass: Harvard University Press, 1960.

[5]There are several translations of the von Clausewitz' treatise *On War* (first published in German in 1832). The classical English translation by J. J. Graham, published in 1908, has been published by Penguin Books in an abridged version edited by Anatol Rapoport in 1968. This edition contains an extensive and thoughtful introduction by Rapoport. A more modern translation of the work, by Michael Howard and Peter Paret, was published by Princeton University Press in 1976.

of pre-battle maneuvering; the gathering of intelligence concerning the enemy's activity; the uses of deception, surprise, and propaganda; and the launching of counterattacks are activities common both to zoning battles and those in real war. The need for preparation is another factor in common. Sun Tzu, a Chinese military philosopher who lived in the fourth or fifth century B.C., suggested that a victorious army won ". . . its victories before seeking battle."[6]

A sense of perspective is also a critical factor, both in military frays and zoning fights. A single combat is frequently part of a larger war; strategy as well as tactics must be studied. A developer may be engaged in numerous zoning conflicts more or less simultaneously over different properties and/or in successive conflicts over the same property. Similarly, a neighborhood may have to deal with attacks from several different directions at the same or different times over diverse parcels, as well as with successive combats over the same parcel. Both developers and neighbors need an understanding of what von Clausewitz referred to as the "economy of forces," which means the expending of sufficient effort for the job at hand without the wasting of resources that might be needed for subsequent battles. In both zoning wars and real wars, it is possible for a stubborn defense to prevail in the long run by forcing the enemy to employ excessive energy in order to win. The object of such a strategy is to wear down the aggressor until the objective is abandoned as being not worth the cost. The aggressor, however, can wear down the defense by repeated attacks and feints that keep the defense off balance.

Zoning wars may, at times, seem to call for the all-out, total approach counseled by von Clausewitz. That is to say, the stakes may be so high for either the developer or the neighbors, or both, that any legal tactics may appear justifiable. Before adopting such an approach, it would be well to read Sun Tzu, who counseled restraint. He wrote, "To subdue the enemy without fighting is the acme of skill."[7] He also said, "To capture an enemy's army is better than to destroy it; . . . ."[8] The developer and the neighbors may need each other at a future date. For example, the developer who wishes a rezoning to build townhouses on a vacant tract surrounded by a neighborhood of single-family, detached homes has a definite interest in not destroying the neighborhood. If the townhouses are approved and built, then the stability of the neighborhood will be important to the developer's investment.

Resolution of Zoning Conflicts

Some zoning conflicts may continue for years in a stalemate costly to both sides, but most get resolved one way or another—by the overpowering of one side by the other, through negotiation, or by a tacit agreement to a standoff. Officially the resolution comes about as a result of a decision by some arm of government—city council, judge, board of adjustment, or zoning administrator.

[6]Sun Tzu, *The Art Of War*, translated by Samuel B. Griffith, New York: Oxford University Press, 1963, p. 87.
[7]*Ibid.*
[8]*Ibid.*

Government, in effect, is playing the role of arbitrator. While providing a resolution of immediate issues, the strong dependence upon governmental arbitration in land-use decisions is not necessarily the best means of resolving conflicts, especially those that are likely to reoccur.

A major reason for the strong reliance on governmental arbitration is the common belief that zoning is a form of public control over private development. However dear this belief may be to the egos of planners, reality seems to say otherwise. In reality, most zoning conflicts tend to be treated as disputes between private parties, and local elected officials tend to view their roles as arbitrators and mediators.

One kind of private zoning conflict is similar to the social conflicts between "in-groups" and "out-groups" that Walter Isard described in his book, *Introduction to Regional Science*.[9] This is the kind that Dan Carter usually faces in trying to get a new project underway. Another kind of private zoning conflict is between members of the "in-group," i.e., between neighbors. This is the kind that Mary Trigg would have faced if she had not been able to resolve her problems short of conflict.

Whatever the nature of a particular zoning conflict, it should be possible for the parties involved to view it constructively as a kind of game in which there may be common interests as well as conflicting interests. Viewed in this light, there would be room for negotiation or tacit bargaining outside the formal zoning framework. There would also be the potential for happier solutions in which everyone might win.

[9]Walter Isard, *Introduction to Regional Science*, Englewood Cliffs, N.J.: Prentice-Hall, Inc., 1975, p. 225.

11
Current Issues and Emerging Concepts

Zoning is not what it used to be for Dan Carter. As recently as ten years ago, he seldom had serious problems in any of the localities where he builds. He did all of the things described in Chapter 7, and it rarely took him more than four months to get zoning approval for a project. Lately, though, the approval process has become more complicated. Approval may take a year or more. More people must be consulted, and time-consuming studies must be made.

In the suburb of Hampshire Woods, where there is a strongly organized group of environmentally sensitive residents, Dan now is required to submit an "environmental impact study" of any proposed project covering more than twenty acres. Dan has to hire a consultant to assess the probable effects of the proposal on wildlife, on trees and other vegetation, on erosion, on flooding and silting, and on the underground water table. The consultant must also estimate noise pollution, air and water pollution, and ground vibrations that might result from the project. The study must be submitted with the rezoning application, and two months are allowed for review by the opposition before the first public hearing is scheduled.

In another fictional suburb, Heathrow, which is similar to the real-life community of Duxbury, Massachusetts, the professional planning staff makes a study of the probable impact that every major rezoning proposal would have on public facilities and services. Sometimes the staff concludes that, although the proposal has no inherent faults, approval should be postponed for two or three years, by which time the sewers or waterlines will have been expanded to a capacity adequate to handle the increased load expected from the projects.

The suburb of Lake Poissy has gone even further. They have decided to limit their growth. Permits for only 300 housing units are issued annually. Who gets these scarce permits? That is not easy to answer, because the decision depends only in part on the order of application. Mostly it depends upon a complex point system. Points are awarded for the availability of sewers, waterlines, and other public facilities, but single-family homes that will be on lots large enough to support septic tanks are given the same number of points as homes that will be served by sewers. This feature gives an advantage to low-density, single-family development as opposed to higher-density, multiple-family housing. All rezonings for housing in Lake Poissy (and all PUD approvals) are made contingent on the awarding of necessary permits within one year. The result is that Dan doesn't build much housing in Lake Poissy. He does, however, build shopping centers and office parks. These are located so that they draw traffic primarily from other suburbs, but Lake Poissy gets the benefit of adding them to the tax rolls, so Dan has little trouble getting the zoning approvals for such commercial developments.

Dan's problems are not found only in the suburbs. In the central city of Metro City, Dan has been accustomed to picking up leftover tracts of land in largely developed areas and getting them rezoned either for commercial use or for the kind of residential use that he sought for the Brady Estate. Occasionally, he would run into the kind of opposition that he encountered with the Brady Estate, but he was usually able to cope with it. Now, however, approval is becoming more involved. Metro City's planning and zoning provisions have been amended so as to divide the entire city into groups of neighborhoods and to establish an official planning advisory committee for each neighborhood group. Each committee has recommended to the city a land-use plan for its area, and each is given a formal place in the rezoning process. Before Dan can get his first hearing scheduled with the Metro City Planning Board, he must first submit the land-use plan formally to the area planning advisory committee and allow forty-five days for them to review it and make recommendations. Worse still for Dan is the fact that the neighborhood committees do not confine their activities to zoning. Dan owns a shopping center that depends upon neighborhood residential streets for an important part of its access. The planning advisory committee for that area is pushing the city council to erect permanent barricades closing off access to the center on those streets.

The new trends are not all to Dan's disadvantage, however. Dan gave up trying to build lower-income housing several years ago, because he found it almost impossible to get zoning approval for the sites. Lately he has discovered that, while still difficult, it is far from impossible. The sites are sometimes not the most desirable ones, either for Dan or for the potential occupants, but the approval can often be obtained. The local councils haven't changed their attitudes, but they are being pressured by the courts and by federal agencies that hand out grants to modify their opposition to low-income housing.

As Dan's recent experiences illustrate, zoning is changing. What we said in the preceding chapters is not the last word on the subject. In those chapters we tried to stick fairly close to a description of what typical property owners might encounter with typical, *present-day* zoning ordinances, bearing in mind that the term "typical" is not easily applied to zoning. We have attempted to explain how the Mary Triggs, the Dan Carters, the Hilda and Fred Pottses, the Dick Smiths, and other property owners might improve their chances of winning a curious game that has been evolving constantly for more than sixty years.

As zoning continues to evolve, the rules will continue to change, and the tactics and strategy necessary to win may well change also. In this chapter, we will provide some brief glimpses of current issues and emerging concepts that are helping to shape the typical zoning ordinance of the future. How far in the future we cannot say. Even though some of the concepts discussed are in limited use at present, it could take many years for them to be used extensively. And, of course, some of them will probably be discarded along the way. We will make no predictions, therefore, about the future forms of zoning or about the timing of the evolutionary process. We will limit ourselves to identifying some of the components of the process.

The reason that zoning is continuing to evolve is that many influential critics are dissatisfied with it. It has been criticized as being *inadequate* for accomplishing needed public objectives and *unfair* in the unequal burdens and benefits that it bestows upon different groups and individuals. It has been called a *parochial* device used by affluent suburban enclaves to exclude low-income and minority groups. It has also been faulted on procedural grounds as having *insufficient checks* on arbitrary and capricious actions by decision makers. Much of the criticism has grown out of basic changes taking place in our society as a whole, a shifting in attitudes toward property rights, an increasing sensitivity to environmental quality, and a growing desire for self-determination by residents of neighborhoods.

Shifting Attitudes Toward Property Rights

In the pioneer days of zoning, advocates of the then-new concept had to contend with critics who viewed it as a threat to the basic rights of property ownership. The use of the police power of government to restrict private property was challenged as a violation of (1) the requirement for due process and (2) the prohibition against taking of private property without just compensation. Zoning itself was further challenged as a denial of the requirement for equal protection, because all property was not being regulated in the same way.

The early promoters of zoning countered these arguments for "property rights" persuasively with assertions that property rights had to be limited in the interest of the public health and safety and for the general welfare of society as a whole. They sometimes quoted the following passage attributed to Theodore Roosevelt:

Ordinarily, and in the great majority of cases, human rights and property rights are fundamentally and in the long run identical, but when it clearly appears that there is real conflict between them human rights must have the upper hand, for property belongs to man and not man to property.

Of course, the reasoning here is specious. Property itself has no rights whatsoever. What we called "property rights" are in reality "human rights in property," and when we speak of a conflict between "human rights" and "property rights," what we really mean is a conflict between two different sets of human rights. Nevertheless, the assertion was popular, and the zoning advocates eventually had their way. Zoning became such an accepted regulation of private property by local government that courts generally placed on a property owner challenging a zoning decision the burden of proving that the decision was unconstitutional. In most states, the burden of proof is still on the property owner. Local governments have great freedom in what restrictions they impose and in what ways they impose them.

The power of local governments to regulate has been strengthened by a widening public acceptance of regulation as a means for accomplishing general social goals. We stated in Chapter 2 that any regulation based on the police power had to be related clearly to the public health, safety, or welfare (and sometimes morals) in order to be constitutional. In recent years there has been a tendency to rely more and more on the *welfare* justification, perhaps because it is more nebulous than *health* or *safety* and therefore less easy for the opponents of a regulation to attack. Under the justification of promoting the general welfare, governments can regulate private property for purpose of (1) achieving greater efficiency in the allocation of resources; (2) achieving greater equity in the distribution of wealth, income and opportunity; and (3) minimizing "social costs," which are costs that society at large must bear as a consequence of private development. For example, a major shopping center served by an inadequate system of access streets is imposing *social costs* on the surrounding neighborhoods through the congestion and pollution created by the traffic that is generated. Regulation has been expanded to minimize social costs and to meet other social objectives.

Although the power to regulate has been expanded, the expansion does not necessarily mean that the power of *local* government is being strengthened. In some respects the power of local government is being threatened. The biggest expansion has been at other levels. The states and the federal government have become increasingly involved. State courts have been intervening in more local decisions. For a time it appeared that the federal courts might intervene, but recently they seem to have pulled back. Even without activity by the federal judiciary, however, it is clear that local governments are not the major beneficiaries of the growing willingness to restrict property rights.

Local governments are not only failing to participate fully in the expansion of regulatory authority, but are under attack for using the authority that they already possess. Their victory in getting zoning upheld as constitutional in the 1920s no longer seems as secure as it once did. The defenders of property rights, despite their overwhelming defeat by the forces of zoning in the 1920s, have never completely given up. Lately there has been a resurgence of sorts in their cause. Bernard Siegan has written a book entitled, *Land Use Without Zoning*,[1] in which he contrasts Chicago, which has zoning, with Houston, which, as every planner knows, is the largest city in the nation without zoning (although it does have some other regulations that serve as partial substitutes). Siegan's conclusion is that the absence of zoning in Houston results in net benefits to the community and that less zoning would also be desirable elsewhere. He has expanded his criticism of zoning with an attack on land-use planning and regulation in general in a more recent book entitled, *Other People's Property*.[2]

One of the most intriguing aspects of Siegan's castigation of zoning is his ability to combine criticisms from two different philosophical streams: the traditional, conservative concern for property rights; and the more recent liberal concern for civil rights. What he has done, in effect, is to consider as one: (1) the freedom of a property owner to build low-income housing in a suburb as

[1]Bernard H. Siegan, *Land Use Without Zoning*, Lexington, Mass.: D.C. Heath and Company, 1972.
[2]Bernard H. Siegan, *Other People's Property*, Lexington, Mass.: D.C. Heath and Company, 1976.

a *property right,* and (2) the freedom of a low-income family to move to the suburb as a *civil right.*

The successes (even though incomplete) of the civil rights movement in achieving equal access to privately owned but public-serving facilities, such as restaurants, hotels, schools, and housing, have given further impetus to changing the concept of private property from a concern solely with the *rights* of the owner or tenant to one that also emphasizes *duties* of ownership. At the same time, the civil rights advocates have been able to overturn many state and local laws that formerly restricted property rights, as, for example, the laws in many states that used to mandate racial segregation even on private property. In the course of overturning these laws, they have caused serious questions to be raised about the defensibility of local regulation of property generally. Thus, while the pursuit of civil rights has limited property rights in some ways, it has expanded them in others by eroding local regulation.

Environmental Sensitivity

Zoning is a form of environmental regulation. Traditionally, however, it has dealt almost entirely with the artificial, or built, environment to the exclusion of the natural environment. The emphasis has been upon *how* land should or should not be developed for urban use—not *whether* or not it should be developed. And except for those ordinances that contain industrial performance standards, there has been little specified concern with the direct effects that a proposed development might have on its surroundings. True, concerns for effects have been brought out in public hearings, and flexible zoning has sometimes been used to limit those effects, but despite all of the flexibility that has been incorporated into it, zoning is still strongly grounded in the concept of preannounced uses-by-right, a concept that does not allow for detailed consideration of the environmental effects of each proposal. Thus, although zoning is an environmental regulation, it is not a very sophisticated one.

Zoning is also a *local* environmental regulation. The officials of a small suburban village or a scenic, rural county are, in their zoning decisions, permitting development that could have widespread effects over an entire metropolitan area or even a larger region. The local decision makers are understandably more sensitive to the perceived needs of the local tax base and local economy than to regional environmental considerations.

The environmental consciousness that has been so prominent in the 1970s has had two general effects on zoning. First, it has increased interest in making zoning itself more sensitive to the environmental consequences of particular developments. Second, it has led to disillusionment with local control of zoning and a push for state and federal control of development having significant environmental impact.

Self-determination

A third contemporary force that is influencing the evolution of zoning is a growing desire for self-determination by the inhabitants of neighborhoods and groups of neighborhoods. This phenomenon is much newer than the shifting attitudes towards property rights and the increasing sensitivity to environmental quality. So far, it has been found almost entirely in the neighborhoods of large cities, where centralized governments for 500,000 or more people may deprive citizens of a sense of influence over their own lives. The "neighborhood movement," as the phenomenon is sometimes called, restores at least some feeling of self-determination. The movement is involved in all matters affecting neighborhoods—not just zoning. It emphasizes initiating proposals rather than simply reacting to other people's initiatives. As the movement is so new, we will not attempt to predict what implications it has for the future of zoning, but the possibilities are something to think about. If successful in the cities, the emphasis on self-determination could spread to the larger suburbs and eventually counter, to some extent, the other currents that we have described as steering land-use regulation toward more centralized control at the state and federal levels.

The future of zoning is being shaped by several underlying forces at work in our society. How they are shaping it is not clear at this time. We think, however, that the reader ought to be aware of some of the special issues being raised and some of the specific techniques that have been devised in response to the underlying changes. We will begin by discussing the issue of *exclusionary zoning.*

Exclusionary Zoning

We pointed out near the beginning of this chapter that Dan Carter had been having trouble finding sites for low-income housing in suburban communities. Dan is not alone. All over the country in our larger metropolitan areas, housing sites for the poor, and even for the not-so-poor, are scarce. One big reason for the scarcity is the local zoning ordinance. By failing to zone any suitable areas for apartments or mobile homes, and by setting very high minimum standards for lot area or residential floor space, a single, individual suburb is not by itself going to stop families with low or moderate incomes from moving to suburbia. When all of the suburbs ringing a central city engage in the same kind of activity, however, the aggregate effect is to exclude those families. Zoning practices that have such an effect are called *exclusionary zoning.*

Exclusionary zoning is criticized because it helps to polarize our society, strengthening the separation between the affluent and the deprived. Specifically, it hinders those who are trying to move up the economic ladder by limiting their access to jobs in the suburbs. And the suburbs are where job opportunities are expanding. The residential exodus from central cities that began after World War II was soon followed by a decentralization of industry and then by retail activity. The completion of beltline freeways around metropolitan areas in the late 1960s, providing the suburban rings with good ground access to major airports, stimulated the decentralization of office employment. The suburbs are no longer dependent upon the central cities for their economic base. The breaking of this former dependency has resulted in a general lessening of the mass transit services available between city and suburb and in a general increase in the fares charged. The ambitious poor, who are trapped in central cities where employment is declining, are discouraged by both the time and the fares involved from commuting to jobs in the suburbs. Their only hope for self-improvement may lie in finding some way to move their residences closer to the job opportunities. When they try to do this, they run up against the barriers erected by exclusionary zoning.

The barriers are now under attack from several quarters but success is uncertain. For a while it was thought by many observers that the federal courts would take action to strike down exclusionary practices. Several recent decisions by the U.S. Supreme Court, however, have made it clear that it is reluctant to become involved in local zoning laws. In 1974, in the case of the *Village of Belle Terre, New York v. Boraas,* the court upheld a local zoning ordinance that defined "family" as not including more than two persons unrelated by blood, marriage, or adoption. Belle Terre is a college community, and several students had jointly occupied a house in a "single-family" zoning district. Although the ordinance might be considered as exclusionary with respect to college students, it is not an example of what is usually thought of as *exclusionary zoning.*

A clearer example of exclusionary zoning was before the court in 1975 in the case of *Warth v. Selden.* Plaintiffs were attacking the zoning ordinance of the town of Penfield, a suburb of Rochester, New York. The ordinance had allegedly zoned ninety-eight percent of the town's undeveloped land for single-family housing with restrictions that raised the cost of new housing above the price that lower-income families could afford. It is interesting to note that the original plaintiffs, who included low-income, inner-city black residents of Rochester and others, were later joined as an ally by the Rochester Home Builders Association. The Supreme Court did not rule directly on the issue of exclusionary zoning, but instead ruled against the plaintiffs on procedural grounds, holding that they had not shown any specific injury by Penfield and that, therefore, they did not have sufficient "standing" in court to entitle them to sue.

The next landmark decision by the U.S. Supreme Court did involve a specific rejection, but did not directly relate to the exclusion of low-income families. The citizens of Eastlake, Ohio, a suburb of Cleveland, had amended their city charter to require that every rezoning had to be approved by a fifty-five percent majority in a referendum before it could take effect. A developer, Forest City Enterprises, got approval from the city council on the rezoning of a tract from an industrial classification to one permitting a high-rise apartment building, but the change was defeated in the subsequent referendum. The developer sued to invalidate the requirement for the referendum on the grounds that the constitutional right of *due process* had been violated. In what had become the case of *City of Eastlake v. Forest City Enterprises, Inc.*, the U.S. Supreme Court upheld the requirement in June 1976. Although not directly related to the exclusion of the poor, the decision could certainly open the way for referenda that did result in such exclusion.

A year later, in 1977, the court heard an appeal that concerned both a specific denial and an allegation of exclusion. The exclusion, however, was not phrased in terms of economic discrimination but rather as racial discrimination against blacks and Mexican-Americans. The case, *Village of Arlington Heights v. Metropolitan Housing Development Corporation,* concerned a non-profit developer that wanted to rezone fifteen acres of vacant land in Arlington

Heights, Illinois, for the purpose of building low-rise multifamily housing for low-income and moderate-income households. The tract was surrounded by an area already developed with single-family homes and like the tract in question was zoned accordingly. The village had zoned sixty other tracts for multifamily use, and some of them were still vacant. The Supreme Court reversed the decision of a lower court that had found the refusal to rezone unconstitutional as racial discrimination, the Supreme Court's reasoning being that a racial motivation for the refusal had not been proven. The case was sent back to the trial court for a decision as to whether or not the refusal was a violation of the Fair Housing Act of 1968. Thus, the court has left open at least a crack in the door to zoning review but on legislative rather than constitutional grounds.

In the case of *Moore v. the City of East Cleveland,* also in 1977, the Supreme Court continued to leave ajar the zoning door. East Cleveland had incorporated a very restricted definition of "family" in its ordinance, limiting not only the number of unrelated people in a household but also the number of certain relatives. A grandmother was convicted of violating the ordinance by allowing her grandson to live with her, and the court overturned this conviction. The court's action should not be construed as a turnabout from the decision in the Belle Terre case, however. In the East Cleveland case, the court seemed to be impressed with the importance of preserving the family as an institution rather than with the issue of exclusionary zoning per se, while in the Belle Terre case the justices seemed to have been concerned with the importance of protecting a single-family neighborhood from the intrusions of a host of un-related individuals.

The courts that have done the most to upset exclusionary zoning practices have been not at the federal level but at the state level, particularly in New Jersey. In 1975, in the case of *Southern Burlington County NAACP v. Township of Mount Laurel,* the Supreme Court of New Jersey upheld a lower court in its decision that Mount Laurel's zoning ordinance had not made sufficient pro-visions for housing for people of low or moderate income. Mount Laurel, a suburb of Philadelphia, was ordered to change the ordinance so as to ac-commodate its "fair share" of the region's needs for such housing. In effect, the court was ordering Mount Laurel to take affirmative action to become a more balanced community in its population and residential land use. In a subsequent case, *Oakwood at Madison v. Township of Madison* (now Old Bridge), decided in 1977, the New Jersey Supreme Court backed away from setting any numerical quotas that might be applied statewide, preferring to leave the exact determination of "fair share" to the lower court involved in each specific case and to state legislation.

No other state supreme court has gone as far as New Jersey's, but several others have struck down various exclusionary practices in particular cases, as, for example, minimum requirements for very large lots. As we explained in Chapter 8, however, the finding that a zoning ordinance is unconstitutional in one case with respect to one tract of land does not automatically change the rules for other properties and other zoning ordinances. Unless courts in other states adopt New Jersey's "fair share" approach, judicial reform of ex-clusionary zoning could take forever. Even in New Jersey, it is likely to take a long time. In the meantime, exclusionary zoning will continue to grow in importance as an issue.[3]

Although exclusionary zoning to date has nearly always meant the exclusion of poor people or racial minorities, it is conceivable that the issue could be expanded to include nonresidential uses. The suburban rings around our major metropolitan areas have the same sort of aversion to certain commercial, industrial, and institutional uses that they have toward low-income housing. Their land-use plans and zoning maps are similarly unbalanced. Each suburb would prefer that mental hospitals, asphalt plants, cemeteries, and junkyards, for example, be located in some other suburb. The aggregate effect of the preferences of all suburbs is that sites are extremely difficult to find for uses that are necessary for the proper functioning of a metropolitan area, even though they may be undesirable in some respects. In a large metropolitan area, it simply is not economical to confine all such uses to locations back in the central city. Junkyards, for example, may well grow in importance in the future as "ecological recycling facilities." If discarded materials are to be collected, sorted, and recycled, there must be at least some collection points in the suburbs, as undesirable as the thought may seem. The issue here is the extent to which suburbs can benefit from their location in large urban areas without, at the same time, putting up with some of the inconveniences required by a balanced pattern of land use.

Growth Controls

Another current issue, and one that is related to the issue of exclusionary zoning, is the subject of *growth controls*. In the past ten years, numerous communities across the nation (including such geographically disparate localities as Ramapo Township, New York; Boca Raton, Florida; Boulder, Colorado; and Petaluma, California) have adopted measures of one sort or another to curb growth. The measures have been varied: moratoriums on sewer connections, refusals to expand public facilities, changes in zoning to lower the density of housing permitted (*up-zoning* or *down-zoning*, depending upon one's point of view), procedures for rationing building permits, outright ceilings on total housing units, and other devices intended either to control the rate of growth or to limit the ultimate size of a community.

The two localities receiving the most publicity for their growth policies have been Ramapo Township, New York, and Petaluma, California, probably because both have survived challenges in the courts. Ramapo, which is located approximately thirty miles northwest of New York City and immediately above the New Jersey state line, adopted in 1969 a set of procedures that coordinated building permits, zoning, and subdivision approvals with the implementation of an eighteen-year capital improvement program. The program provided for the completion of sewers, drainage improvements, recreational facilities, road improvements, and firehouses throughout the township by the end of the eighteen-year period.

[3]For readers who wish to learn more about the subject we suggest the following book: Richard R. Babcock and Fred P. Bosselman, *Exclusionary Zoning*, New York: Praeger, 1973.

In order to keep private development in line with the improvement program, Ramapo has adopted a system of awarding points to proposed residential projects on the basis of their nearness to adequate facilities. If a proposed project does not have enough points for approval (1) the developer can wait until the township has provided sufficient improvements under its eighteen-year program; or (2) the developer can provide the capital for making the improvements.

Petaluma has a more complicated set of controls that combines a point system, a total limit on dwelling permits to 500 per year, a moratorium on annexation, and limitations on the expansion of public facilities. Located approximately thirty-five miles north of San Francisco, Petaluma, like Ramapo, is a developing suburb near the outer edge of a large metropolitan area.

Both Ramapo and Petaluma's controls are likely to be emulated by other suburbs similarly located. The extent to which this will occur, however, is not yet clear. In some states, the courts may prove unfriendly to the concept. Boca Raton, Florida, for example, has been trying unsuccessfully for several years to win litigation upholding its ceiling of 40,000 housing units. The subject will continue to be controversial for some time to come.

For a better understanding of the motives involved in growth control, we will refer again to our fictional composite suburb of Lake Poissy, where Dan Carter used to build houses, but doesn't anymore. Lake Poissy, which is twenty-five miles from the center of Metro City, was originally developed in the 1920s as a pleasant summer resort and weekend retreat for the moderately well-to-do. By the early 1950s, more and more affluent families were residing there year-round. It had lovely woods and rolling hills, clean air, and a chain of four clear lakes. It also featured the kinds of golf, tennis, and other club facilities that helped to make life worthwhile.

Lake Poissy doubled in population during the Fifties, going from 1500 to 3000 permanent residents. The newcomers were absorbed with little difficulty, however. The additional people caused only a modest expansion of retail business. Their homes were on lots large enough to permit septic tanks, so no system of public sewers was required. Many of them had their own private wells, so there was no significant increase in the load on the local water distribution system. All of the newcomers with children sent them to private schools, so the local public schools were unaffected by the influx. In brief, the idyllic way of living continued much as it had in the past.

The decade of the sixties brought a different kind of change to Lake Poissy. Population jumped from the 1960 figure of 3000 to a new total of 11,000, and the increase was accelerating. By 1969, permits were being issued for more than 1500 homes annually. The new residents of the sixties were not as affluent on the average as those of earlier years. Some were top executives with the corporate offices that had begun moving to Lake Poissy and nearby suburbs around 1963, but others were employees of lesser rank in those same offices. Most, however, were fairly well-off, middle-class households having at least one member who commuted daily to a job in Metro City. These families were fleeing from the pollution, high taxes, worsening public services, and perceived threats from rising crime rates in Metro City. For the most part, they liked what they found in Lake Poissy.

By the end of the Sixties, Lake Poissy was experiencing some problems. Land prices had risen to such an extent that homes were now being built on smaller lots. Septic tanks did not work properly on these smaller lots, and as a result the lakes were becoming polluted. Bonds had to be floated for a sewer system and treatment plant. The high cost of commuting to the city forced many of the new families to enroll their children in the local public schools, overcrowding them and necessitating another bond issue. The operating budget of the village soared as demands for more police, fire, and sanitation services grew substantially. The village employees, who could not afford to live in Lake Poissy, formed a union and were successful in getting big boosts in wages every two years. Fortunately for the homeowners of Lake Poissy, the additional tax revenue generated by the new corporate offices and shopping centers locating in the village was adequate to cover all of the rising expenditures, thereby forestalling any need for an increase in the tax rate.

In other respects, the growth was presenting problems that were not being forestalled. Traffic congestion was one such problem. The state was willing to spend money to widen village roads, but strong objections were raised every time a specific widening was proposed. There was simply no way to increase the width of any important road without destroying beautiful old trees or quaint buildings. Another problem was use of the lakes. Long-time residents liked to sail; newer residents tended to have powerboats, and some of them went in for water skiing. The village council debated an ordinance to restrict powerboats to certain lakes, but agreement could never be obtained as to which lakes.

The Sixties also brought several major zoning controversies. There were pressures for more commercial zoning and for amendments to permit smaller residential lots. Near the end of the decade, there were several applications for apartment developments, and three of them were granted. One of the projects was located on Lake Nancy. Following the project's completion, use of the lake increased threefold, much to the irritation of the owners of single-family homes around the lake.

Early in the 1970s, growth and problems in Lake Poissy accelerated dramatically. By the middle of 1974, population had jumped to an estimated 31,000. An abnormally hot and dry summer accentuated a rising demand for water that the overloaded system could not supply. At the height of the water crisis, the village council approved four hotly contested rezonings, one for apartments and three for small-lot subdivisions. That was the last straw. In the September election, the entire village council was replaced by advocates of a moratorium on rezonings. Within six weeks of taking office, the new council had adopted the moratorium. Two months later, they passed the growth control ordinance, limiting housing permits to 300 units annually. They then modified the moratorium to make all residential rezonings and PUD approvals contingent upon getting the necessary permits within one year after approval.

From the point of view of Lake Poissy, their reaction to uncontrolled growth was perfectly rational. They were being overwhelmed, and something had to be done quickly to prevent a complete loss of the kind of living environment that had attracted the refugees from the city. Lake Poissy's action got favorable publicity from ecology circles, and other suburbs around Metro City began to copy them. Then civil rights activists began to chastise Lake Poissy for "snobbery" and "selfishness." Exclusionary zoning was charged. Lake Poissy pointed out that it was't being exclusionary; it was just trying to bring order into its growth.

Lake Poissy is a fairly good illustration of the motives for growth control. The motives may be selfish in a way, but they have some justifiable basis in their concerns for upholding environmental quality end for local determination of community character. As we mentioned earlier, many localities around the country have adopted policies similar to Lake Poissy's, and some have gone even further by clamping absolute ceilings on their ultimate population, taking the position that no more permits will be issued after the ceiling is reached. In a society that is becoming increasingly sensitive to environmental degradation, enamoured with the idea of zero population growth, and rebellious against the erosion of self-determination, the possibility of limiting the size of a pleasant community is appealing. The limit would protect the good life for those fortunate enough to have entered before the gates shut. Those arriving late and finding the entrance barred would simply have to look elsewhere for a place to live.

The exclusionary aspect of growth controls raises a serious question about their ethics. It also raises questions similar to those involved in exclusionary zoning. If most suburbs in a given metropolitan area adopt growth controls, then how can the ambitious poor escape the central city and move out where the jobs are going? In the case involving Petaluma, California, the federal district court held that Petaluma's growth controls, if copied throughout the San Francisco region, would tend to drive up housing costs and make it more difficult for people to move to the suburbs. The court concluded that such a restriction would constitute a violation of a fundamental right under the constitution: the freedom to travel and live in any state or municipality in the nation. The growth controls were, therefore, unconstitutional. This case, *Construction Industry of Sonoma County v. the City of Petaluma*, is another example of an alliance between developers and civil rights advocates.

The decision of the federal district court was reversed, however, by the circuit court of appeals, which used the precedent of *Warth v. Selden* to rule that the plaintiffs did not have the "standing" that would entitle them to use. The U.S. Supreme Court refused to review the case, again demonstrating that they would rather not get involved in constitutional challenges to local development controls.

Fiscal Zoning

Lake Poissy's officials have not been as strict about commercial development as they have about new housing. They are selective in what they approve, but they like to approve office parks, research parks, and shopping centers as long as these developments do not harm residential areas in the village. So far they have not been harmful—at least not to Lake Poissy. In the northwest corner of the village is an area of about 3000 acres that is separated from the rest of the village by a major creek and a freeway. Nearly all of Lake Poissy's commercial uses are in this area. They add considerably to Lake Poissy's property tax base but present few problems except to the neighboring village of Parkhurst. Residential areas in Parkhurst have to put up with a lot of extraneous traffic generated by the commercial uses, and many of the office and retail employees live in Parkhurst, sending their children to the public schools there and using the village services. Unfortunately, Parkhurst gets no tax revenue from the commercial area to support these services. It consequently has a much higher tax rate than does Lake Poissy, whose lower rate helps to attract more commercial uses that, in turn, help to perpetuate the low rate. Lake Poissy's use of zoning to boost its tax base is an example of what is called *fiscal zoning.*

Fiscal zoning is practiced by many suburbs around the country. Some, like Lake Poissy, are mainly interested in zoning so as to encourage "clean" additions to the tax rolls, even if neighboring municipalities will have to suffer from the external effects of the additions. Other suburbs go further and also use zoning as a device for keeping down expenditures. They do this by drawing the zoning map so as to minimize the land available for those uses that tend to demand more in services than they produce in revenue—uses such as apartments for families with children, mobile homes, houses on small lots, and tax-exempt institutions. Used in this way, *fiscal zoning* becomes *exclusionary zoning.*

Like growth controls, fiscal zoning makes sense from the narrow viewpoint of the suburb applying it. Viewed from the perspective of the entire metropolitan area, it is harmful, because it accentuates the imbalances between the different parts of the metropolis. Some local governments have the greater needs for expenditures, while others have the tax base that might support those needs. When the better-off suburbs practice fiscal zoning, they worsen this disparity.

Fairness to Property Owners

Although the validity of zoning has generally been upheld by the courts, some aspects of it seem basically unfair even if they are constitutional. The unfairness mainly has to do with the inequitable impact of zoning on different property owners. Some receive benefits amounting to windfalls, while others are burdened with restrictions that border on the taking of their property without compensation. When a local government uses the power of *eminent domain* to take property for a public purpose, it must pay just compensation. On the other hand, as we pointed out in Chapter 8, when it uses the *police power* to restrict use of the property, then it does not have to compensate. The local government, therefore, is tempted strongly to use the police power in marginal situations when funds are insufficient for acting under the power of eminent domain.[4]

Preservation is one current issue that may involve pushing the police power to its limits. There is growing interest in the United States in preserving natural features that are scenic or ecologically sensitive and buildings that are architecturally or historically significant. Interest in preserving a specific site sometimes arises suddenly and unexpectedly just as a developer is about to act. Witness Karla Petersen's experience.

[4]For a more thorough discussion of problems in achieving fairness in zoning, we suggest the following: Daniel R. Mandelker, *The Zoning Dilemma,* Indianapolis: Bobbs-Merrill Company, Inc., 1971.

Karla purchased a 200-acre tract, intending to subdivide it into 15,000-square-foot lots for home sites. At the time of purchase, the tract was zoned "R-3 Residential," a category that permitted lots of that size. Shortly after Karla bought the land, the county supervisors were all defeated for reelection and replaced by a group of fervent conservationists. Only a few weeks after they took office, Karla applied for a preliminary approval of her subdivision plat, so that she could begin grading the land and constructing streets. When Karla's intention to develop came to the attention of local environmental groups, they quickly noted that Karla's tract contained a fifty-acre stand of virgin hardwood forest. They also commented that the entire property was on top of a "recharge" area where rainwater entered the ground and recharged the underground water aquifer tapped by the numerous wells in the county. Karla's application for subdivision approval was deferred while the new board of supervisors had a study made of the problem. The result was the creation of a new zoning district called "A-C Agricultural-Conservation." Karla's land was "up-zoned" to this classification, which allowed one residence on the whole tract plus farming and recreation but which prohibited any cutting of the trees unless they were dead or diseased. Karla couldn't understand why this was called "up-zoning." She and her associates all referred to it as a case of "down-zoning." She thought that her property had been "taken" without compensation.

Dan Carter had a similar experience in Metro City. He assembled a block of old buildings and prepared to demolish them to create a site for a new office building. Dan had a copy of the Metro City zoning map on his wall, and he had been careful to avoid assembling land in the "Old and Historical District." He paid little attention to a provision in the text of the ordinance that allowed the city to delay for one year the demolition of a significant building outside of the designated district. When Dan's plans came to the public's attention, a letter to the newspaper pointed out that one of Dan's buildings had been a plush theater built in the 1880s and that the interior was a treasure of late-nineteenth-century design that had been covered up, but not destroyed, by subsequent remodeling. The letter aroused interest in preserving the structure, and when Dan's contractor applied for the demolition permit, the review of the application was delayed long enough for the city council to designate the old theater as a "landmark" and thereby justify withholding the permit for one year, thus providing those interested in keeping it time to negotiate with Dan.

The year passed, and the preservationists could produce neither the money for buying out Dan nor a feasible proposal for incorporating the existing building in Dan's new project. In the meanwhile, Dan lost considerable money because of the delay.

Preservation is a needed undertaking. Zoning and other regulations based on the police power can be effective and justifiable in carrying out preservation objectives. The regulations can also be unfair, however, in their unequal impact on different property owners, and in particular instances they can become almost confiscatory.

The examples just cited also illustrate another unfair aspect of current zoning practices—delay. Both Karla and Dan set out to do things that were permissible. Before they could begin, their applications were delayed, and then the rules were changed. They could challenge their treatment in court as denials of procedural due process, and perhaps they would be successful, but there is no guarantee of success, and while the litigation is pending, there will be further costly delay.

As we pointed out in Chapter 8, each parcel of property is different in the eyes of most courts. The fact that owner A was successful in litigation does not necessarily mean that owner B, whose property is across the street from A's, is going to benefit from the decision. If the court ordered A's land rezoned, then the local council is not bound to grant the same zoning to B unless B goes through the same litigation that A went through. This hardly seems fair. The general precedent has been set, and the local government is ignoring it, choosing to fall back on a technicality to delay the development in the hope that the developer will give up.

Other complaints of unfairness involve the inconsistencies in many local decisions and the failure to keep adequate written records. Local boards are often charged with granting or denying approvals according to the extent of opposition rather than on the merits of the proposals. In the same meeting, a board might turn down a strongly opposed application that would seem reasonable to an impartial observer and approve three others having dubious merit but little or no opposition. On occasion, an application that draws no opposition from the surrounding area might have grave citywide implications. For example, a neighborhood of white homeowners on the edge of a racial transition area banded together and requested a rezoning of their entire subdivision to apartments, expecting that the apartment zoning would raise the value of their property so that they could sell out at a good price and move to the suburbs. The city council, noting that all of the property owners favored it and that there was no opposition from the vicinity, ignored the possible effects of the rezoning on the future of the neighborhood and granted it.

Although the inconsistencies of zoning decisions may be apparent to an on-the-spot observer, they do not always appear in the written records. Even where a fairly accurate set of minutes is kept, the reasons for actions may not appear in them simply because the decision makers fail to state them.

Lack of Uniformity Between Localities

Dan Carter builds in several different communities. Each has a different zoning ordinance with different procedures and different terminology as well as different regulations. Keeping up with these differences is not only a problem for builders. It also confuses brokers, architects, retailers with branches or franchises, and lawyers. Dispelling the confusion takes time and thus adds to the cost of developing. Wherever possible, the additional costs are passed on to the purchaser or tenant who occupies the development. The lack of uniformity, therefore, should not be considered as merely a selfish concern of builders.

As a matter of fact, some of the builders' most persistent critics, the environmentalists, are also concerned about the multiplicity of ordinances in single metropolitan areas. As they see the situation, a smart builder can shop around to find suburbs with weak regulations or friendly officials. What is permitted in those suburbs, however, may adversely affect the entire metropolitan area. For example, a developer was refused permission by a county government to build at the density allowed by the zoning ordinance, because the temporary sewage treatment plant that would handle the development's wastewater was overloaded. The county would permit only single-family houses on lots large enough for the use of septic tanks. The developer went to the officials of a nearby village, who agreed to let him connect to their sewer system and build at the higher density if he would agree to the annexation of his project by the village. The site was annexed, developed, and connected to the sewer. The county officials were furious. It seems that the village turns all of its wastewater over to the county for disposal. The project ended up overloading further the very treatment plant that had led to the county's original disapproval of the higher density.

Drift of Controls to Higher Levels of Government

The growing dissatisfaction with local zoning practices by influential movers and shakers in our society has resulted in pressure for greater regulation at local, state, and federal levels. The new controls at these higher levels are of two basic kinds:

1. Controls on activities not previously regulated locally to any great extent

2. Constraints on local regulations to protect the interests of society as a whole

The first set mainly involves pollution controls and prohibitions against despoliation of environmentally sensitive areas, such as wetlands. Although a few states have been active in adopting these new environmental regulations, the federal government has had the dominant role to date. The principal vehicles used at the federal level have been the National Environmental Policy Act of 1969, the Clean Air Act of 1970, and the Water Pollution Control Act Amendments of 1972. Taken together, these acts have considerable potential for regulating land use. For example, under the Clean Air Act, a use that would be a direct source of pollution can be prohibited by the Environmental Protection Administration (EPA) from locating in certain areas. In 1974, the EPA proposed a set of controls called "Indirect Source Regulations" that would have required EPA approval for proposed uses contributing indirectly to air pollution. Among the private uses that would have been regulated were new developments having parking facilities for 1000 or more cars and additions to existing uses that provided parking for 500 or more. The Indirect Source Regulations were supposed to become effective on December 31, 1974, but there were so many complaints to members of Congress that the EPA postponed the effective date to June 30, 1976, and then forgot about them.

Under the Water Pollution Control Act Amendments, the EPA has further potential for strong influence over private development. In addition to providing for direct regulation of uses that might involve significant pollution, the act authorizes major federal grants to local governments for trunk sewer lines and treatment plants. The capacity of these facilities will determine the intensity of development that will be possible in the areas served by them. Thus, in approving grants for their construction, the EPA will be having a say in local land-use policy.

Federal agencies also have an influence over development in floodplains and development in high-noise areas (as, for example, in the vicinity of an airport). Development in such areas, and especially housing construction, is discouraged through the withholding of federally assisted financing.

Although the federal government has had the dominant role to date in the new environmental regulations, covering as it does all fifty states, several states have taken actions that individually are more stringent than federal controls. Massachusetts and Wisconsin, for example, have state control over the development of wetlands. California regulates development along its coastline and, in addition, has created a San Francisco Bay Conservation and Development Commission to regulate filling and construction around the shoreline of the bay. Maine and Vermont have rather broad provisions for state review of proposed projects.[5]

The current trend is toward increased state involvement in land-use and development regulations. The kind of involvement that is emerging, however, is not so much one of *direct state control* as it is one of *state review* of local decisions. For several decades, the states have been giving broad regulatory powers to local governments with a minimum of constraints attached. Now, the states are no longer content to play the role of a passive partner. More and more of them, including Florida, Colorado, Massachusetts, Minnesota, Oregon, Utah, and Washington, have put reins to local powers. The reins applied have been adapted generally from a document prepared by the American Law Institute and entitled the "Model Land Development Code."

The Model Land Development Code provides for state review of two kinds of development:

1. Developments in "areas of critical state concern," which include mainly areas of environmental, historical, or archaeological significance but also areas experiencing, or about to experience, major public investment, such as the vicinity of a major airport or freeway interchange.

2. "Developments of regional impact or benefit," which basically include those projects that, for any reason, substantially affect the residents of more than one local government.

The term "regional benefit" would presumably encompass uses that might be the objects of exclusionary zoning. It may, therefore, be expected to generate some controversy as states consider its adoption. Perhaps it is significant that the Florida Environmental Land and Water Management Act of 1972 incorporates the Model Land Development Code's concept of "development of regional impact" but omits the words "or benefit."

The Model Land Development Code does not represent the only vehicle for attacking exclusionary zoning. In Massachusetts, for example, a more specific action was taken in 1969 with the passage of the Massachusetts Zoning

---

[5]Although it is several years old and does not include some important state controls enacted since its publication, a good introduction to the subject of state regulation is the following: Fred Bosselman and David Callies, *The Quiet Revolution in Land Use Control*, Washington, D.C.: U.S. Government Printing Office, 1971.

Appeals Law, popularly known as the "Anti-Snob-Zoning Law." This law consolidates all of the approvals required for subsidized housing into a single "Comprehensive Application to Build Housing." The would-be developer of subsidized housing may submit such an application to a local board of zoning appeals. If the application is denied, approved with unacceptable conditions, or simply not acted on within a certain period of time, the developer may appeal to a state body, the Housing Appeals Committee, which has the power to override the local action. The intent of the law is to overcome delaying tactics by a local government as well as outright exclusionary zoning.

Another approach to breaking down exclusionary barriers to subsidized housing has been for metropolitan or regional councils to promote "fair share" plans. Under such a plan, each local government agrees to zone for its fair share of the low-income and moderate-income housing needs of the region. In turn, each locality is assured that it will not have to provide for more than its fair share. A *fair-share plan* is, to some extent, voluntary on the part of the locality, but there is an element of coercion. Under the Intergovernmental Relations Act of 1968, any substantial project involving federal money, including federal grants to local governments, must be reviewed in the proposal stage by a metropolitan or regional "clearing house." The so-called clearing houses go under various names, including "councils of governments" (COGs) and "regional planning commissions," but basically they are planning and review bodies. Although they have little power other than the power to recommend, the power to make a negative recommendation on a local application for federal aid should not be taken lightly.

Under the Community Development Block Grant program contained in the Housing and Community Development Act of 1974, a local government's application for funds must be accompanied by a "housing assistance plan." As a result of a 1976 federal court decision involving suburbs of Hartford, Connecticut (*City of Hartford v. Hills*), it appeared for a while that the "fair-share" concept was going to have added teeth. A more recent decision, however, has made the addition of teeth less certain (*City of Hartford v. Towns of Glastonbury, West Hartford and East Hartford*).

Impact Studies

Federal and state environmental regulations, and the growing popularity of the Model Land Development Code's concept of "developments of regional impact and benefit," have stimulated the making of studies on the probable impacts of particular developments. Under environmental regulations, the studies are called "environmental impact statements" (EISs) and are supposedly assessments regarding the effects that a proposed project would have on the natural environment. The statements in themselves do not determine whether or not a project will be approved, but they are supposed to aid the decision makers in arriving at their judgments.

Unfortunately, the aid that EISs can give is no better than the studies on which they are based, and the studies are often little more than ritualistic exercises. It is the developer who usually has the responsibility for preparing an EIS. A developer is not likely to retain a consultant who has a reputation for finding adverse impacts. The result is that a "reasonable" consultant is often retained, and the report issued tends to be self-serving.

The task of assessing environmental impact is a complex one, properly requiring the services of experts in several different fields. These experts are not always used in practice, and resulting inadequacies are sometimes obscured through "overkill," i.e., overwhelming readers of the report with masses of trivial and even irrelevant information. If environmental impact statements are ever to realize their potential as means for assessing impact, then some way must be found for having them made by impartial, competent experts.

Impact Zoning

The use of impact studies has now moved beyond the consideration of just the natural environment. Some communities are studying the probable impacts of proposed projects on public facilities and services as well as their impacts on the natural environment. The term "impact zoning" is sometimes used to denote an approach that makes use of such studies to minimize the subjectivity involved in major zoning decisions. Under this approach every major change in land use is handled somewhat like a PUD or a floating zone but with an important difference. The difference is that much more factual information is considered in arriving at a judgment. The developer must submit detailed data on probable impacts that the development would have on the natural environment, public facilities, public services, the growth rate of the locality, and the locality's progress toward inclusion of a reasonable share of housing for lower-income groups and metropolitan-serving land uses.

The burden for obtaining the specific data is not entirely on the developer. The local government must have matching data for the community as a whole, so that a proper evaluation can be made by an impartial planning staff. For example, the planning staff must have available overall information about the capacity of sewers and treatment plants if the impact of additional load from a proposed project is to be assessed adequately. The data file amassed by the local government is sometimes stored in a computer, from which it can be retrieved quickly. The computer can also be used in assessing the impacts of a particular project. Duxbury, Massachusetts, and Bern Township, Pennsylvania, are two examples of communities that are making such use of computers.[6]

The store of information maintained by the local government has another function in addition to that of aiding in the assessment of impact. Developers can have access to it *before* they begin the planning of a specific project. Thus, they can anticipate many of the subsequent findings of the public planners.

Once the impact assessments have been made, a judgment must be made by the elected decision makers of the locality as to whether or not to approve the proposal and, if so, what conditions, if any, should be added. The need

[6]For further information on the application of impact zoning in these communities, see: John Rahenkamp, "Land Use Management: An Alternative To Controls," in Robert W. Burchell and David Listokin (eds.), *Future Land Use*, New Brunswick, N.J.: Center for Urban Policy Research, 1975, pp. 191–199; and "Impact Zoning." *House and Home*, August 1972, pp. 58–67.

for human judgment has not been eliminated, but the potential for an informed judgment with minimum of subjectivity has been greatly enhanced.

An impact assessment that is factually based also enhances the possibility for open and aboveboard negotiations. For example, if the assessment indicated that an off-site sewer line would be overloaded by a proposed project, then the developer and the government would have a rational basis for discussing a financial contribution by the developer toward the cost of replacing it as a condition of approval.

Performance Zoning

Another concept that embodies impact assessment is *performance zoning*. Performance zoning involves less judgment than *impact zoning*. The gist of performance zoning is preannouncement of the level of impacts to be tolerated. A developer who could meet the performance standards specified could be assured of approval. In a way, performance zoning is a further development of the industrial performance standards described in Chapter 2. It encompasses much more, however, taking into consideration the impact of a proposed project on drainage, traffic, and the other factors evaluated in impact zoning, as well as pollution, noise, glare, and vibration.

Conflicting Goals in Impact Assessment

The use of impact assessments is becoming more and more important in the making of zoning decisions. The more widely they are used, the more likely the possibility that their use will become mired in controversy over two conflicting goals. One goal of zoning is to minimize subjectivity in decision making and to maximize the reliance on factual information. Another is to make the process of decision making understandable to the average citizen. These two goals are difficult to reconcile. The goal of greater objectivity seems to require increasingly sophisticated analysis involving terms and quantities intelligible only to expert technicians. The goal of greater understanding by the citizenry apparently demands a much lower level of sophistication. What this conflict will do to zoning is anybody's guess. The clamor for more rational development of our resources can only be satisfied by greater sophistication in analysis. The clamor for self-determination and participatory democracy, together with the widespread popular distrust of technological decisions, can be placated only be a simpler process.

Ironing Out the Inequities in Rezoning

As we pointed out earlier in this chapter, zoning often seems unfair in the unequal burdens and benefits that it confers upon different property owners. The trend toward impact assessment and performance zoning is not likely to alleviate this problem. In fact, it may worsen it. Consequently, there is much discussion these days among planners and lawyers concerning possible ways for ironing out the seeming inequities. Followers of Henry George, the early twentieth-century reformer, still favor taxing away the site value of real estate as an "unearned increment" or windfall conferred on lucky property owners by society. The tax is being applied in some countries under the name of "betterment charge." Britain, for example, enacted such a charge in 1947, later repealed it after it appeared to be stymieing private development, and then reimposed it, but only at forty percent of the "unearned increment." The concept in its original form never seems to have gained much support in the United States and is not now the subject of much serious discussion. Three other concepts for ironing out inequities are being discussed seriously, though. These are *land banking,* the *transfer of development rights,* and *zoning by eminent domain.*

Land Banking

The term "land banking" has more than one meaning. In its simplest and least controversial sense it means the acquisition of undeveloped land for future *public* use before the best sites can be gobbled up by private developers and before speculation can drive up the cost substantially. In the sense in which we are using it here, however, it means the acquisition of large areas of undeveloped land for future public and *private* use.[7] The land thus acquired would be released for private development according to a comprehensive plan that would include statements as to the desired sequence and timing of growth as well as to its other characteristics.

When the public land-banking agency disposed of a tract, it would impose restrictive covenants binding on the purchaser and all subsequent owners just as a private developer would impose. These restrictions would be in greater detail than zoning restrictions normally are. Thus, a purchaser would know at the time of purchase what could and could not be done with the property. The purchase price of the land would reflect the use potential. Property benefiting from restrictions that permitted a high use potential would command a high price; property burdened by restrictions that severely limited its use potential would be available at a comparatively low price. Theoretically, the inequities that now exist in the sharing of benefits and burdens would thereby be eliminated.

The ironing out of inequities is only one motivation for land banking. Proponents also advocate it as a means of curbing speculation, overcoming exclusionary zoning (the land banking agency would be able to override local restrictions), regulating the timing of growth, coordinating public and private investment, and controlling the price of raw land to developers. As Harvey Flechner points out in his book, *Land Banking in the Control of Urban Development,*[8] there are some serious built-in conflicts between the various goals of land banking. Unless these conflicts can be resolved, the future of the concept will remain uncertain at best.

Transferring Development Rights

Unlike land banking, proposals for transferral of development rights (TDR) have a single objective: the sharing of burdens and benefits. As with other new

---

[7]Although land banking in this sense does not exist in the United States, two Canadian cities—Edmonton, Alberta, and Saskatoon, Saskatchewan—are making use of the concept.

[8]Harvey L. Flechner, *Land Banking in the Control of Urban Development,* New York: Praeger, 1974.

concepts relating to zoning, this one has not crystallized into a single coherent package. We will not attempt to summarize the different versions of it but instead will present a very simplified description of how it might work.

Let's assume that Shawnee County has just completed the preparation of a new comprehensive plan and zoning ordinance. The ordinance is drafted so as to carry out the plan's conservation objectives. Several large marshes and one notably scenic outcropping of granite, for example, have been zoned in the proposal so as to permit almost no private development. Two areas, on the other hand, have been zoned as commercial districts permitting floor/area ratios of up to 6.0. [The reader will recall from Chapter 2 that a floor/area ratio (F.A.R.) of 6.0 allows the buildings on a site to contain no more than six times the area of the site.] In the proposed Shawnee County ordinance, every zoning district has been assigned an intensity rating that is based primarily on the F.A.R. permitted but that also incorporates parking, open space, and density provisions.

Now if the proposed ordinance were to be adopted in this form, it is obvious that owners of land zoned for a F.A.R. of 6.0 would benefit greatly, while owners of land zoned for preservation or conservation would experience no benefits. In fact an owner of property zoned effectively for no use might justifiably complain of confiscation. Owners of land having intensity ratings in between these two extremes would receive varying degrees of benefits. (If the assumption that zoning confers benefits is philosophically offensive to some readers, then we suggest that they view the owner of a marsh as receiving the burden of maximum restriction while the lucky owner of the 6.0 F.A.R. has been given the least burden. Either way the problem is viewed, there are inequities.)

To offset the inequities that would be created if the zoning stood alone, Shawnee County has put in its ordinance a section on "development rights." On the effective date of the zoning ordinance every owner of land in the county will be given a certain number of development rights based on the acreage owned. In a very simple version of this concept, the rights might be expressed as so many square feet of floor area, every owner receiving, say, 4500 square feet per acre. In order to develop to a particular intensity, the developer would need *both* the proper *zoning* and the required number of *development rights*. For example, on a five-acre site zoned for a F.A.R. of 6.0, the zoning would permit the construction of 1,306,800 square feet of floor space. (One acre = 43,560 square feet; five acres = 217,800 square feet; and the floor area allowed = 6.0 × 217,800). If each owner is given development rights of 4500 square feet of floor space per acre, then the developer of the five-acre site would have rights to only 5 × 4500 square feet, or 22,500 square feet.

What good is a site where the zoning permits 1,306,800 square feet of floor area if the developer, in acquiring the site, only gets 22,500 square feet in development rights? If the developer acquired the site and nothing else, the answer would be "very little." Something else can be acquired, however— more development rights. They can be bought from another landowner who has a surplus of rights. Take, for example, the owner of a 500-acre marsh zoned for conservation. This owner has 500 × 4500 square feet, or 2,250,000 square feet, of development rights. If 1,284,300 of this amount could be sold to the developer of the 5-acre site and then added to the 22,500 already belonging to the 5-acre site, then there would be enough rights for building to the maximum intensity permitted by the zoning. The owner of the marsh would still possess 965,700 square feet of development rights for sale to other developers. It is conceivable that a bank of sorts could be established for trading in surplus rights.

Zoning by Eminent Domain

Another proposal for offsetting the unequal benefits and burdens experienced by property owners under zoning is called "zoning by eminent domain," or "ZED." Under a ZED system, the property gaining in value from a zoning decision would be subject to special assessment similar to what is often imposed on property benefiting from a public improvement, such as a sewer line, a sidewalk, or a nearby neighborhood park. The special assessment for improvements is based on the argument that a property owner should pay at least a portion of the costs of benefits received from public activity to the extent that such benefits are in excess of those shared by the public at large. An analogous argument is used to justify the special tax assessments under a ZED system. The proceeds of the special ZED assessment would be used to compensate the owners of property that lost value as a result of zoning actions. As would be the case with a system of *transferring development rights,* the payments under a system of *zoning by eminent domain* would compensate property owners for loss of value by transferring resources from one set of land owners to another set. Under ZED, the transfer would have to be administered by an agency of government. Under TDR, on the other hand, development rights might be traded privately.

The Future of Zoning

Zoning by eminent domain and the *transfer of development rights* are only two of several emerging concepts that may alter the nature of zoning over the next decade or so. Just how these new concepts are going to interact with each other to change zoning as we know it, and how they are going to help or hinder in resolving the conflicts and issues that we have described, is not at all certain. Despite Houston's experience, we do not think that zoning will be abolished. It is too popular. Even with its inequities and inefficiencies, zoning is likely to be around for a long time to come. It is sure to change, but we suspect that the change will come slowly. Dramatic change may occur from time to time in a few localities, or in a few states, but several decades might be required for such changes to permeate the many hundreds of ordinances now in existence. We will not attempt, therefore, to predict the rate or form of the future change. The future of zoning belongs in another book.

What we have tried to do in this book is to explain present-day zoning— what it is and how it works—with due regard for the changes that are taking place, but with primary emphasis on the kinds of ordinances that property owners are most likely to encounter now and in the near future. The ordinances now in use have many faults, but they are a concrete reality, and property owners must learn to cope with them. We hope that our book will help the Mary Triggs and the Dan Carters of our society in dealing successfully with a difficult and complex subject.

A Zoning Ordinance from the 1920s

Present-day zoning is a product of years of evolution, and most of today's ordinances still contain significant traces of the earliest models. A reader who wishes to understand why contemporary ordinances are as they are may therefore find some enlightenment in a typical product of the 1920s. Although the first comprehensive zoning was adopted by New York in 1916, the 1920s were the period when most important cities embraced the concept for the first time. We are reproducing, therefore, the text of the ordinance adopted by Memphis, Tennessee, in 1922. This ordinance, although modified for conditions peculiar to Memphis, was much like those enacted by numerous other cities. It differs from most present-day regulations in that there are two zoning maps— one for *use districts* and one for *height, area, and yard districts*. In many respects, however, it is remarkably similar to current ordinances.

The original Memphis ordinance was replaced in 1955 by one that retained some of the original. In 1975, work was begun on a replacement for the 1955 version.

If the reader wonders why we are reproducing a 1922-model ordinance and not a typical one from the present, the answer is simple. Current models are easy to obtain; the classic ones are not.

CITY OF MEMPHIS, TENNESSEE
ZONING ORDINANCE
(As Passed November 7, 1922.)

AN ORDINANCE to regulate and restrict the location of trades and industries and the location of buildings designed for specified uses, to regulate and limit the height and bulk of buildings hereafter erected or altered, to regulate and determine the area of yards, courts and other open spaces surrounding buildings, to regulate and limit the density of population, and for said purpose to divide the city into districts and prescribe penalties for the violation of its provisions and to provide for its enforcement.

WHEREAS, by the provisions of Chapter 165 of the Private Acts of the General Assembly of the State of Tennessee for the year 1921, authority is conferred upon the

City of Memphis to establish districts or zones within its corporate limits for the purpose of better regulating the use of land and controlling the density of population to the end that congestion upon the public streets may be lessened, the public health, safety, convenience, and general welfare promoted; and,

WHEREAS, the City Planning Commission, created under the provisions of Chapter 162 of the Private Acts of 1921, pursuant to the provisons of Section 4 of said Chapter 165 and resolutions of the Board of Commissioners of the City of Memphis duly adopted, has recommended boundaries or districts, and appropriate regulations to be enforced therein, and public hearings having been held, at which all owners of property affected were given ample opportunity, after public notice by advertisement, to file their protests or criticisms, if any they had; and,

WHEREAS, the passage, promulgation and enforcement of the provisions hereinafter contained are deemed to be necessary to the carrying out of the governmental powers delegated to and possessed by the City of Memphis for securing the objects hereinbefore expressed: therefore:

SECTION 1. DEFINITIONS

Be it ordained by the Board of Commissioners of the City of Memphis, that for the purpose of this ordinance certain terms and words are herewith defined, as follows:

Words used in the present tense include the future; words in the singular number include the plural number, and words in the plural number include the singular number; the word "building" includes the word "structure"; the word "shall" is mandatory and not directory. Any words not herein defined shall be construed as defined in the building code.

ALLEY: A public thoroughfare not over twenty (20) feet wide.

APARTMENT HOUSE: A building or portion thereof used or intended to be used as the home of three or more families or households living independently of each other.

BASEMENT: A story partly under ground, which, if not occupied for living purposes by other than the janitor or his family, shall not be included as a story for purpose of height measurements.

BOARDING HOUSE: A building, other than a hotel, where lodging and meals, for five or more persons, are served for compensation.

BUILDING: A structure having a roof supported by columns or walls for the shelter, support or enclosure of persons, animals or chattels; and when separated by division walls from the ground up, and without openings, each portion of such building shall be deemed a separate building except as provided in Section 16.

CURB LEVEL: The mean level of the established curb in front of the building.

DEPTH OF REAR YARD: The minimum horizontal distance between the rear line of a building other than a building for an accessory use, and the center line of the alley, where an alley exists, otherwise the rear lot line.

DEPTH OF LOT: The mean horizontal distance between the front and rear lot lines.

HEIGHT OF BUILDING: The vertical distance measured from the curb level to the highest point of the roof surface, if a flat roof; to the deck line of mansard roofs, and to the mean height level between eaves and ridge for gable, hip and gambrel roofs. For buildings set back from the street line the height of the building may be measured from the average elevation of the finished grade along the front of the building, provided its distance from the street line is not less than the height of such grade above the established curb level.

HEIGHT OF COURT OR YARD: The vertical distance from the lowest level of such court or yard to the highest point of any bounding wall.

HOTEL: A building occupied as the more or less temporary abiding place of individuals who are lodged with or without meals, in which, as a rule, the rooms are occupied singly for hire, in which provision is not made for cooking in any individual apartment, and in which there are more than twelve (12) sleeping rooms, a public dining room for the accommodation of more than twelve (12) guests, and a general kitchen.

INNER COURT: An open, unoccupied space surrounded on all sides by walls, or by walls and a lot line.

LENGTH OF OUTER COURT: The mean horizontal distance between the open and closed ends of the court.

LODGING HOUSE: A building, other than a hotel, where lodging for five (5) or more persons is provided for compensation.

LOT: Land occupied or to be occupied by a building and its accessory buildings, and including such open spaces as are required under this ordinance, and having its principal frontage upon a public street or officially approved place.

LOT, CORNER: A lot situated at the junction of two or more streets, and having a width not greater than fifty (50) feet.

LOT, INTERIOR: A lot other than a corner lot.

LOT, THROUGH: An interior lot having frontage on two streets.

LOT LINES: The lines bounding a lot as defined herein.

NON-CONFORMING USE: A building or premises occupied by a use that does not conform with the regulations of the use district in which it is situated.

ONE-FAMILY DWELLING: A detached building having accommodations for and oc-cupied by only one family.

OUTER COURT: An open reserved space on the same lot with a building, extending to and opening upon a street, alley or yard.

PLACE: An open unoccupied space reserved for purposes of access for abutting property.

PORCH: A roofed space open on three sides; one or two stories in height.

PRIVATE GARAGE: A garage with capacity for not more than three (3) steam or motor-driven vehicles, for storage only, for private use and not more than one space in which shall be rented to persons not occupants of the premises. Of the vehicles allowed not more than one shall be a commercial motor-driven vehicle. A private garage may exceed a three (3) vehicle capacity, provided the area of the lot whereon such a private garage is to be located shall contain not less than twenty-five hundred (2,500) square feet for each vehicle stored.

PUBLIC GARAGE: Any premises, except those described as a private garage, used for housing or care of more than three (3) steam or motor-driven vehicles, or where any such vehicles are equipped for operation, repaired, or kept for remuneration, hire or sale.

PRIVATE STABLE: A stable with a capacity for not more than four horses or mules.

PUBLIC STABLE: A stable with a capacity for more than four horses or mules.

REAR YARD: A space, unoccupied except by a building or accessory use as hereinafter permitted, extending for the full width of the lot between a building other than a building of accessory use and the rear lot line.

ROW HOUSE: A row of attached dwellings erected simultaneously, each dwelling having accommodations for one family only.

SETBACK: The minimum horizontal distance between the front line or any projection of the building, excluding steps and unenclosed porches, and the street line.

SIDE YARD: An open, unoccupied space on the same lot with a building between the building and the side line of the lot and extending from the street line to the rear yard.

STREET: A public thoroughfare more than twenty (20) feet wide.

STORY: That portion of a building included between the surface of any floor and the surface of the floor next above it, or if there be no floor above it, then the space between such floor and the ceiling next above it.

STORY, HALF: That portion of a building, in the "A" Height and Area District, between the surface of the floor above the second story and the finished ceiling line underneath the roof. This half story shall not have an average height of more than eight feet covering a floor area of more than seventy-five (75) per cent of the area of the floor on the first story below.

STRUCTURAL ALTERATIONS: Any change in the supporting members of a building, such as bearing walls, columns, beams or girders.

TENEMENT HOUSE: See "Apartment House."

TWO-FAMILY DWELLING: A detached or semi-detached building having separate accommodations for and occupied as a dwelling by two (2) famillies.

SECTION 2.   USE DISTRICT REGULATIONS

Be it further ordained, that in order to regulate and restrict the location of trades and industries and the location of buildings erected or altered for specified uses, the City of Memphis is hereby divided into "USE DISTRICTS," of which there shall be five, known as:

"A" Residence District.

"B" Residence District.

"C" Commercial District.

"D" Industrial District.

"E" Unrestricted District.

The City of Memphis is hereby divided into five (5) districts, aforesaid, and the boundaries of such districts are shown upon the map attached hereto and made a part of this ordinance, being designated as the "USE DISTRICT MAP," and said map and all the notations, references and other things shown thereon shall be as much a part of this ordinance as if the matters and things set forth by said map were all fully described herein.

Except as hereinafter provided, no building shall be erected or altered, nor shall any building or premises be used for any purpose other than is permitted in the Use District in which such building or premises is located.

SECTION 3. "A" RESIDENCE DISTRICT

Be it further ordained, that in the "A" Residence District no building or premises shall be used and no building shall be hereafter erected or structurally altered, unless otherwise provided in this ordinance, except for one or more of the following uses:

1. One-Family Dwellings.

2. Two-Family Dwellings.

3. Churches.

4. Schools.

5. Libraries.

6. Farming and Truck Gardening.

7. Accessory buildings, including one private garage or private stable when located not less than 60 feet from the front lot line, or a private garage in a (fireproof) compartment as a part of the main building.

8. Uses customarily incident to any of the above uses when located on the same lot and not involving the conduct of a business; including also home occupations engaged in by the occupants of a dwelling not involving the conduct of a business on the premises, and including also the office of a physician, surgeon, dentist, musician or artist, when situated in the same dwelling used by such physician, surgeon, dentist, musician or artist as his or her private dwelling; provided no name plate exceeding one (1) square foot in area, containing the name and occupation of the occupant of the premises, nor a sign exceeding eight (8) square feet in area appertaining to the lease, hire or sale of a building or premises, nor advertising sign of any other character shall be permitted in any "A" residence district.

SECTION 4. "B" RESIDENCE DISTRICT

Be it further ordained, that in the "B" Residence District no building or premises shall be used and no building shall be hereafter erected or structurally altered unless otherwise provided in this ordinance, except for one or more of the following uses:

1. Any use permitted in the "A" Residence District.

2. Apartment Houses.

3. Hotels.

4. Private Clubs, Fraternities, Lodges, excepting those the chief activity of which is a service customarily carried on as a business.

5. Boarding and Lodging Houses.

6. Hospitals and Clinics.

7. Institutions of an educational, philanthropic or eleemosynary nature.

8. Nurseries and Greenhouses for the propagating and cultivation and growing of plants only.

9. Accessory buildings and uses customarily incident to any of the above uses when located on the same lot and not involving the conduct of a business.

10. Public garages, for storage purposes only, and where no repair facilities are maintained, when located not less than sixty (60) feet from the front lot line, and not less than

thirty (30) feet from any other street line on which the property faces; provided that before permit is issued there are on file in the office of the Commissioner of Public Utilities, Grounds and Buildings the written consents of the owners of seventy-five (75) per cent of the property within five hundred (500) feet of any part of the premises whereon such public garage is to be established, and not separated therefrom by more than one (1) street or one (1) alley; provided, further, that no public garage shall have an entrance or exit for motor vehicles within two hundred (200) feet of an entrance or exit for motor vehicles within two hundred (200) feet of an entrance or exit of a public or private school, playground, public library, church, hospital, children's or old people's home, or other similar public or semi-public institutions.

SECTION 5. "C" COMMERCIAL DISTRICT

Be it further ordained, that in the "C" Commercial District, all buildings and premises, except as otherwise provided in this ordinance, may be used for any use permitted in the "B" Residence district or for any other use except the following:

1. Bakery (employing more than five (5) persons).

2. Blacksmith or Horseshoeing Shop.

3. Bottling Works.

4. Building material storage yard.

5. Carting, express, haulting or storage yard.

6. Contractor's plant or storage yard.

7. Coal, coke or wood yard.

8. Cooperage works.

9. Dyeing and cleaning works (employing more than five (5) persons).

10. Ice Plant or Storage House of more than five (5) tons capacity.

11. Laundry (employing more than five (5) persons).

12. Livery Stable.

13. Lumber Yard.

14. Machine Shop.

15. Milk Distributing Station.

16. Stone Yard or Monument Works.

17. Storage Warehouse.

18. All uses excluded from the "D" Industrial District.

19. Any kind of manufacture or treatment other than the manufacture or treatment of products clearly incidental to the conduct of a retail business conducted on the premises.

20. Public Garages: Provided, however, that special permits for the location and maintenance of public garages shall be granted by the Commissioner of Public Utilities, grounds and Buildings, when there shall be on file with said Commissioner the written consents of the owners of 75 per cent of the area of all the property within two hundred (200) feet of any part of the premises whereon such public garage is to be established, erected or enlarged. Provided, further, that no public garage shall have an entrance or exit for motor vehicles within two hundred (200) feet of an entrance or exit of a public or private school,

playground, public library, church, hospital, children's or old people's home, or other similar public or semi-public institutions.

SECTION 6. "D" INDUSTRIAL DISTRICT

Be it further ordained, that in the "D" Industrial District all buildings and premises except as otherwise provided in this ordinance may be used for any use permitted in the "C" Commercial District or for any other use except the following:

1. Abattoirs.
2. Acetylene gas manufacture.
3. Acid manufactures.
4. Ammonia, Bleaching Powder or Chlorine manufacture.
5. Arsenal.
6. Asphalt manufacture or refining.
7. Blast Furnace.
8. Boiler Works.
9. Brick, Tile or Terra Cotta manufacture.
10. Candle manufacture.
11. Bag cleaning.
12. Celluloid manufacture.
13. Coke Ovens.
14. Cotton Gin.
15. Crematory.
16. Creosote treatment or manufacture.
17. Disinfectants manufacture.
18. Distillation of Bones, Coal or Wood.
19. Dyestuff manufacture.
20. Exterminator and Insect Poison manufacture.
21. Emery Cloth and Sand Paper manufacture.
22. Fat Rendering.
23. Fertilizer manufacture.
24. Fireworks or Explosive manufacture or storage.
25. Fish Smoking and Curing.
26. Forge Plant.
27. Gas (illuminating or heating) manufacture.
28. Glue, Size or Gelatine manufacture.
29. Gunpowder manufacture or storage.

30. Incineration or Reduction of Garbage, Dead Animals, Offal or Refuse.

31. Iron, Steel, Brass or Copper Foundry.

32. Lamp Black manufactures.

33. Oilcloth or Linoleum manufacture.

34. Oiled, Rubber or Leather Goods manufacture.

35. Ore Reduction.

36. Paint, Oil, Shellac, Turpentine or Varnish manufacture.

37. Paper and Pulp manufacture.

38. Petroleum Products, refining or wholesale storage of Petroleum.

39. Plating Works.

40. Potash Works.

41. Printing Ink manufacture.

42. Pyroxylin manufacture.

43. Rock Crusher.

44. Rolling Mill.

45. Rubber or Gutta Percha manufacture or treatment.

46. Salt Works.

47. Sauer Kraut manufacture.

48. Sausage manufacture.

49. Ship Yard.

50. Shoe Blacking manufacture.

51. Smelters.

52. Soap manufacture.

53. Soda and Compound manufacture.

54. Stock Yards.

55. Stone Mill or Quarry.

56. Storage or Baling of Scrap Paper, Iron, Bottles, Rags or Junk.

57. Stove Polish manufacture.

58. Sulphuric, Nitric, or Hydrochloric Acid manufacture.

59. Tallow, Grease or Lard manufacture or refining from animal fat.

60. Tanning, Curing or Storage of Rawhides or Skins.

61. Tar Distillation or manufacture.

62. Tar Roofing or Water Proofing manufacture.

63. Tobacco (chewing) manufacture or treatment.

64. Vinegar manufacture.

65. Wool Pulling or Scouring.

66. Yeast plant.

67. And in general those uses which have been declared a nuisance in any court of record, or which may be obnoxious, or offensive by reason of the emission of odor, dust, smoke, gas or noise.

SECTION 7. "E" UNRESTRICTED DISTRICT

Be it further ordained, that in the "E" Unrestricted District buildings and premises may be used for any purposes whatsoever, not in conflict with any ordinance of the City of Memphis regulating nuisances.

SECTION 8. NON-CONFORMING USES

Be it further ordained, that the lawful use of land existing at the time of adoption of this ordinance, although such use does not conform to the provisions hereof, may be continued, but if such non-conforming use is discontinued, any future use of said premises shall be in conformity with the provisions of this ordinance.

The lawful use of a building existing at the time of the adoption of this ordinance may be continued, although such use does not conform with the provisions hereof, and such use may be extended throughout the building, provided no structural alterations, except those required by law or ordinance, are made therein. If no structural alterations are made, a non-conforming use of a building may be changed to any use permitted in the same use district as that in which the use existing at the time of the adoption of this ordinance is permitted, according to the provisions of this ordinance. Whenever a use district shall be hereafter changed, any then existing non-conforming use in such changed district may be continued or changed to a use permitted in the same use district as that in which the existing use is permitted, provided all other regulations governing the new use are complied with. Whenever a non-conforming use of a building has been changed to a more restricted use or to a conforming use, such use shall not thereafter be changed to a less restricted use.

SECTION 9. BILL BOARDS AND SIGN BOARDS

Be it further ordained, that it shall be unlawful for any person, firm or corporation to erect or construct any bill board or sign board in the "A" Residence District as defined in this ordinance. It shall be unlawful for any person, firm or corporation to erect or construct any bill board or sign board in the "B" Residence District as defined in this ordinance, without first obtaining the consent in writing from the owners or duly authorized agents of said owners owning at least seventy-five per cent of the frontage of the property on both sides of the street in the block in which said bill board or sign board shall be erected, constructed or located. It shall be unlawful for any person, firm or corporation to erect or construct any bill board or sign board in the "C" Commercial District as defined in this ordinance, without first obtaining the consent in writing from the owners owning the majority frontage of the property on both sides of the street in the block in which said bill board or sign board shall be erected, constructed or located. The written consent required in the "B" Residence District and the "C" Commercial District shall be filed with the Commissioner of Public Utilities, Grounds and Buildings before a permit shall be issued for the erection, construction or location of such bill board or sign board.

SECTION 10. HEIGHT AND AREA DISTRICT REGULATIONS

Be it further ordained, that in order to regulate and limit the height and bulk of buildings hereafter erected or altered; to regulate and determine the area of yards, courts and other open spaces surrounding buildings, and to regulate and limit the density of population, the City of Memphis is hereby divided into districts, of which there shall be five (5), known as:

"A" Height and Area District.

"B" Height and Area District.

"C" Height and Area District.

"D" Height and Area District.

"E" Height and Area District.

The boundaries of such districts, shown upon the map attached hereto and made a part of this ordinance, are hereby established, said map being designated as the "Height and Area District Map," and said map and all the notations, references and other information shown thereon shall be as much a part of this ordinance as if the matters and information set forth by said map were all fully described herein.

Except as hereinafter provided, no building shall be erected or structurally altered except in conformity with the regulations herein established for the height and area district in which such building is located.

No lot area shall be so reduced or diminished that the yards or open spaces shall be smaller than prescribed by this ordinance.

SECTION 11. "A" HEIGHT AND AREA DISTRICT

Be it further ordained, that in the "A" Height and Area District the height of buildings, the minimum dimensions of yards and courts, and the minimum lot area per family shall be as follows:

HEIGHT: No building hereafter erected or structurally altered shall exceed thirty-five (35) feet or two and one-half (2 1/2) stories. See Section 16 (a) and (b).

REAR YARD: There shall be a rear yard having a minimum depth of twenty-five (25) feet. See Section 16 (i).

SIDE YARD: There shall be a side yard on each side of a building of not less than five (5) feet in width, provided, however, that on a lot having a width of less than forty (40) feet and held under a distinct ownership from adjacent lots, and of record at the time of the passage of this ordinance, there shall be a side yard on each side of a building of not less than three (3) feet in width. See Section 16 (g) and (i).

OUTER COURT: The least dimension of an outer court shall be not less than five (5) feet, nor less than two (2) inches for each foot of height of such court, nor less than two (2) inches for each foot of length of such court from the closed end. See Section (i).

INNER COURT: The least dimension of an inner court shall not be less than six (6) feet, nor less than two and one-half (2 1/2) inches for each foot of height of such court, nor shall its area be less than twice the square of its required least dimension.

SETBACK: There shall be a setback line of not less than thirty (30) feet for the building line and a minimum of twenty (20) feet for the front line of any porch, provided that when twenty-five (25) per cent or more of all the frontage on one side of a street between two intersecting streets at the time of the passage of this ordinance has been built up with buildings having a minimum setback line of more, or of less, than thirty (30) feet from the street line, no building hereafter erected or structurally altered shall project beyond the minimum setback line so established; provided, further, that this regulation shall not be so interpreted as to reduce the buildable width of a corner lot facing an intersecting street, held under a separate and distinct ownership from adjacent lots and of record at the time of the passage of this ordinance, to less than thirty-four (34) feet.

LOT AREA PER FAMILY: Every building hereafter erected or structurally altered which is located in the "A" Residence District and the "A" Height and Area District shall provide a lot area of not less than three thousand seven hundred and fifty (3,750) square feet per family; provided, however, that where a lot held under a distinct ownership from adjacent lots and of record at the time of the passage of this ordinance has less area than herein required, this regulation shall not apply.

Every building hereafter erected or structurally altered which is located in the "B" Residence District and the "A" Height and Area District shall provide a lot area of not less than two thousand (2,000) square feet per family.

SECTION 12. "B" HEIGHT AND AREA DISTRICT

Be it further ordained, that in the "B" Height and Area District the height of buildings, the minimum dimensions of yards and courts, and the minimum lot area per family shall be as follows:

HEIGHT: No building hereafter erected or structurally altered shall exceed forty-five (45) feet or three stories. See Section 16 (a).

REAR YARD: There shall be a rear yard having a depth of not less than twenty-five (25) feet. See Section 16 (i).

SIDE YARD: There shall be a side yard on each side of a building of not less than five (5) feet in width, provided, however, that on a lot having a width of less than forty (40) feet and held under a distinct ownership from adjacent lots, and of record at the time of the adoption of this ordinance, there shall be a side yard on each side of a building of not less than three (3) feet in width. A side yard shall in no case be less than one (1) inch in width for each foot of building length. See Section 16 (g) and (i).

OUTER COURT: The least dimension of an outer court shall be not less than five (5) feet, nor less than two (2) inches for each foot of height of such court, nor less than two (2) inches for each foot of length of such court from the closed end. See Section 16 (i).

INNER COURT: The least dimension of an inner court shall not be less than six (6) feet, nor less than two and one-half (2 1/2) inches for each foot of height of such court, nor shall its area be less than twice the square of its required least dimension.

SETBACK: There shall be a setback line of not less than thirty (30) feet for the building line and a minimum of twenty (20) feet for the front line of any porch; provided, that when twenty-five (25) per cent or more of all the frontage on one side of a street between two intersecting streets at the time of the passage of this ordinance has been built up with buildings having a minimum setback line of more, or of less, than thirty (30) feet from the street line, no building hereafter erected or structurally altered shall project beyond the minimum setback line so established; provided, that no building shall be required to set back more than forty (40) feet in any case; and provided further, that this regulation shall not be so interpreted as to reduce the buildable width of a corner lot facing an intersecting street, held under a separate and distinct ownership from adjacent lots and of record at the time of the passage of this ordinance, to less than thirty-four (34) feet. Where all the frontage on one side of a street between two intersecting streets is located in a "C" Commercial, "D" Industrial, or "E" Unrestricted District, and a "B" Height and Area District, the setback regulations may be waived.

LOT AREA PER FAMILY: Every building hereafter erected or altered shall provide a lot area of not less than one thousand (1,000) square feet per family.

SECTION 13.   "C" HEIGHT AND AREA DISTRICT

Be it further ordained, that in the "C" Height and Area District the height of buildings, the minimum dimensions of yards and courts, and the minimum lot area per family shall be as follows:

HEIGHT: No building hereafter erected or structurally altered shall exceed ninety (90) feet or eight (8) stories.

REAR YARD: There shall be a rear yard of not less than twenty-five (25) feet. See Section 16 (i).

SIDE YARD: There shall be a side yard on each side of the building having a width of not less than six (6) feet. A side yard shall in no case be less than one (1) inch wide for each foot of building height nor less than one and one-half (1 1/2) inches wide for each foot of building length. See Section 16 (g) and (i).

OUTER COURT: The least dimension of an outer court shall not be less than five (5) feet, nor less than two (2) inches for each foot of height of such court, nor less than two (2) inches for each foot of length of such court from the closed end. See Section 16 (i).

INNER COURT: The least dimension of an inner court shall not be less than six (6) feet, nor less than two and one-half (2 1/2) inches for each foot of height of such court, nor shall its area be less than twice the square of its required least dimension.

SETBACK: There shall be a setback line of not less than thirty (30) feet for the building line and a minimum of twenty (20) feet for the front line of any porch, provided that when twenty-five (25) per cent or more of all the frontage on one side of a street between two intersecting streets at the time of the passage of this ordinance has been built up with buildings having a minimum setback line of more, or less, than twenty (20) feet from the street line, no building hereafter erected or structurally altered shall project beyond the minimum setback line so established; provided, that no building shall be required to set back more than forty (40) feet in any case; and provided, that this regulation shall not be so interpreted as to reduce the buildable width of a corner lot facing an intersecting street, held under a separate and distinct ownership from adjacent lots and of record at the time of the passage of this ordinance, to less than thirty-four (34) feet; provided, however, when all the frontage on one side of a street between two intersecting streets is located in a "C" Commercial, "D" Industrial, or "E" Unrestricted District, and a "C" Height and Area District, the setback regulations may be waived.

LOT AREA PER FAMILY: Every building hereafter erected or structurally altered shall provide a lot area of not less than six hundred twenty-five (625) square feet per family.

SECTION 14.   "D" HEIGHT AND AREA DISTRICT

Be it further ordained, that in the "D" Height and Area District the height of buildings and the minimum dimensions of yards and courts shall be as follows, provided, however, all buildings or parts of buildings hereafter erected or structurally altered for residential purposes shall conform to the regulations of the "C" Height and Area District (Section 13).

HEIGHT: No building hereafter erected or structurally altered shall exceed ninety (90) feet or eight (8) stories.

REAR YARD: There shall be a rear yard of not less than ten (10) feet. Section 16 (i).

SIDE YARD: A side yard, if provided, shall be not less than five (5) feet. See Section 16 (i).

OUTER COURT: The least dimension of an outer court shall be not less than five (5) feet wide, nor less than two (2) inches wide for each foot of height of such court, and not less than two (2) inches wide for each foot of length of such court from the enclosed end. See Section 16 (i).

INNER COURT: The least dimension of an inner court shall be not less than six (6) feet wide, nor less than two (2) inches wide for each foot of height of such court, nor shall its area be less than twice the square of its required least dimension.

SECTION 15. "E" HEIGHT AND AREA DISTRICT

Be it further ordained, that in the "E" Height and Area District the height of buildings and the minimum dimensions of yards and courts shall be as follows; provided, however, all buildings, or parts of buildings, hereafter erected or structurally altered for residential purpose shall conform to the regulations of the "C" Height and Area District (Section 13).

HEIGHT: No building hereafter erected or structurally altered shall exceed one hundred and fifty (150) feet or twelve (12) stories.

SIDE YARD: A side yard, if provided, shall be not less than five (5) feet wide. See Section 16 (i).

OUTER COURT: The least dimension of an outer court shall be not less than five (5) feet wide, nor less than two (2) inches wide for each foot of height of such court, nor less than two (2) inches wide for each foot of length of such court from the enclosed end. See Section 16 (i).

INNER COURT: The least dimension of an inner court shall be not less than six (6) feet wide, nor less than two (2) inches wide for each foot of height of such court, nor shall its area be less than twice the square of its required least dimension.

SECTION 16. HEIGHT AND AREA DISTRICT EXCEPTIONS

Be it further ordained, that the foregoing requirements in the height and area district shall be subject to the following exceptions and regulations:

HEIGHT: (a) That in the "A" and "B" Height and Area Districts, public or semi-public buildings, hospitals, sanitariums or schools may be erected to a height not exceeding seventy-five (75) feet, when set back from all lot lines not less than one foot for each foot such buildings exceed thirty-five (35) and forty-five (45) feet, respectively, in height.

(b) One- and two-family dwellings in the "A" Height and Area District may be increased in height by not more than ten (10) feet when two (2) side yards of not less than fifteen (15) feet each are provided. Such dwellings, however, shall not exceed three (3) stories in height.

(c) Parapet walls not exceeding four feet in height, chimneys, cooling towers, elevator bulkheads, fire towers, gas tanks, grain elevators, pent houses, stacks, stage towers or scenery lofts, sugar refineries, tanks, water towers, radio towers, ornamental towers, monuments, cupolas, domes and spires and necessary mechanical appurtenances may be erected as to their height in accordance with existing or hereafter adopted ordinances of the City of Memphis.

(d) In the one hundred fifty (150) foot height district, towers for occupancy may be erected above the height limit herein established, provided the largest horizontal dimension of any such tower shall not exceed sixty (60) feet, provided the total area shall not exceed twenty-five (25) per cent of the area of the lot, and provided that each such tower shall be removed at least twenty-five (25) feet from every lot line other than a street line, and at least fifty feet from any other tower.

(e) On through lots one hundred (100) feet or less in depth the height of a building may be measured from the curb level on either street. On through lots more than one hundred (100) feet in depth the height regulations and basis of height measurements for the street permitting the greater height shall apply to a depth of not more than one hundred (100) feet from that street.

AREA: (f) For purposes of the area regulations a semi-detached dwelling, or row house, in the "B" Residence District may be considered as one building and occupying one lot.

(g) A commercial building in the "A," "B" and "C" Height and Area Districts may waive the requirements for side yards, but if a side yard be provided it shall have a minimum width as required.

(h) Buildings on through lots and running through from street to street may waive the requirements for a rear yard by furnishing an equivalent open space in lieu of such required rear yard.

(i) In computing the depth of a rear yard or the width of a side yard or outer court for any building where such yard or court opens onto an alley or street, one-half of such alley or street may be assumed to be a portion of the yard or court.

(j) Every part of a required yard or court shall be open from its lowest point to the sky unobstructed, except for the ordinary projections of skylight above the bottom of such yard or court, and except for the projection of sills, belt courses, cornices and ornamental features not to exceed four (4) inches.

(k) No cornice shall project over the street line more than five (5) per cent of the width of such street, and shall in no case project more than four (4) feet.

(l) Open or lattice enclosed fire escapes, fireproof outside stairways and balconies opening upon fire towers, projecting into a yard not more than five (5) feet or into a court not more than three and one-half (3 1/2) feet, and the ordinary projections of chimneys and flues, may be permitted by the Commissioner of Public Utilities, Grounds and Buildings, where same are so placed as not to obstruct the light and ventilation.

SECTION 17.   ADMINISTRATIVE BOARD

Be it further ordained, that an Administrative Board is hereby established. The word "Board" when used in this section shall be construed to mean the Administrative Board. The City Planning Commission shall be the Administrative Board.

MEETINGS: Meetings of the board shall be held at least once a month. There shall be a fixed place of meeting and all meetings shall be open to the public. The Board shall adopt its own rules of procedure, and keep a record of its proceedings, showing the action of the Board and the vote of each member upon each question considered. The presence of five (5) members shall be necessary to constitute a quorum.

APPEAL: Appeal from the ruling of the Commissioner of Public Utilities, Grounds and Buildings concerning the enforcement of the provisions of this ordinance may be made to the Administrative Board within such time as shall be prescribed by the Board by general rule. The appellant shall file with the Commissioner of Public Utilities, Grounds and Buildings and with the Administrative Board a notice of appeal, specifying the grounds thereof. The Commissioner of Public Utilities, Grounds and Buildings shall forthwith transmit to the Administrative Board all the papers constituting the record upon which the action appealed from was taken.

JURISDICTION: In specific cases the Administrative Board may authorize by permit a variation of the application of the use, height and area district regulations herein established in harmony with their general purpose and intent, as follows:

(1) Grant a permit for a temporary building for a commerce or industry in a residence district which is incidental to the residential development, such permit to be issued for a period of not more than one (1) year.

(2) Grant a permit for the reconstruction, within twelve months, of a building located in a district restricted against its use, which has been destroyed by fire or other calamity, to the extent of not more than seventy-five (75) per cent of its assessed value.

(3) Grant a permit for the extension of a use or height and area district for a distance of not more than twenty-five (25) feet, where the boundary line of a district divides a lot in a single ownership at the time of the adoption of this ordinance.

(4) Grant a permit for the alteration or enlargement of an existing building located in a district restricted against its use, where such alteration or enlargement is a necessary incident to the business existing at the time of the adoption of this ordinance; provided, however, that such alteration shall not unduly prolong the life of the building, and provided further, that any such enlargement shall be in no case more than fifty (50) feet from an existing structure and on property in the same ownership as the existing structure at the time of the passage of this ordinance.

(5) Grant a permit for the erection and use of a building or the use of a premises in any location to a public service corporation or for public utility purposes which the Board admits reasonably necessary for the public convenience or welfare.

(6) Grant a permit in an industrial district for a building or use otherwise excluded from such district, provided such building or use is distinctly incidental and essential to a use permitted in an industrial district, provided such incidental building or use occupies nor more than ten per cent of the lot, provided that no more than ten per cent of the employes of the building or plant are engaged therein, and provided that such building or use is not located within fifty feet of any street or lot line.

(7) Interpret the provisions of this ordinance in such a way as to carry out the intent and purpose of the plan, as shown upon the maps fixing the several districts accompanying and made a part of this ordinance where the street layout actually on the ground varies from the street layout as shown on the maps aforesaid.

(8) Interpret the provisions of this ordinance in harmony with their fundamental purpose and intent where practical difficulties or unnecessary hardships occur.

(9) Adopt from time to time such rules and regulations as may be deemed necessary to carry into effect the provisions of this ordinance.

SECTION 18. CERTIFICATE OF OCCUPANCY AND COMPLIANCE

Be it further ordained, that no building hereafter erected or altered shall be occupied, used or changed in use until a cerficate of occupancy and compliance shall have been issued by the Commissioner of Public Utilities, Grounds and Buildings, stating that the building or proposed use of a building, or premises, complies with all the building and health laws and ordinances and with the provisions of these regulations.

Certificates of occupancy and compliance shall be applied for coincident with the application for a building permit and shall be issued within ten (10) days after the erection or structural alteration of such buildings shall have been completed in conformity with the provisions of these regulations. A record of all certificates shall be kept on file in the office of the Commissioner of Public Utilities, Grounds and Buildings, and copies shall be furnished, on request, to any person having a proprietary or tenancy interest in the building affected. No fee shall be charged for an original certificate, but for copies of any original certificate there shall be a charge of fifty cents each.

No permit for excavation for any building shall be issued before application has been made for certificate of occupancy and compliance.

The use of no building already erected at the passage of this ordinance shall be changed from one class of use to another unless and until a certificate of occupancy and compliance with the provisions of this ordinance shall have been obtained from the Commissioner of Public Utilities, Grounds and Buildings.

SECTION 19. PLATS

Be it further ordained, that all applications for building permits shall be accompanied by a plat in duplicate drawn to scale, showing the actual dimensions of the lot to be built upon, the size of the building to be erected, and such other information as may be necessary to provide for the enforcement of these regulations. A careful record of such applications and plats shall be kept in the office of the Commissioner of Public Utilities, Grounds and Buildings. No yard, court or other open space provided about any building for the purpose of complying with the provisions of these regulations shall again be used as a yard, court or other open space for another building.

SECTION 20. INTERPRETATION, PURPOSE AND CONFLICT

Be it further ordained, that in interpreting and applying the provisions of this ordinance, they shall be held to be the minimum requirements for the promotion of the public safety, health, convenience, comfort, prosperity and general welfare. It is not intended by this ordinance to interfere with or abrogate or annul any easements, covenants or other agreements between parties; provided, however, that where this ordinance imposes a greater restriction upon the use of building or premises or upon height of building, or required by other ordinances, rules, regulations or permits, or by easements, covenants or agreements, the provisions of this ordinance shall control.

SECTION 21. VIOLATION, PENALTY

Be it further ordained, that any person, firm or corporation who violates, disobeys, omits, neglects or refuses to comply with or who resists the enforcement of any of the provisions of this ordinance shall be fined not less than five (5) dollars or more than fifty (50) dollars or more than fifty (50) dollars for each offense. Each day that a violation is permitted to exist shall constitute a separate offense.

SECTION 22. BOUNDARIES OF DISTRICTS

Be it further ordained, that where uncertainty exists with respect to the boundaries of the various districts as shown on the maps accompanying and made a part of this ordinance, the following rules shall apply:

(a) The district boundaries are either streets or alleys, unless otherwise shown, and where the designation on the maps accompanying and made a part of this ordinance indicating the various districts are approximately bounded by street or alley line, said street or alley shall be construed to be the boundary of such district.

(b) Where the district boundaries are not otherwise indicated and where the property has been or may hereafter be divided into blocks and lots, the district boundaries shall be construed to be lot lines, and where the designations on the maps accompanying and made a part of this ordinance indicating the various districts are approximately bounded by lot lines, said lot line shall be construed to be the boundary of such district, unless said boundaries are otherwise indicated on the maps.

(c) In unsubdivided property the district boundary lines on the maps accompanying and made a part of this ordinance shall be determined by use of the scale contained on such maps.

SECTION 23. VALIDITY

Be it further ordained, that should any section, clause or provision of this ordinance be declared by the courts to be invalid, the same shall not affect the validity of the ordinance as a whole or any part thereof, other than the part so declared to be invalid.

SECTION 24. CHANGES AND AMENDMENTS

Be it further ordained, that the Board of Commissioners of the City of Memphis may, from time to time, amend, supplement or change by ordinance the boundaries of districts or regulations herein established. Any proposed amendment, supplement or change shall first be submitted to the City Planning Commission for its recommendation and report.

A public hearing shall be held by the Board of Commissioners before adoption of any proposed amendment, supplement or change, notice of which hearing shall be given by publishing three (3) times in some daily newspaper of general circulation, stating the time and place of such hearing, not earlier than ten (10) days from the last date of such publication.

If a protest against any proposed amendment, supplement or change be presented in writing to the city clerk, within ten days from date of last publication, duly signed and acknowledged by the owners of twenty (20) per cent or more of any frontage proposed to be altered, or by the owners of twenty (20) per cent of the frontage immediately in the rear thereof, or by the owners of twenty (20) per cent of the frontage directly opposite the frontage proposed to be altered, such amendment, supplement or change shall not be passed except by a four-fifths vote of the Board of Commissioners.

SECTION 25.   ENFORCEMENT

Be it further ordained, that it shall be the duty of the Commissioner of Public Utilities, Grounds and Buildings to see that this ordinance is enforced through the proper legal channels. Appeal from the decision of the Commissioner of Public Utilities, Grounds and Buildings may be made to the Administrative Board, as provided by Section 17.

SECTION 26.   CONFLICTING PROVISIONS REPEALED

Be it further ordained, that all ordinances or parts of ordinances in conflict with any of the provisions of this ordinance are hereby repealed.

*SECTION 27.   WHEN EFFECTIVE

Be it further ordained, that this ordinance shall be in effect from and after its passage, the public welfare requiring it.

Index